Assembly Language Progra
for the BBC Microcomp

Macmillan Microcomputer Books

General Editor: Ian Birnbaum
(General Adviser (Microelectronics in Education)
Education Department, Humberside County Council))

Other books of related interest

Assembly Language Programming
for the
BBC Microcomputer

Ian Birnbaum

*General Adviser
(Microelectronics in Education)
Education Department,
Humberside County Council*

Second Edition

MACMILLAN
EDUCATION

First edition 1982
Reprinted 1982, 1983 (three times)
Second edition 1984
Reprinted 1985, 1986, 1987

Published by
Higher and Further Education Division
MACMILLAN PUBLISHERS LTD
Houndmills, Basingstoke, Hampshire RG21 2XS
and London
Companies and representatives
throughout the world

Typeset by Photo-Graphics, Honiton, Devon.

Printed in Great Britain by Camelot Press Ltd, Southampton

British Library Cataloguing in Publication Data
Birnbaum, Ian
Assembly language programming for the BBC
Microcomputer.—2nd ed.—(Macmillan microcomputer books)
1. BBC Microcomputer.—Programming
I. Title
001.64′2   QA76.8.B3
ISBN 0–333–37096–1

The accompanying cassette is
ISBN 0–333–38267–6

Dedicated to Theresa

Contents

Preface to the First Edition

Every BBC Microcomputer, whether model A or model B, comes equipped with an immensely powerful and very fast assembler. What is more, assembly language statements and BASIC statements can be freely mixed, so hugely increasing the programmer's potential control over the machine.

This book shows you how to establish that control. It assumes that you are proficient in BASIC, for if you are not this is probably not the best time to learn assembly language. But it assumes no knowledge of assembler at all, taking you step by step from the basics to their complex implementation.

Since every user of the BBC Microcomputer assembler will have a working knowledge of BASIC, it is possible to use that knowledge to motivate and illustrate the ideas in assembly language. This book takes that approach, and this should help you to master assembly code, for you will always be acquainted with the fundamental concepts by seeing their connection with BASIC.

I had three types of readers in mind in writing this book. Firstly, all current owners of BBC Microcomputers who want to extend their knowledge into machine code. To help them with self-instruction, this book contains a considerable number of exercises and *a full solution is provided for every one*. Secondly, the teacher or student of computer science who wants to use this text in a structured course. The book is the result of many years of teaching experience, and it is designed according to a teaching strategy that the author has found to be very successful.

And thirdly, those people, already experienced BASIC programmers, who are wondering whether to buy the BBC Microcomputer, when there seems to be so much competition from cheaper and seemingly comparable computers. This book should help to convince them that the BBC Micro is worth the extra expense. Quite apart from its superb BASIC, the Micro possesses an assembler that turns it into a potential 6502 development system in its own right! It also possesses an operating system that is designed to mesh with assembly language programming in an extraordinarily simple way. One of the aims of this book is to show you how to exploit these features to the full.

The book contains more than 75 listings of programs, many of which will be found to be useful utilities in their own right, quite apart from their value in teaching you assembly language. In particular, it contains a full machine code monitor, a suite of machine code sorting programs which you can use on BASIC variables, a high-resolution screen copy to the Epson printer and a program compactor. There is a companion cassette available with the book if you do not feel you want to type in the programs yourself. The cassette also contains two useful extra utility programs. One is a machine code program which will find the locations of any segment of code in a BASIC program (equivalent to the FIND command found in some utility packages); the other is a machine code program which will replace any segment of code in a BASIC program by any other segment; so, for example, you can change any variable's name in the whole program in an instant.

The book is completely self-contained: full information on the 6502 instruction set is provided throughout and summarised in an appendix. Other appendixes cover floating-point and the user port.

May 1982
Ian Birnbaum
Needingworth

Preface to the Second Edition

For this new edition I have incorporated all the extra features of OS 1.2 and of BASIC version 2. In particular, much of chapter 9 on interrupts has been rewritten to take advantage of the event-handling facilities of OS 1.2; and throughout the book, all the powerful OS 1.2 calls have been used where relevant. The useful pseudo-instructions of BASIC 2 have been used where they are appropriate, but equivalent methods for BASIC 1 are also included.

The book has been completely reset and any errors in the first edition corrected.

February 1984   Ian Birnbaum
                                                   Kingston-upon-Hull

1 Preliminary Ideas

1.1 What is a Computer?

In its simplest form, a computer can be considered in four sections: *input, output, microprocessor* and *internal memory*. Figure 1.1 shows the inter-relationship

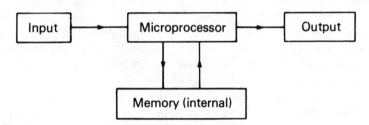

Figure 1.1: Simplified diagram of a computer

Most *input* is through the keyboard, but other input devices and channels include: cassette tape system, disc system and sensor devices connected to an input port.

Most *output* is through the TV or monitor (the VDU), but other output devices and channels include: cassette tape system, disc system, printer and control devices connected to an output port.

Notice that the cassette and disc systems are both input and output devices. These are sometimes referred to as backing store. Printers and suchlike are sometimes referred to as peripherals—things outside the main system.

All input must pass through the *microprocessor*, at some time or other. It may reside temporarily in some internal memory (often referred to in this context as a buffer or latch), but the microprocessor will deal with it when it can. Similarly, all output will be directed by the microprocessor and all will pass through it. The microprocessor is the 'brain' of the system, and this book is concerned with how to program it directly. There are also other 'lesser brains' to be found in a computer, but these are not usually under our control and correspond roughly, following the metaphor, to the autonomic nervous system.

Internal memory can be divided into two parts: *ROM* (read only memory) and *RAM* (misleadingly called random access memory—read/write memory is a better name). ROM contains information that is fixed: the microprocessor is unable to modify it. Usually it contains instructions and data that the microprocessor will need in the same form when a specific task is demanded. In particular, in the BBC Micro it contains the Operating System (OS) and the BASIC Interpreter. A considerable advantage of ROM is that information in it does not disappear when the computer is switched off.

Information in RAM will, by contrast, disappear if power is removed. It has the advantage, however, of allowing information to be modified. It is in RAM that all the programs and data that we input will reside.

Some RAM is given a special function. Some, for example, will be used by the microprocessor as a sort of 'scratch pad' (this is called the stack and is covered in chapter 9). Other parts are reserved for the OS or the BASIC Interpreter in which to store results and information. And some parts are connected to input/output channels. RAM used in this way is often referred to as *memory mapped*. For example, the BBC Micro has a memory-mapped VDU, each character on the screen corresponding to a specific portion of memory that is fixed for each graphics mode chosen (this is not strictly true, as we shall see in chapter 9).

There are some specialised chips in the computer that act as RAM, though they are not usually referred to in this way. The best example of these are the input/output chips, going under a variety of names (PIO—programmable input/output, PIA—peripheral interface adapter, VIA—versatile interface adapter). PIO is the most descriptive: the chip consists of a series of memory locations in which data passing in or out can be latched; certain locations contain information on whether a particular channel is to be conceived as input or output, and this information can be changed by the microprocessor. Although these chips contain more than just memory (for example, some contain a timer, results of which are available at a specific location), they are most conveniently thought of as RAM because they are *addressable*, an idea to which we now turn.

1.2 How Memory is Organised in a Computer

If we want to refer to a specific location of memory, it will need to have a name. Since we may want to refer to any part of memory at some time, we must make sure that memory is organised in such a way that every location has a name and that this name is unique.

When computers are built they are wired up in such a way that the microprocessor can refer to a specific location by outputting a series of pulses called an *address*. The set of wires through which they pass is called the *address bus*.

Since each wire will either have a pulse or not have a pulse there are two states which we may label 1 (pulse) and 0 (no pulse). A microprocessor is a *digital device* because it always understands things and communicates with other parts of the computer in this *two-state* way. Thus: a switch is either on or off; an element either has a positive or negative field, etc.

The microprocessor in the BBC Micro can accept 16 wires on its address bus. Since each wire can either be 1 or 0 this gives a total of $2^{16} = 65536$ addresses, that is from 0000000000000000 to 1111111111111111. Hence there can be at most 65536 locations of memory.

Now writing 16 ones and/or zeros like this is very hard to read, and so we will adopt a notation that makes it easier. We will divide our 16 digits into four groups of four. So for example in 0111101101000010 the four groups are:

$$0111 \quad 1011 \quad 0100 \quad 0010$$

Now each group of four can have one of sixteen different forms, from 0000 to 1111 (2^4). We can use the numerals 0 to 9 for the first ten; after that we will use A, B, C, D, E, F. Table 1.1 gives the details. In that table we can conceive of the four digits on the left as the display on a rather odd car odometer (the meter measuring the distance covered). Each cog on the dial has just two numerals, 0 and 1. As the cog revolves through one revolution it pushes the next one on half a turn. In this way, the first sixteen numbers (0–15, decimal) are generated in the order shown.

Using this notation we can write the number above as 7B42. The number 0010010101000000 will be written 2540, but this is rather misleading because it looks like two thousand five hundred and forty, which it is not. So to prevent confusion, we precede these hexadecimal numbers, as they are called, by the ampersand sign (&). Thus we write them as &7B42 and &2540 (some computers use the dollar sign, $, but not the BBC Micro).

You will notice that the terms *binary* and *hexadecimal* are used in table 1.1. Binary means two (there are two possible numerals, 0 and 1) and hexadecimal means sixteen (there are sixteen possible numerals, 0 to F). In the same way decimal, our usual system of representing numbers, means ten (numerals 0 to 9).

Many books spend ages explaining how to convert from one system to another, but this is a complete waste of time. Your BBC Micro will do it for you.

For example, type into your computer

P.   &7B42

and see what you get. This is the decimal equivalent of &7B42.

Table 1.1 Relationship between binary and hexadecimal

Binary	Hexadecimal
0000	0
0001	1
0010	2
0011	3
0100	4
0101	5
0110	6
0111	7
1000	8
1001	9
1010	A
1011	B
1100	C
1101	D
1110	E
1111	F

Similarly, type in

P.   ~14321

and see what you get. This is the hexadecimal equivalent of 14321.

If you wish, you can write a program to convert either way but it is hardly worth it; you might as well operate in direct mode, as above. It is worth experimenting a little with various numbers to see the equivalence operating for yourself.

It should be clear to you by now why it is convenient for the computer to work in binary and why it is convenient for us to work in hex (the usual abbreviation for hexadecimal). From now on we will think of all the memory locations in terms of hex.

Now in order to make the wiring as simple as possible, a simplifying concept called *pageing* is used. The 65536 addresses of memory are conceived as a series of *pages*. The page number is given by the top two digits of the hexadecimal number; the bottom two digits give the location in that page. The best image is that of a book with 256 pages, each page having 256 lines, each line being a memory location. Rather eccentrically, the book's first page is labelled zero, and is called *zero page*. It is a very important area of memory as we shall see in the next chapter. Figure 1.2 should make the idea clear. Thus address &F1B2 refers to location 178 in page 241; that is, address number 61874. We can think of this in the following way: the high byte &F1 accesses all the locations in page 241; then the low byte &B2 picks out a particular location in that page, location 178. The top half of the address bus is thus wired up to access pages, and the lower half to access one of 256 locations in any page.

When referring to memory *en masse*, it is conventional to work in units of 4 pages and refer to this as a *K of memory* locations. Thus the microprocessor in the BBC Micro can address 64K of memory locations; your machine will have 32K of RAM.

So far we have talked rather vaguely about a memory location; we must now ask what we can put in such a location.

As we have already said, the microprocessor outputs only ones or zeros and can understand only ones and zeros. Hence it comes as no surprise to find that what exists in these locations is a series of ones and zeros.

The microprocessor in the BBC Micro communicates with the *contents* of a memory location through a set of eight wires called a *data bus*. Since there are eight wires, this allows any one of 2^8 or 256 different numbers in one location, that is from &00 to &FF.

We have referred so far to an 8-wire data bus and a 16-wire address bus, but the term usually used is *bit* not wire (bit standing for *b*inary dig*it*). Thus the data bus is 8-bit and the address bus 16-bit. A bit is simply either a 1 or 0. With their usual good humour, computer scientists have called a memory location consisting of eight bits a *byte* (you will meet the 'nybble' later, so be warned!).

Thus a byte consists of 8 bits in sequence. These bits are usually numbered from right to left, zero to seven, the seventh being called the most significant bit (MSB) and the zeroeth the least significant bit (LSB); see figure 1.3.

We can say, then, that the microprocessor can address 64K bytes, but that the memory contains 512K bits. The memory is therefore *byte-addressable* (that is, each byte can be addressed) but not *bit-addressable* (that is, an individual bit cannot be addressed except by addressing the byte of which it is a member).

1.3 How the 6502 Microprocessor is Organised

The microprocessor in the BBC Micro is a 6502 manufactured by MOS

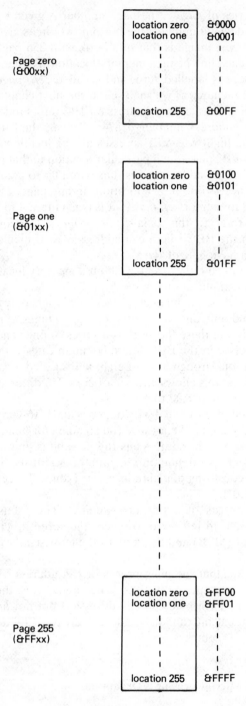

Figure 1.2: Pageing

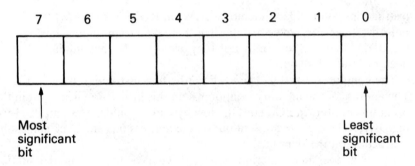

Figure 1.3: Diagram of a memory location, a byte

Technology. It is an 8-bit microprocessor in that it can accept and transfer only 8 bits of data at a time.

The diagram in figure 1.4 is a very simplified block diagram of the organisation or *architecture*, as it is usually called, of the 6502 micro-processor.

In subsequent chapters the box labelled 'Other Registers' will be opened out to reveal further aspects of the architecture when they are needed. By chapter 9 all the architecture will have been revealed. For now, we should note the difference between a *register* and a RAM location. The essential point is that a register is internal to the microprocessor and can be accessed without having to output an address on the address bus. As a consequence, accessing registers is relatively faster than accessing other memory locations.

We shall focus on the *program counter* at this stage. In order to operate, the microprocessor needs a sequence of instructions to follow. These

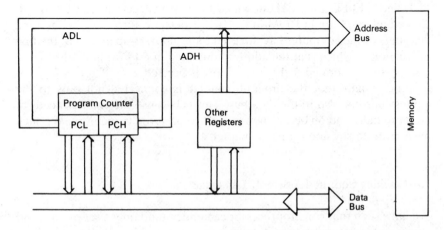

Figure 1.4: Partial block diagram of 6502 architecture

instructions will reside in memory, either in ROM or in RAM. If they are in ROM they will have been deposited there by the computer's designer (in the BBC Micro's case, Acorn); if they are in RAM they might well have been put there by you.

The computer needs to know where the first instruction is to be found. The address of the memory location where this instruction lies is put in the program counter: in PCL goes the low byte of the address and in PCH the high byte. These bytes are sent out on the address bus and back comes the instruction on the data bus.

But what does an instruction look like? We have already said that all that can be sent on the data bus is a set of 8 bits. So long as the microprocessor expects to get an instruction it will decode the particular 8 bits in a special register (the instruction register and decoder) and respond to the instruction according to the instruction set details fixed in the circuitry of the microprocessor. It is these instructions that we will be looking at in the rest of the book.

After it has decoded the first instruction it will know what to expect next. The program counter will automatically increment by one and put out the next address in sequence on the address bus. Back will come the next byte on the data bus. How this byte is interpreted will depend on the instruction previously decoded, as we shall see in later chapters.

The function of the program counter, then, is to fetch, one by one, a sequence of bytes from a section of memory, the starting address of which is put in the program counter initially. You may be wondering how this initial address gets there, since the microprocessor needs an instruction to put it there in the first place! The answer is that there is a special line connected to a pin of the microprocessor called a *reset line*. When a pulse is sent to this line, as it is when the computer is turned on, the microprocessor is preprogrammed to obtain an address from a fixed location (&FFFC for PCL and &FFFD for PCH) in which the first instruction is to be found. These addresses are in ROM in the BBC Micro (as they must be) and the designers of the computer have written a special start-up program, the first instruction of which is at the address contained in &FFFC and &FFFD. A reset is also generated if the 'break' key is pressed.

Notice finally that the program counter is connected not only to the address bus but also to the data bus. This is because the counter needs to be set initially and on occasion may need to be saved in memory. We shall have more to say about this in chapter 9.

1.4 Machine Code and Assembly Language

We have seen that a microprocessor can understand only a set of ones and zeros; that is, information at its level is expressed in bits. We have also seen that an instruction is received through the data bus as a set of 8 bits, a byte. A sequence of bytes, stored consecutively in memory, can be accessed by the microprocessor using the program counter and constitutes a *program*. This program is said to be in *machine code*, since it is in the form directly comprehensible to the microprocessor.

It is not directly comprehensible to humans however. &8D as an instruction does not mean much to us; we would have to continually look up tables or else commit the entire set of instructions to memory. And this would lead to errors.

In the early days of computing a brilliant but now commonplace insight occurred: why not write a program that would allow humans to communicate with computers in a more accessible way. This gave rise to the idea of *assembly language*. Each instruction is given a *mnemonic*, an 'aide memoire', and the programmer can work solely with these mnemonics. So, for example, &8D becomes STA, which is easy to remember. It means 'store a copy of the accumulator somewhere', an idea that we will meet in the next chapter.

Thus a program already written and stored in ROM in the computer, called an *assembler*, translates each mnemonic into its machine code equivalent. Some assemblers are more powerful still and allow the programmer to use variables as in BASIC; the BBC Micro's assembler is like this. In the following chapters we will be learning to program in this assembly language.

There are a few concepts connected with assembly language that are worth mentioning now. We have already met the idea of a mnemonic. The instruction that this represents often needs to act upon some information contained in the next byte (or sometimes the next two bytes). In such cases, the next byte (or bytes) is called the *operand field* or usually just the *operand*. (This is an ugly Latinate word, and not one I particularly like, but it is in common usage and so needs to be known.) In effect it means that a byte or bytes are being understood by the microprocessor as an item of data or as an address of where some data is stored, rather than as an instruction. We will expand upon this idea in the next chapter.

We have already mentioned that a program written in assembly language needs to be translated by the assembler. It is usual to call the program to be translated (that is, the one written in assembly language) the *source code* and the machine code program corresponding to it (that is, the one produced when the assembler makes the translation) the *object code*. The object code is thus just the machine code program corresponding to our assembly language program. Figure 1.5 should make this clear.

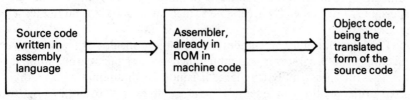

Figure 1.5: Translation of source code into object code by the assembler

1.5 Compilers and Interpreters: Why Use Assembly Language?

Assembly language is a vast improvement on machine code but it is still a
very *low-level language*. By this we mean that each mnemonic in assembly
language corresponds to one and only one machine code instruction. By
contrast, if we write in a *high-level language*, each high-level instruction
will correspond to a whole set of instructions in machine code.

High-level language translators fall into two groups: *compilers* and
interpreters. A compiler takes the source code written in the high-level
language and translates it into object code. This object code may itself be
machine code or may be what is called a pseudo-code which will itself be
translated into machine code. The important point here is that, once the
object code is produced, the source code is no longer necessary for the
running of the program.

By contrast, an interpreter cannot dispense with the source code. A
program written in BBC BASIC for example, needs to reside in the
computer memory while the program is being run. If BBC BASIC were a
compiled language, once the translation was over we would remove the
BASIC program and use the object code instead. This is because in a
compiled language translation and execution take place at quite separate
times. In an interpreted language, however, each statement is first
translated and then executed. Thus, every time the interpreter meets the
statement GOTO 100 it needs first to translate this into machine code
before executing it. The advantage of an interpreted language over a
compiled language is that it is much easier to edit and debug programs. The
disadvantage is that programs run more slowly.

The advantage that high-level languages in general have over assembly
languages is that it is easier to learn a high-level language and writing a
program is both simpler and quicker than in assembly language. Also,
assembly is specific to the microprocessor used: the 6502 assembly code
that you will learn in this book will not work on a Z80 microprocessor for
example. High-level languages are generally portable between machines,
although different machines will need different compilers or interpreters.

Then why use assembly language at all? There are four principal
reasons: programs written in assembly language will generally be more
efficient and shorter than those written in a compiled language; they will be
very much faster to execute than those written in an interpreted language
like BBC BASIC; working with assembly language gives you great insights
into the operations of a computer and allows you to exploit some of its
special features not easily accessible at high level; and, last but not least, it
is fun!

However, one must not underestimate the difficulties of writing even
medium-sized programs in assembly language. For this reason, while it is
fun to write in assembly language, it is not worth attempting a medium-
sized project entirely in assembly language unless one or both of the two

middle reasons above are of particular importance in your chosen application. This is because the BBC Micro allows you to mix BASIC and assembly language in a particularly easy way. This means that you can use assembly language to do things that need to be done quickly or that cannot be realistically accomplished by BASIC or that will need to be accomplished when the BASIC interpreter is not in use, while you can use BASIC to do all those things for which assembly language is unnecessary.

There is nothing to be gained in using assembly language when BASIC will do (except perhaps a rather peculiar one-upmanship). Nevertheless, for pedagogical reasons, I have used some examples in this book which could be programmed in BASIC without too much loss; and again for pedagogical reasons I will use BASIC statements to motivate the introduction of new instructions in the 6502 instruction set. But, where possible I mix BASIC and assembly language in programs in proportion to their relevance to the particular task. Indeed the great advantage of the BBC Micro lies in this freedom to mix the two languages; and one of the aims of this book is to show you how to exploit that freedom.

Exercise 1.1

1. The following concepts have been introduced in this chapter. Try to write a brief description of each one.

   ROM; RAM; memory mapping; PIO; addressable memory; address bus; two-state device; binary numbers; hexadecimal numbers; pageing; zero page; data bus; bit; byte; 64K bytes; bit- and byte-addressability; register; program counter; reset; machine code; assembly language; mnemonic; operand; assembler; source code; object code; low-level language; high-level language; compiler; interpreter.

2. Why is it that a memory-mapped VDU cannot be in ROM and that the address of the start-up instruction cannot be in RAM?

3. If it is generally regarded as a disadvantage to have an 8-bit data bus instead of a 16-bit data bus, can you think of reasons why the 6502 microprocessor was not designed with a 16-bit data bus?

4. Referring to figure 1.4 explain why the data bus is bidirectional (that is, data can pass in both directions) but that the address bus is unidirectional.

5. Why is a program executed under an interpreter slower than one compiled and then executed?

2 Assignments

2.1 The Accumulator

The first and the most important of the 'Other Registers' in figure 1.4 that we will consider is the *Accumulator*. This is an 8-bit register, like all the 'Other Registers', and communicates with both the address bus and the data bus. The principal feature of the accumulator is that all arithmetic and most logical operations must take place using it. So, for example, if two numbers are to be added, one of them must be in the accumulator. The result of this addition will also be placed in the accumulator.

We will cover these arithmetical and logical operations in the next chapter, but here we will concentrate on the other function of the accumulator: as a temporary storage location used when moving data from one memory location to another. The 6502 does have other registers for this purpose as we shall see in chapter 5, but the accumulator is the most important of these. We can view the accumulator, then, as an interim storage location inside the microprocessor, being the place through which movements of data pass and where intermediate results are stored.

Let us look now at some of the simplest assignment statements involving the accumulator. To motivate ideas in this and some of the later chapters we will try to find assembly language equivalents to some common BASIC statements.

2.2 What is the Assembly Language Equivalent of LET NUM1 = 17?

In BASIC, this statement directs the computer to put the number 17 into a storage location labelled NUM1. What is the equivalent in assembly language? Consider the following statements in assembly code

```
LDA    #17
STA    NUM1
```

This does not quite suffice, as we shall see in a moment, but let us first examine what this code does.

LDA is an instruction which means 'load the accumulator' and #17 means 'with the number seventeen'.

STA is an instruction which means 'store a copy of the accumulator' and NUM1 is the name of the storage location where it is to be stored. So, taken together these statements store the number 17 in a location labelled NUM1, via the accumulator.

The problem is, however, that we need to tell the computer *where* this storage location called NUM1 is. In BASIC this is not necessary: the interpreter, a complex machine code program already in the computer, sorts this out for us. We do not need to tell the computer where NUM1 should go; and it does not need to tell us where it has put it. (In fact it puts it into five bytes, not one, but this need not concern us now.)

In assembler things are different, however. Without a directive from us, the computer will not know where NUM1 is. As it stands, then, the computer will give us an error message telling us that the label NUM1 is undefined.

We define it by preceding the first line with

$$NUM1 = \&0DFF$$

The computer will now store 17 in the location &0DFF. We must be careful in our choice of memory location so that it cannot be contaminated by other operations in the computer. If necessary we may have to protect the area of memory by suitably redefining portions of memory. We will have more to say about this later in this chapter.

Even with this protection, it may well be that our choice for NUM1 is not the best. The 6502 is designed to give special preference to memory locations in page zero (which, as we saw in the last chapter, is between &0000 and &00FF). To understand how this gains, we need first to understand how our simple program is stored in the computer.

We have to tell the assembler where the first instruction will go. We do this by writing

$$P\% = \&0C00$$

at the beginning (again making sure this is a protected area). When we now get the assembler to translate our mnemonics into machine code, the very first instruction goes into memory location &0C00. Let us see what the machine code translation looks like.

LDA #17 takes up two bytes: &A9 in &0C00 and &11 in &0C01. &A9 is the *op code*, as it is called, for LDA when the number to be loaded is contained in the next byte. This is signified by the symbol # in the assembly code, and is called, for obvious reasons, *immediate addressing*. The number to be loaded is immediately available; it does not need to be fetched from another part of memory first.

When NUM1 = &0DFF, STA NUM1 takes up three bytes: &8D in &0C02, &FF in &0C03 and &0D in &0C04. Notice that the lower byte of the address is stored first; fortunately the assembler does this automatically so we need not worry too much about it now. This sort of addressing, where a two-byte address indicating where the contents are to be found follows the instruction, is called *absolute addressing*.

By contrast, when NUM1 = &70, say, STA NUM1 takes up only two bytes: &85 in &0C02 and &70 in &0C03. Only the lower byte, &70, of the address needs to be supplied; the computer knows that the higher byte is &00. Note that the op code, &85, is different from &8D, the one above. This reflects the different mode of addressing. Here, the addressing mode is called *zero page addressing*. Fortunately again, the assembler sorts all this out, so we do not need to change the mnemonic code in any way for zero page addressing. STA NUM1 is coded &8D, &FF, &0D if NUM1 = &0DFF, and &85, &70 if NUM1 = &70, quite automatically by the assembler.

Hence by using a zero page location we save one byte of memory. This can be crucial in large programs. Even more importantly, the zero page operation is faster than the absolute one; and again this can be crucial.

So, to summarise, if our symbolic code is this

```
         P%    =    &0C00
       NUM1    =    &0DFF
        LDA         #17
        STA         NUM1
```

it goes into memory thus

Location	&0C00	&0C01	&0C02	&0C03	&0C04
Contents	A9	11	8D	FF	0D

If we change line two to NUM1 = &70, it goes into memory as

Location	&0C00	&0C01	&0C02	&0C03
Contents	A9	11	85	70

2.3 More on the Immediate, Absolute and Zero Page Addressing Modes

In the last section we met three modes of addressing. These ideas are so important that it is worth elaborating upon them further.

We have seen in chapter 1 that when the microprocessor first receives a byte which it expects to be an instruction, it decodes it and then acts upon it. Whether it interprets the next byte as a piece of data, a zero page address or the least significant byte of a non-zero page address depends on the particular instruction that it has received. Thus, the address mode information is contained in the op code of the instruction. This is a crucial aspect of the 6502's operation and it must be thoroughly grasped.

The assembler obscures this fact somewhat, since the same mnemonic is used for all the address modes. Thus LDA #17, LDA &0070, LDA &0DFF all use the mnemonic LDA. The # in the first case means immediate addressing (op code &A9) where the next byte is to be treated as data. In the second case (LDA &0070), because the address is in zero page it will be coded as zero page addressing (op code &A5), and the next byte is treated as a zero page address. In the last case (LDA &0DFF), the address is not in zero page so it will be coded as an absolute address (op code &AD) and the next byte will be the lower byte of this address. In this case the following byte will be interpreted as the higher byte of the address; by contrast, in the first two cases this following byte will be interpreted as a new instruction.

The use of a single mnemonic for different address modes is a relief to our human memories, but we must be aware that, depending on the operand, it is encoded in different ways in the computer's memory.

2.4 What is the Assembler Equivalent of LET NUM2 = NUM1?

We assume that a value has already been put into NUM1, a zero page location. We code this further statement in assembler as follows

```
LDA    NUM1
STA    NUM2
```

Of course we need to tell the assembler the address of NUM2. If we can, we should again choose zero page, say &71. Putting everything together we have

```
P% = &0C00
NUM1 = &70
NUM2 = &71
LDA    NUM1
STA    NUM2
```

When translated into machine code by the assembler, the following is produced

Location	&0C00	&0C01	&0C02	&0C03
Contents	A5	70	85	71

Notice that LDA is coded as &A5 and not &A9 as before. This reflects the change in addressing mode, here zero page, before, immediate. In this case the number to be loaded, 17, has to be fetched from the memory location &0070. The computer puts the address &0070 out on to the address bus, and back comes the contents, 17, on the data bus. All this is initiated automatically by the op code &A5.

There is an ambiguity in the BASIC statement which needs to be resolved. When we write LET NUM2 = NUM1 we usually regard NUM2 and NUM1 as the names of variables, just as we do in algebra. Hence it is often conceptualised as equivalent to let $y = x$, but this is not in fact what it means. The precise meaning of this statement is: assign to memory location NUM2 the contents of memory location NUM1. This may seem to be splitting hairs, and in many practical applications of BASIC perhaps it is, but when using assembly language the distinction is crucial, although the ambiguity remains. So, LDA NUM1 means load the accumulator with the *contents* of memory location NUM1, whereas STA NUM1 would mean store a copy of the contents of the accumulator into memory location NUM1. The same label is used in two different ways: in the first case NUM1 refers to the *contents* of a memory location, in the second NUM1 refers to the *address* of a memory location. There is no *real* ambiguity here, however, since the mnemonics LDA and STA provide the distinction in meaning.

A useful way to resolve real ambiguities though is to put brackets round a label if we mean to refer to its contents: thus (NUM1) refers to the contents of the memory with address NUM1. When we wish to make this distinction clear in our *discussion* of the various instructions we are quite free to use the convention, and this we will do. Moreover, the 6502 assembler does use the convention itself on certain occasions, as we shall see later, but it makes very specific use of it and so we are *not* free to put brackets round our labels when *writing* assembly language.

Note finally that we do not have to use labels like NUM1 and NUM2 at all. We could instead write directly

```
LDA    &70
STA    &71
```

At this stage it does not matter, but as our programs become more complex, the use of labels becomes more convenient and important.

Exercise 2.1

1. State which form of addressing is used in each case. Assuming the first instruction in each statement begins at &C00, show how the assembler would translate each statement into machine code.

✓(a) LDA #14   A9   0E   (f) LDA #&12   A9 12 ✓
✓(b) LDA &7F40   AD 40 7F   (g) STA &0002   8D 02 ✓
✓(c) LDA &20   A5 20   (h) LDA #14   A5 0E
✓(d) STA &7A72   8D 72 7A   (i) STA #1024   85 00 04
✓(e) STA &00   85 00

2. If we combine the two programs in sections 2.2 and 2.4 into a single program, explain why LDA NUM1 can be omitted.

Write out the program in assembly code, and show what the machine code translation would be.

3. Code this BASIC program into assembly language (assume NUM2 and NUM3 already have values).

P% = &0C00

LET NUM1 = NUM3   LDA NUM3
LET NUM3 = NUM2   STA NUM1
LET NUM2 = NUM1   NUM2
                             LDA NUM3
                             STA NUM1
                             LDA NUM2
                             STA

2.5 Where to Put Machine Code Programs in the BBC Micro

We have already seen that we have to tell the assembler where our first instruction will go: we do this by setting the variable P% equal to some value. There are six principal ways of doing this.

(a) Putting the machine code above the BASIC program
As we shall see in a moment, assembly language programs are entered into the machine in BASIC programs. We could put the machine code translation of the program above this program. There are four ways to do this.

(i) P% = TOP + 1000. TOP is a BASIC function which gives the location following the last memory location occupied by the program text. By adding 1000 to it we reserve adequate space for any dynamic variables used in the program.

(ii) LOMEM = LOMEM + 250. LOMEM is a BASIC 'pseudo-variable' which controls where the first dynamic variable is to be placed. By setting it to 250 above its default value (which is TOP), we reserve 250 bytes for our machine code program. This statement must precede all references to dynamic variables (that is, any except α% and A%–Z%). We can then write P% = TOP.

(iii) DIM P% 250. This reserves 250 bytes in the dynamic variable region above the program text and automatically sets P% equal to the address of the first location of this reserved block.

(iv) HIMEM = HIMEM−250. HIMEM is a BASIC 'pseudo-variable' which specifies the highest point in memory available to any program. Usually it is set to the first location of screen memory, &5800 in Mode 4. BASIC programs use the top of memory to store information about procedures and functions, etc., so we cannot just put a machine code program at the top of memory. However, by resetting HIMEM, we reserve 250 bytes at the top of memory for our program. This statement should be the first one in the program. Note that changing from a smaller to a higher resolution mode (for example, MODE 4 to MODE 0) will destroy the machine code program.

(b) Putting the machine code below the BASIC program
(i) PAGE = PAGE + 256. PAGE is a 'pseudo-variable' which controls the starting address of a BASIC program. It is always a multiple of 256 (reference to section 1.2 will remind you why) and its default value is &E00 on the ordinary BBC Micro (that is, a system without discs, etc.). This instruction should be performed *before* loading the program. We can then safely set P% to PAGE−256 in the program.

(ii) Using memory below &E00: The locations from &900 to &AFF are used by the cassette system when the OPENIN, OPENUP and OPEN-OUT commands are used but not by the system to save and load programs. They are also used by the RS423 port, and &900 to &9FF is in certain circumstances used by the sound system (some of &900 to &9BF if five or more envelopes are in use; &9C0 onwards if the speed chip is fitted). Hence, in certain circumstances these locations may be safe.

The locations &C00 to &CFF are reserved for programmed characters (ASCII codes 223–255 inclusive). If you do not expect to use these at the same time as a machine code program then this area is free.

Finally, locations &D01 to &DFF are untouched by the operating system, but only in the standard models. This means that this area is safe for machine code programs on the standard models. However, with some types of extra ROMs (for example, VIEW) in the paged ROM sockets, some of the memory locations &D9F onwards store addresses which may be accessed by these ROMs. Hence, do not use these locations if you intend in the same session to use any such ROMs (and note that BREAK will reset the relevant locations to their correct values). &D00 itself is unsafe, however, and should not be used. The reason for this will be explained in section 9.3.

Other areas are best left alone. &B00 to &BFF, for example, is used for the programmable keys and, even if you do not intend to use them, accidentally pressing one with machine code in this area can have strange effects. Even stranger things happen if you put code into the sound buffer at &800 to &8FF!

Of these six options for machine code location, (a) (iii) is useful when a machine code program is to be used in conjunction with a BASIC program, since they are kept together in a simple way. Wherever the BASIC program is loaded into memory, the machine code will run. Moreover, unlike most other micros, the BBC Micro allows us to store many programs in memory at the same time, using the PAGE command. Hence, we can use a machine code program contained in one BASIC program in a second BASIC program.

(b)(ii) is most useful for stand-alone machine code programs. Clearly &D01–&DFF is the safest area, but in many cases if more than 256 bytes are needed &C00–&DFF (with D000 left out) is reasonable. The only disadvantage here might be the effects when non-standard BBC Micros are used (with discs, etc.).

In this book option (a)(iii) will be followed in the earlier chapters, where BASIC and machine code are often linked, usually for pedagogical purposes. In later chapters, and especially in chapter 10, option (b)(ii) with &D01 will be used. The one exception to this is the Monitor program which requires &330 bytes: in this case option (a)(iv) will be used.

Finally in this section, note that the designers of the BBC Micro have reserved 32 zero page locations for assembly program use. This is very useful, for we have already seen the saving involved in using zero page. These locations are from &70 to &8F inclusive.

2.6 How to Input Assembly Language Programs into the BBC Micro

Listing 2.1 shows how to input the solution to question 2 of exercise 2.1 into the computer. Put it in and run it. Try different numbers and convince yourself that it works; press ESCAPE when you have tried a few.

Listing 2.1

```
  10 NUM1=&70:NUM2=&71:NUM3=&72
  20 DIM P% 50
  30 [OPT3
  40 .START
  50 LDA NUM3
  60 STA NUM1
  70 LDA NUM2
  80 STA NUM3
  90 LDA NUM1
 100 STA NUM2
 110 RTS:]
 120 REPEAT
 130    INPUT"Contents of NUM2",?NUM2
 140    INPUT"Contents of NUM3",?NUM3
 150    CALLSTART
 160    PRINT?NUM1,?NUM2,?NUM3
 170    UNTIL FALSE
```

Let us look at the listing in detail. In line 10, we give zero page addresses to the three labels that we shall use. In line 20 we set the program counter as recommended in the last section. As a rule of thumb, allow 3 bytes for every instruction. This will always be ample, and will usually give some room for any editing and insertion required later. There is no need to count the instructions, though; a rough estimate is all that is required, and rounding up to the nearest fifty will do. Line 30 is the beginning of the assembly code: the open square bracket, [, tells the interpreter that .OPT3 is what is called a pseudo-operation: it is not strictly part of the 6502 assembly language. Its function is to specify whether and how the translation into machine code will be listed on assembly. In this case, 3 indicates that the translation will be listed, and any errors displayed (the possible errors at this stage are syntax error or unknown label).

In line 40 we begin with .START. This label will automatically be given the address into which the first instruction will be put. Any label will do, so long as it begins with a full stop, and otherwise conforms to all the rules for BASIC variables. (Some assemblers restrict the length to six, but not the BBC Micro's assembler.) Clearly START is a sensible label, and we should endeavour to use labels that are as meaningful as possible. We shall have much more to say about labels like these, having the function of referring to an address within the program, in chapter 4.

The assembly program proper is in lines 50 to 110. The assembly program is translated into machine code line by line through to line 110. In line 150 control is passed to the machine code program, located at the address referenced by START. The function of the new instruction RTS in line 110 is to return control to the statement following this call, when the machine code program has finished. Every assembly program must end with RTS. We shall have much more to say about RTS in chapter 9, but for now we regard it as an essential terminator to the assembly program. The close square bracket,], indicates to the interpreter that the assembly program has finished (note the colon before it, which is essential if it does not begin a line).

In lines 130 and 140 we put values into address locations NUM2 and NUM3 prior to calling the machine code program, and in line 160 we print out the values in the three address locations after returning from the machine code program. The query operator ? means the 'contents of the memory location whose address is the value of the variable attached'. Thus P.?NUM2 prints the contents of the memory location with address NUM2 (that is, the contents of &71).

It is possible to extend the notation to a binary operation and write NUM?1 instead of ?(NUM+1), but this is less readable, in my view, and saves very little.

Using the query operator, we can pass values to the machine code program and output results from that program. It is possible to do this directly from the machine code program—essential if speed is an important factor—but the details of this must wait until chapter 9.

It is important to understand that when lines 10 to 110 of the program are run, all that happens is that the assembly code is translated into machine code and placed in memory above the BASIC program text. *The machine code program itself is not executed during this process.* To execute the program, we must CALL it, as in line 150. Hence *assembly (that is, translation) and program execution are two distinct processes:* we assemble the mnemonics into machine code and then, if required, execute that machine code afterwards.

The REPEAT...UNTIL in lines 120 and 170 is a standard way of producing an infinite loop. Notice that we need assemble the program only once: after that we use the technique of passing values to the machine code program using the query operator. It is good programming practice always to design our programs in this way: we should never have to reassemble a program to give it new values to work on.

This last point brings us to the subject of saving programs on tape. Since we should not need to assemble a program more than once into machine code, it is possible in principle to save the machine code on tape, using the instruction *SAVE. Then we need only save lines 120 to 170 of the BASIC program. However it is not generally convenient to store programs in two parts like this. We shall, in general, recommend saving the unassembled program, such as all of listing 2.1, and assembling it once each time we load it. This is not likely to be unreasonably slow, and is very much more convenient.

Moreover, this method results in automatically 'relocatable programs' which can be amended in exactly the same way as any other BASIC program. All we need to do is to adjust PAGE prior to loading the program. This is a very powerful feature of the BBC Micro.

Even if we are producing a stand-alone machine code program which we will load with the *LOAD command, we should still keep a copy of the program in assembly language. If we need to add, delete or change a line it then becomes almost as easy as with a BASIC program.

In using an assembler as comprehensive as this one, we do not need to worry very much about what the machine code translation looks like. We can be sure that if our assembly language is correct, the machine code translation will be correct. It follows that if our program fails to work, we should try to mend the assembly language version and not try to delve into the machine code. (We will have more to say about 'debugging' in chapter 10.) You will have noticed that OPT3 provides us with a listing that includes the machine code translation. This is of some pedagogical interest, and occasionally in this book we will consider the machine code representation of assembly instructions to deepen our understanding. But, in general, our main focus should be at the assembly language level.

2.7 Storing Numbers Larger than 256 in Assembly Language

Listing 2.2 illustrates how to load the hex number &D5C3 (decimal 54723) into memory. We need two bytes for this and we use the labels NUML for the low byte and NUMH for the high byte. It is conventional on the 6502 microprocessor to put the low byte in a lower memory location than the high byte and to store them consecutively.

Listing 2.2

```
 10 NUML=&70:NUMH=&71
 20 DIM P% 50
 30 COPT3
 40 .START
 50 LDA #&C3
 60 STA NUML
 70 LDA #&D5
 80 STA NUMH
 90 RTS:]
100 CALLSTART
110 ?&72=0:?&73=0
120 PRINT!NUML
```

Lines 110 and 120 need some explanation. Line 120 prints out the number represented by the four bytes in &70, &71, &72 and &73, with &73 being the most significant. Since zero is in &72 and &73 (allocated in line 110), the number is &0000D5C3, and line 120 will print out this in decimal. This 'pling' operator (!) is a way of referencing four consecutive memory locations at one go, and we will find it useful later. We could, of course, have printed out the number by writing 256*?NUMH + ?NUML, but listing 2.2 serves to introduce the ! operator.

Finally, there is a useful symbolic convention that we can introduce now. NUML and NUMH should really be taken together, since they present one number, and we can usefully write these locations as NUMH;NUML. The semicolon between the two serves to separate two *ordered* bytes, the first being the higher byte and the second the lower byte. We can refer to the *contents* of these locations, and so to the number that they jointly represent, as (NUMH;NUML) using the bracket notation we introduced in section 2.4. As a decimal number, (NUMH;NUML) is 256*(NUMH) + (NUML). Remember, though, that this notation is to be used for the purposes of *discussion*: it is not part of the 6502 instruction set, and should *not* be used in the assembly programs themselves.

3   *Addition and Subtraction*

3.1 The Arithmetic Unit

At the beginning of the previous chapter we mentioned that all arithmetic must take place in the accumulator. The part of the microprocessor used to perform the arithmetic is called the Arithmetic Logic Unit (Arithmetic Unit or ALU for short). Figure 3.1 shows the simplified architectural details.

Notice that the ALU has two inputs: one fron. the accumulator and one from the data bus. (In certain internal operations, one of the program counter bytes is used as an input instead of the accumulator, but in order not to complicate things, this is not shown on figure 3.1.) The output from the ALU always passes back to the accumulator (again, with certain internal operations, the output can pass directly to the address bus but this need not concern us now). From the accumulator it can go out on the data bus to a memory location whose address is on the address bus.

Also included on figure 3.1 is a new register, the Processor Status

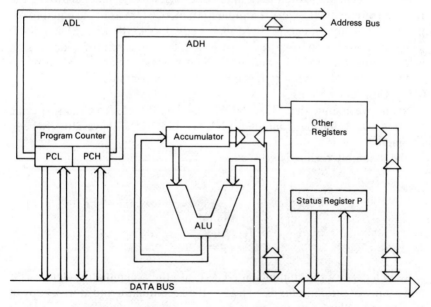

Figure 3.1: Partial block diagram showing the ALU and Status Register

Register, usually labelled P. The function of this register will become clear in this and the next chapter.

3.2 What is the Assembly Language Equivalent of Some Simple BASIC Statements Involving Addition?

(a) Consider first LET SUM = 14 + 29.

As usual, we will assume that SUM has already been given a specific memory location in zero page, for example SUM = &70. Thus we require the result of adding 29 to 14 to be put in memory location &70 which we have labelled SUM.

The assembly coding is

```
LDA    #14
CLC
ADC    #29
STA    SUM
```

The first statement is familiar by now: put the number 14 into the accumulator. The next one, CLC, means 'clear carry'; we shall come back to the meaning of this later. ADC #29 means add 29 to the contents of the accumulator storing the result in the accumulator. STA SUM stores a copy of this result in SUM.

Notice again the potentially ambiguous use of the label SUM in the BASIC statement. It is very tempting to think of SUM as being equal to 43, whereas it is the *contents* of SUM that is equal to 43 (that is, (SUM) = 43, using the convention discussed in section 2.4). The assembly code version is less ambiguous since the mnemonic STA makes it clear that SUM refers to the *address* of a memory location and not its contents.

(b) Consider now LET SUM = NUM1 + NUM2.

Again, we assume that SUM, NUM1 and NUM2 refer to already specific locations, and that the contents of NUM1 and NUM2 have already been assigned.

The assembly coding is

```
LDA    NUM1
CLC
ADC    NUM2
STA    SUM
```

Load a copy of the contents of NUM1 into the accumulator, clear carry, add a copy of the contents of NUM2 to the accumulator and store a copy of the result in SUM.

We can represent this process symbolically thus

$$(NUM1) + (NUM2) \rightarrow SUM$$

Thus the contents of NUM1 and NUM2 are added and stored in the memory location SUM. This symbolic representation is much less ambiguous than the BASIC statement, and we shall be using it a great deal. (Note that some authors reverse this notation; that is, SUM ← (NUM1) + (NUM2).)

3.3 The Importance of Carry

In section 3.2(b) we have implicitly assumed that the result of adding (NUM1) and (NUM2) will not exceed 255 or &FF. This is because the final result will not fit into the one byte SUM otherwise. Does this mean that we are restricted to adding numbers whose sum is less than 256?

Let us consider the situation when (NUM1) = 87 and (NUM2) = 194. The result will be 281, but let us examine the arithmetical process as it occurs in the microprocessor—in binary.

We have

```
        01010111          87
        11000010          194
       _____        ____
   [1]  00011001          25      ?
       _____        ____
```

The result is 25, which is of course wrong. What has happened is that a carry occurred on adding the two most significant bits. Fortunately, however, this carry digit is preserved in one of the bits of the Processor Status Register. This bit is referred to as the *carry flag, C*. Hence, if after performing an addition the carry flag contains 1, we know that a carry has occurred. If no carry has occurred the carry flag will contain zero, regardless of what it contained before the addition took place.

Now 281 in hex is &0119, that is, 256 + 25. So if there is a carry we need to store our result in two bytes, not one, the higher byte containing 1. How can we access the carry bit, however? The answer is that the carry bit is automatically added in when we perform the next addition.

Consider the assembly coding in lines 50 to 120 of listing 3.1.

Listing 3.1

```
10 NUM1=&70:NUM2=&71:SUML=&72:SUMH=&73
20 DIM P% 50
30 [OPT3
```

```
 40 .START
 50 LDA NUM1
 60 CLC
 70 ADC NUM2
 80 STA SUML
 90 LDA #0
100 STA SUMH
110 ADC SUMH
120 STA SUMH
130 RTS:]
140 REPEAT
150    INPUT"First number to be added",?NUM1
160    INPUT"Second number to be added",?NUM2
170    CALLSTART
180    PRINT?NUM1+?NUM2,256*?SUMH+?SUML
190    UNTIL FALSE
```

The first four instructions are as before except that the result is stored in memory location SUML. Then we put zero in the accumulator, store zero in SUMH, and then add SUMH to the accumulator, finally storing the result in SUMH. Why on earth should we want to add zero to zero?

The point is that we have done more than this. Look at the mnemonic ADC—what is the C? ADC actually means *add with carry*. So ADC M really means

$$A + (M) + C \rightarrow A$$

This always happens automatically. It follows that if we do not want to add the carry we should set C to zero. This is the purpose of the instruction CLC.

Notice that the second ADC (ADC SUMH) is not preceded by CLC. This is quite deliberate: if there is a carry from the previous addition we want it included in this addition.

The consequence of this is that if (NUM1) = 87 and (NUM2) = 194, SUML will contain &19 and SUMH will contain 1. Put listing 3.1 into your computer and try some values. Convince yourself that the coding works and then press ESCAPE.

Exercise 3.1

Write a program to add three numbers together, each number being less than 256. Remember that the final result may be anything up to 765. Type in your program in the same way as in listing 3.1 and try it out.

3.4 Adding Numbers that are Greater than 256: Multiple Precision Arithmetic

How would we program the microprocessor to add two numbers, at least one of which lay between 256 and 65535?

Consider for example 3929 + 52667 or in hex &0F59 + &CDBB. The 6502 microprocessor can only deal with a byte at a time so we consider the lower bytes first. In binary and hex we have

01011001	&59
10111011	&BB

| 1 | 00010100 | & | 1 | 14 |

We have generated a carry of 1, which we carry over to the higher bytes. We then obtain

00001111	&0F
11001101	&CD
1	1
11011101	&DD

Thus the final result is &DD14 or 56596, which is correct, of course.

To produce a general coding for this we will put the first number in bytes NUM1H NUM1L, and the second in NUM2H NUM2L. The result is stored in SUMH SUML. Listing 3.2 gives the details. As before put it into your computer and convince yourself that it works. Notice that we cannot print out (NUM1) and (NUM2) by using !NUM1L and !NUM2L, since neither bytes 3 nor 4 of either of these will be zero. We could if we wished output (SUM) by using !SUML so long as &76 and &77 contained zeros.

Listing 3.2

```
 10 NUM1L=&70:NUM1H=&71:NUM2L=&72:NUM2H=&73:SUML=&74:
    SUMH=&75
 20 DIM P% 50
 30 [OPT3
 40 .START
 50 LDA NUM1L
 60 CLC
 70 ADC NUM2L
 80 STA SUML
 90 LDA NUM1H
100 ADC NUM2H
110 STA SUMH
120 RTS:]
130 REPEAT
140   INPUT"First number to be added",!NUM1L
150   INPUT"Second number to be added",!NUM2L
160   CALLSTART
170   PRINT256*?NUM1H+?NUM1L+256*?NUM2H+?NUM2L,
      256*?SUMH+?SUML
180 UNTIL FALSE
```

You will have noticed that this coding is not quite general enough. It is possible that the result will need three bytes, not two. This will happen if we try to perform 57922 + 37130, for example. However the coding is easily modified for this case, and this is set as an exercise in exercise 3.2.

Before doing that, let us extend the notation introduced in section 2.7 a little. You will recall that we write NUM1H;NUM1L to denote a two-byte number. We can extend this to three or more bytes very easily. In this example, if the result is stored in SUM2, SUM1 and SUM0 we can express the whole thing symbolically as

$$(NUM1H;NUM1L) + (NUM2H;NUM2L) \rightarrow SUM2;SUM1;SUM0$$

Exercise 3.2

1. Write a program to perform the operation described symbolically above.

2. Write a program to add together two four-byte numbers. Assume that neither number exceeds &7FFFFFFF so that only four bytes are needed for the result.

Set up the addresses using arrays and a loop as follows

```
10    DIM NUM1(3) , NUM2(3), RESULT(3)
20    FOR I% = 0TO3: NUM1(I%) = &70+I%
30    NUM2(I%) = &74 + I% :RESULT(I%) = &78 + I% : NEXT
      I%
```

What is the symbolic representation of this process?

Test the program by using on INPUT, !NUM1(0) and !NUM2(0). Print out the result by using !RESULT(0).

3.5 Subtraction

Consider the equivalent assembly code to LET DIFF = NUM1 − NUM2, where both numbers are less than 256 and NUM1 > NUM2.

```
LDA    NUM 1
SEC
SBC    NUM2
STA    DIFF
```

The two new instructions are SEC, set the carry flag, and SBC, subtract.

You will be wondering why we need to set the carry flag in this case. In order to understand this we need to understand how the microprocessor subtracts.

In fact the microprocessor does not subtract at all—it adds! Thus it treats

98 − 41 as 98 + (−41). The advantage of this is that no additional circuitry is needed for subtraction.

But the problem now is how to represent −41. What we require of the representation for (−41) is that (−41) + 41 = 0. Consider the binary representation of 41: 00101001. Suppose we now reverse all the ones and zeros to get 11010110—this is called the *one's complement*, or often just the *complement*. If we add 41 and its complement we get

$$
\begin{array}{c}
00101001 \\
11010110 \\
\hline
11111111 \\
\hline
\end{array}
$$

If we now add one to this we obtain

$$\boxed{1} \quad 0000\ 0000$$

Hence, if we ignore the carry, we get zero. It follows that by complementing 41 and adding one, we obtain a representation of −41, that is, 11010111. This is because it performs just as −41 should perform (−41 + 41 = 0) so long as we ignore the carry obtained.

The process of complementing a number and adding one is called finding the *two's complement* of a number.

Now the microprocessor gets the one it is to add on from the carry flag—this is why we must set the carry flag to 1 before we subtract. What happens if the carry flag is zero will be considered in a moment.

Let us just convince ourselves that this works. In two's complement form 98 + (−41) is

$$
\begin{array}{cc}
\begin{array}{c}
01100010 \\
11010111 \\
\hline
\end{array}
&
\begin{array}{c}
98 \\
-41 \\
\hline
\end{array}
\\
\boxed{1} \quad 00111001 & 57
\end{array}
$$

and ignoring the carry, this is correct. All that has happened here is that we have performed (57 + 41) + (−41); the last two numbers added together give zero carry 1, and hence we obtain the result.

Notice that the usual understanding of 11010111, namely as the number 215, is replaced by its interpretation as −41. This change in interpretation follows simply because we suppress the usual meaning of the carry flag. If we understand the carry flag in the usual way we would get &139, or 313, which is indeed the sum of 98 and 215. By not treating carry as the 'ninth bit' as we do in addition, we can treat &D7 as −41.

If you have followed all this you will see that when the microprocessor performs the subtraction 215 − 158, it will perform precisely the same sum as above, but in reverse order. Thus 158 is 10011110, its complement is 01100001 and so its two's complement is 01100010. We then get

$$
\begin{array}{cc}
11010111 & 215 \\
01100010 & -158 \\
\hline
00111001 & 57 \\
\end{array}
$$

with a box showing **1** to the left of 00111001

as before.

3.6 The Function of the Carry Flag in Subtraction: Multiple Precision Subtraction

We have just seen that the microprocessor obtains the one it needs to perform the two's complement from the carry flag. But what happens if zero is in the carry flag?

In this case instead of adding on one it adds on zero. It follows that the number obtained will be one less than it would otherwise have been (since if we add one to a negative number it gets bigger, although it becomes numerically smaller). Thus the effect of having the carry flag zero is to *make the number subtracted one greater*. The *result* of the subtraction will thus be *one less* than would otherwise have been the case.

It is in this way that the carry flag plays a crucial role in multiple precision subtraction. Consider the sum, &732E − &6492. As usual we need to consider the lower bytes first. So we have &2E − &92. The two's complement of &92 is &6E (since &92 + &6E = &100). So in binary we have

$$
\begin{array}{cc}
00101110 & \&2E \\
01101110 \ + & -\&92 \\
\hline
10011100 & \&9C \\
\end{array}
$$

with a box showing **0** to the left of 10011100

Notice the crucial point: the carry flag is zero. When we worked out 98 − 41 before, it was one. Hence, *if we attempt to subtract a larger byte from a smaller byte the carry flag is reset to zero*.

What do we make of the final result &9C? There are two ways to look at it: one is to treat it as a negative number (we shall return to this in a moment). The other way is to consider it as the result that we get if we have borrowed one from the next column.

Thus

$$\begin{array}{r} \&12E \\ 92\ - \\ \hline \&\ 9C \\ \hline \end{array}$$

(remember &12 = 18 and 18 − &9 = &9).

This second way of treating things is what is required here. The carry being reset to zero indicates that we have needed to borrow. Now as we have seen, if the carry is zero this is equivalent to subtracting a number one greater. Hence when we subtract the higher bytes we will 'pay the borrow back'. Thus, the one's complement of &64 is &9B (&64 + &9B = &FF), and this is the two's complement of &65. We then have

$$\begin{array}{cc} \&73 & \&73 \\ \&9B\ + & \&65\ - \\ \hline \boxed{1}\quad \&0E & \&0E \\ \hline \end{array}$$

The final result is &0E9C, which is correct, of course.

Now, can we always be sure that when we try to take a larger byte from a smaller one the carry flag will be reset to zero? Indeed so. The two's complement of a number is 256 minus that number. Hence V − U gives V + (256 − U). Now if U > V this must be less than 256 since we can write it 256 − (U − V). Similarly if V > U it must be more than 256 since we can write it 256 + (V − U). It always works.

Exercise 3.3

1. Write a program to perform two-byte multiple precision subtraction as described above.

The symbolic representation is

$$(\text{NUM1H;NUM1L}) - (\text{NUM2H;NUM2L}) \rightarrow \text{DIFFH;DIFFL}$$

2. Using the same labels as in question 2 of exercise 3.2, write a program to subtract two four-byte numbers.

3.7 Positive and Negative Numbers: Signed Arithmetic

We have seen that any byte can be considered as negative or positive: the interpretation we (or the microprocessor) give to it depends on how we obtained the number, and the various conditions applying at the time.

Above we said that in &2E − &92 = &9C, we could consider &9C as a negative number. In that case it is −&63 or −99. But we would have got &9C as an answer to &ED − &51, and this time it would have been positive, that is, +157. We know which is which because in the first case the carry flag is reset to zero, and in the second case it is set to one.

Now suppose that, instead of obtaining a negative number as a result of a subtraction sum, we just wanted to input a negative number straight away. In principle there seems to be no problem: if we want −17 we need the two's complement of &11 which is &EF and we can use this; similarly if we want −150 we use &6A. As long as we remember that in both cases the numbers are to be understood as negative then there is no problem, it seems. Unfortunately, this is totally impracticable. Almost all the time, we will want to do arithmetic with such numbers, and it would defeat the object of using a microprocessor if we had to work through all the sums first so that we could tell the microprocessor whether a result is to be understood as positive or negative! Thus, for example, the micro may at one point perform the sum &6A + &12 = &7C. Is this 124 or −132? The microprocessor has no clues, since it has taken the byte &6A from memory and there is no room for us to attach a sticky label to the byte indicating that it is negative (if that is what we require it to be)!

We are going to have to introduce a convention to deal with this. If a number is going to be considered negative then its most significant bit must be one; otherwise it is a positive number. This means that using a single byte to represent a number, &00 to &7F are positive; and &80 to &FF are negative. This gives us a range of −128 to +127. This convention is an easy one to use since if a number is greater than 127 we need to subtract it from 256 and treat the result as negative; for example, &AB is −&55, which is −85. It is usual to call the most significant bit in this case the *sign* bit.

Remember that this convention is necessary only if we want to treat some numbers as negative *from the outset*; in all other cases, there is other information in the microprocessor (like the state of the carry flag) to provide the clue as to the sign of the result.

Let us consider a couple of examples.

(a) 70 + (−90)
```
01000110
10100110 +
————————
11101100
```

Since the MSB is a 1, the number is negative, namely −20.

(b) (−24) + (−58)
```
11101000
11000110 +
————————
10101110
```
$\boxed{1}$

Again the result is negative, namely −82. The carry flag here has no significance. This is because we are effectively dealing only with seven bits; any carry will go into the eighth bit, though even then it may not always be relevant.

This last point leads us to a problem called overflow. Consider

(c) 83 + 54

```
01010011
00110110 +
```
———
```
10001001
```

The result is −119, which is plainly ridiculous. Moreover, the micro-processor knows that it is ridiculous too, since it has added two positive numbers. It therefore flags the problem by setting another bit in the status register called the overflow bit, and labelled V (oVerflow).

It should be obvious that overflow can occur only when adding two positive or two negative numbers, that is, when adding two numbers of the same sign. In those cases, and *only* in those cases, can V be set to one. Overflow is often erroneously thought of as a carry taking place from bit 6 to bit 7, but a glance at example (b) will show you that this is *not* so.

The overflow flag is set to one by the microprocessor only if the sign bit of the result is different from the sign bits of the two numbers added (assuming, of course, that the numbers have the same sign bit); in all other cases it is reset to zero. Overflow can occur without there being any carry from bit 6 to bit 7 (consider for example (−65) + (−65)).

What happens if V is set to 1? Then we know that the result is either greater than 127 or less than −128. Which it is will depend on the value of the MSB: if it is one, the result is greater than 127; if it is zero, less than −128. We will consider how to deal with these cases in the next chapter.

Let us end this section by considering how we can represent signed numbers in two bytes. Using two bytes we have &0000 to &7FFF as positive (MSB=0), and &8000 to &FFFF as negative (MSB=1). This gives us a range of -2^{15} to $2^{15} - 1$, that is, from −32768 to +32767. Let us consider as an example 18548 + (−25239).

In hex we have

&48	&74
&9D +	&69 +
&E5	&DD

The result is &E5DD, which is negative since the MSB=1 (E=1110), and this is −6691. A simple way to calculate this is −(255 − &E5) * 256 − (256 − &DD)=−6691, or −(&10000−&E500).

Notice that the arithmetic on the low bytes is interpreted quite normally. The V flag *will* be set, but *we* choose to take no notice of it because the sign bit is not bit 7 but bit 15. The microprocessor will always set V when treating the bytes as single byte signed numbers would result in overflow: it does not know whether we are treating them this way or not in any particular case. In this case it is the higher pair of bytes (&48 and &9D) that are being considered this way, but in this case overflow does not occur. Remember, then, that overflow is a problem to *us* only when we are considering the bytes that contain the sign bit. The microprocessor will always flag overflow when appropriate in case the particular pair of bytes that we have just added *does* contain the sign bit: it is up to us to make the right interpretation in the way we construct our programs, as we will see in the next chapter.

Exercise 3.4

1. Show how the computer would perform the sums $24 - (-18)$ and $(-86) - 35$. Under what circumstances would overflow occur in the case of signed subtraction?

2. What is the range of signed numbers with 4 bytes?

3. What adjustments, if any, would you need to make to the program of question 2 in exercises 3.2 and 3.3 to perform signed addition and subtraction, assuming that there is no overflow? Give a BASIC statement to print out the result from the four bytes.

3.8 Logical Operations

Suppose we have a number in the accumulator and we wish to change its sign; that is, we want to perform the operation $-A \rightarrow A$. One way to do this is to subtract the accumulator from zero, but to do this we need to put the accumulator into a memory location. The coding is

```
STA    TEMP
LDA    #0
SEC
SBC    TEMP
```

where TEMP is the temporary memory location.

It would be helpful if there was a way of doing this that does not need any temporary memory location; and indeed there is. We need a new operation called the exclusive-OR. Actually this operation exists in BASIC and indeed has the same mnemonic, EOR.

EOR operates only on the accumulator and the final result is put in the accumulator. EOR M takes each bit of the accumulator and exclusive-ORs it with the corresponding bit of (M), according to the following table

Ⅴ	0	1
0	0	1
1	1	0

where Ⅴ is the symbol for EOR. Like bits give a zero, unlike bits a 1. For example, 11010100 Ⅴ 10111101 = 0110100.

It follows that to complement the accumulator we need only write EOR #&FF: every zero in the accumulator becomes 1 and every 1 becomes zero. To give the two's complement we need to add 1. So the full coding to perform $-A \to A$ is

```
EOR    #&FF
CLC
ADC    #1
```

For completeness let us now mention the other two logical operations that the microprocessor can perform, both on the accumulator (and both also present as BASIC operations).

First ORA M. This takes each bit of the accumulator and ORs it with the corresponding bit of (M), according to the following table

V	0	1
0	0	1
1	1	1

where V is the symbol for OR. The final result is put in the accumulator. Only two zeros give a zero; all the other combinations give one. For example, 11010100 V 10111101 = 11111101.

The main use of ORA is to set one or more bits to one in the accumulator without affecting the rest. For example, ORA #&42 will ensure that bits 1 and 6 are both 1, and that the others are unchanged.

The final operation is AND M. This takes each bit of the accumulator and ANDs it with the corresponding bit of (M), according to the following table

Λ	0	1
0	0	0
1	0	1

where Λ is the symbol for AND. The final result is put in the accumulator. Only two ones give a 1; all the other combinations give zero. For example, 11010100 Λ 10111101 = 10010100.

The main use of AND is to *mask* off one or more bits in the accumulator, that is, to set them to zero, without affecting any other bits. For example, AND #&ED will ensure that bits 1 and 4 are zero, and that the other bits are unchanged. AND #&0F will ensure that the top four bits are zero, the bottom four remaining unchanged.

The uses of these operations will become more apparent in the later chapters of this book.

Exercise 3.5

Write the coding to
  (a) set bits 3 and 7 to one and to mask bits 0 and 4, all other bits remaining unchanged;
  (b) reverse bit 7, set bit 6 to 1 and mask off all the rest of the bits except bit 5.

3.9 A New Addressing Mode: Implied Addressing

The instructions CLC and SEC illustrate a new form of addressing. All instructions must refer to some part of memory or to some register, and this includes the instructions CLC and SEC. In this case, it is the carry flag in the Processor Status Register that is addressed and the value to be deposited in that flag is included in the instruction. This is implicitly the case, however, since we do not need to specify what is being addressed nor what value is to be deposited, aside from writing down the instruction itself. Instructions like these, where the address and contents referred to are included implicitly in the instruction, are said to use the *implied addressing mode*. All such instructions are single byte, for no data is required to accompany the instruction. Note that instructions like EOR are not implied: for while one of the addresses is implicit—the accumulator—a second one is needed, namely the memory location with whose contents the accumulator will be EORed. Everything must be included in the instruction for it to be implied addressing.

4 Decision-making in Assembly Language

4.1 The Processor Status Register

In the previous chapter (section 3.1) reference was made to a new register: P, the status register. Figure 3.1 shows it in relation to the rest of the architecture that we have met so far. Each of the eight bits of this register has a separate function: each operates as a *flag*, indicating that certain conditions have or have not occurred. If the bit is 1, the flag is said to be *set*, if the bit is 0, the flag is said to be *clear* (or sometimes *reset*). We have already considered two flags: C, the carry flag, and V, the overflow flag. Figure 4.1 shows all the flags in the P register. There are five new ones, N, B, D, I, Z. Of these, we will defer discussion of B, D and I until later chapters.

The N flag is set to one whenever the most significant bit of the result of any arithmetic or logical operation is one. It is also set to one if data moved into the accumulator has an MSB of one. (It is also affected by movements concerning the X or Y registers, as we shall see in chapter 5.) It is called the negative flag because if a byte is to be interpreted as a signed integer, then a negative integer will have an MSB of one. This concept of negativity has no meaning outside of the signed integer representation, but the negative flag has uses outside signed arithmetic. Since N = 1 when the MSB of a result is one, and N = 0 when the MSB of a result is zero, the N flag allows us easily to test whether the MSB of a location is set or not. This has particular uses in monitoring input from an external device. In this context,

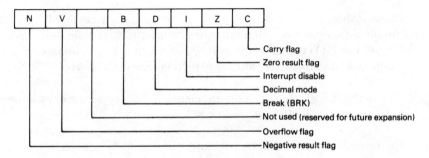

Figure 4.1: Processor Status Register

it is often used with the BIT instruction, which we will consider in chapter 9.

The Z flag is set to one whenever the result of any arithmetic or logical operation is zero. It is also set to one if data moved into the accumulator is zero (and if data moved into the X or Y registers is zero, as we shall see in chapter 5). Thus the Z flag is affected by exactly the same operations as the N flag, but it reflects a result of zero rather than an MSB of one.

One particular use of the N, V, Z and C flags is in the monitoring of branching within the microprocessor, and this is the concern of this chapter.

4.2 Decision-making Using the Microprocessor

You will know from your work with BASIC that the real power of a computer lies in its ability to take simple decisions. This is the conditional IF...THEN jump in BASIC; what corresponds to it in assembly language? The general concept involved is one of *branching*.

Usually, the program counter moves consecutively through a portion of memory. However, there is a series of instructions which cause it to stop doing this and instead to jump forward or backward by a certain amount if a particular flag is set or clear. These instructions are called the branch instructions, and all their mnemonics have a first letter of B, for 'branch'. Here they are

BEQ	branch if	$Z = 1$ (result EQual to zero)
BNE	branch if	$Z = 0$ (result Not Equal to zero)
BMI	branch if	$N = 1$ (data MInus; MSB $= 1$)
BPL	branch if	$N = 0$ (data PLus; MSB $= 0$)
BCS	branch if	$C = 1$ (Carry Set)
BCC	branch if	$C = 0$ (Carry Clear)
BVS	branch if	$V = 1$ (oVerflow Set)
BVC	branch if	$V = 0$ (oVerflow Clear)

These instructions are all *conditional*: the branch occurs only if the condition is true (that is, if the relevant flag has the state indicated). You will recall the GOTO statement in BASIC, which is *unconditional*, since the jump is always made. A similar instruction exists in assembly language

JMP   jump to a new location in memory and commence program execution from there

The program counter has its contents replaced by a new address, and this, in effect, causes a jump to a new section of the program.

Clearly all the above instructions need an operand: they all need to have attached a reference which points to the location where the branch or jump should go. In BASIC this is done by using line numbers: in assembly language, the corresponding concept is the *label*. We have already met this idea in chapter 2 with .START: this label marked the beginning of the program since it was put next to the very first instruction. You will recall that a label can be any BASIC variable, but that it must begin with a dot. It is very useful to make these labels as meaningful as possible (.START is better than .X2Y96T, though both would serve the same purpose).

The best way to illustrate the concept of branching and of labels is to see how we can translate simple BASIC statements into assembly language.

4.3 The Assembly Language Equivalents of some BASIC Conditional Statements. I: Use of the N and Z Flags

(a) IF NUM = 0 THEN GOTO 50

```
           LDA   NUM
           BEQ   ZERO
                  .
                  .
                  .
                  .
.ZERO             .
                  .
                  .
                  .
```

There are a number of points to make here. Notice first the way the label, ZERO, is put in the first column; the second column contains the instruction and the third the operand. This is a standard way to write down assembly language programs. Notice next that the dot in front of the label is necessary only if the label is put in the first column; when ZERO is an operand (as it is in BEQ ZERO) the dot is not required. As we will see later, the dot is used by the BBC Micro to differentiate labels from instructions; it is not a standard requirement of assemblers. Indeed, very few assemblers use this convention. For this reason, unless we are displaying a program that is to be typed directly into the microcomputer, we will not include the dot notation either. We shall have more to say about this in section 4.6.

Notice the choice of label here: ZERO is a meaningful choice since the branch is made only if the result is zero. Again, any legal label will do, but we should try to find labels that indicate to us what is going on. The program works as follows: we load the contents of the location with address NUM into the accumulator. BEQ ZERO looks at the Z flag and branches to the line with the label ZERO if $Z = 1$. If $Z = 0$, the branch is not made and the next instruction is obeyed as usual. Thus this assembly program does exactly the same as the BASIC statement.

In the program shown, the line labelled ZERO is further down in memory than the branching instruction, but this is not essential. Branches can occur backward as well as forward. In that case the program would be

```
ZERO            .
                .
                .
                .
                .
                LDA   NUM
                BEQ   ZERO
```

(b) IF NUM <> 0 THEN GOTO 50

```
                LDA   NUM
                BNE   NTZERO
                .
                .
                .
                .
NTZERO          .
```

Here a branch is made to the line labelled NTZERO if $Z = 0$ (that is, if (NUM) $\neq 0$). Again the labelled line could be earlier rather than later than the branching instruction: this is true of all the branching instructions, in fact. Notice again the use of the meaningful label. Remember that in some assemblers labels are confined to a length of six symbols, but the BBC Micro allows us to use labels of whatever length we like.

(c) IF NUM < 0 THEN GOTO 50

```
                LDA   NUM
                BMI   NEGATIVE
                .
                .
                .
                .
NEGATIVE        .
```

This assumes, of course, that we are working with the signed integer representation, otherwise it would not make sense to test for a number to be less than zero. This and the next two examples are valid only if numbers are in signed integer format.

(d) IF NUM >= 0 THEN GOTO 50

```
                LDA   NUM
                BPL   GTEQUAL
                        .
                        .
                        .
                        .
    GTEQUAL             .
```

(e) IF NUM > 0 THEN GOTO 50

```
                LDA   NUM
                BEQ   ZERO
                BPL   POSITIVE
    ZERO                .
                        .
                        .
                        .
                        .
    POSITIVE            .
```

In (d) we note that if a number is zero or positive, then $N = 0$, and so BPL will result in a branch if (NUM) is greater than or equal to zero. If we want the branch to occur only if (NUM) is greater than zero, as here, we must first eliminate the case when (NUM) equals zero. This is the function of BEQ ZERO. If we get through to BPL POSITIVE then either (NUM) is more than zero or less than zero. If the former, then the branch to the line labelled POSITIVE will occur; otherwise the next instruction will be performed and this, of course, is the one labelled ZERO. Hence the set of instructions beginning with the line labelled POSITIVE is performed if (NUM) > 0; in all other cases, the set of instructions beginning with the line labelled ZERO is performed.

(f) IF NUM = 0 THEN NUM = 1

```
                LDA   NUM
                BNE   NTZERO
                LDA   #1
                STA   NUM
    NTZERO    _____
```

Many IF...THEN statements in BASIC do not involve jumps at all. In assembly language, however, conditional statements must always be effected by a branch, as here. The most economical way to encode this is to branch to what is in effect the next statement (at NTZERO) if (NUM) $\neq 0$. Then, if no branch occurs (NUM) must be zero, and then the second part of the conditional statement is enacted. Here is another example.

(g) IF NUM < 0 THEN NUM = −NUM

```
              LDA   NUM
              BPL   NTMINUS
              EOR   #&FF
              CLC
              ADC   #1
              STA   NUM
NTMINUS       _____
```

(h) IF NUM = 0 THEN NUM1 = 3: NUM2 = 4 ELSE NUM1 = 4: NUM2 = 3

```
              LDA   NUM
              BNE   NTZERO
              LDA   #3
              STA   NUM1
              LDA   #4
              STA   NUM2
              JMP   OVER
NTZERO        LDA   #4
              STA   NUM1
              LDA   #3
              STA   NUM2
OVER          _____
```

An IF...THEN...ELSE structure in BASIC can be accommodated in assembly language only by using an unconditional jump, for this separates the THEN... from the ELSE... . Some authorities on assembly language dislike the use of the JMP instruction and prefer if possible to replace it by a branch instruction that always branches. In the example here BNE OVER would do that, since the accumulator always contains &04 which is non-zero. They have two reasons for doing this: firstly, as we shall see later in this chapter, the branch saves a byte of storage (though it executes no quicker); secondly, as we shall also see later, the branch is intrinsically relocatable, in that its addressing mode is relative, whereas the jump uses an absolute address.

These points are valid, but must be offset against the unnaturalness of the coding. Using such 'tricks' as these needs very careful documentation, otherwise disasters occur. If we use the coding as a model and then try to implement IF NUM = 0 THEN NUM1 = 3: NUM2 = 0... , the branch will not work.

Exercise 4.1

Encode these BASIC statements using assembly language with suitable labels (in all the questions (NUM1) and (NUM2) occupy single byte locations—in 1 assume signed integer representation).

1. IF NUM1 + NUM2 > 0 THEN GOTO 50.

2. IF NUM1 − NUM2 <> 0 THEN NUM3 = NUM2: NUM2 = NUM1: NUM1 = NUM3.

3. IF NUM1 + NUM2 > 255 THEN SUM = 0 ELSE SUM = NUM1 + NUM2.

4.4 The Assembly Language Equivalents of Some BASIC Conditional Statements. II: Use of CMP Instruction

(a) IF NUM1 = 2 THEN GOTO 50

Here is the way to encode this using the instructions learnt so far

```
        LDA   NUM1
        SEC
        SBC   #2
        BEQ   EQUAL
          .
          .
          .
          .
EQUAL     .
```

This coding is fine if we do actually want to reduce (NUM1) by 2. But if our sole aim is to *compare* (NUM1) to 2 then putting the result of subtracting 2 into the accumulator, as we have done here, is a waste of time. What we require is an instruction that will do the subtraction and set the appropriate flags *without* affecting the accumulator. This is the function of the CMP instruction. The coding using CMP is

```
            LDA    NUM1
            CMP    #2
            BEQ    EQUAL
                    .
                    .
                    ..
                    .
EQUAL               .
```

This is much neater and leaves (NUM1), unaffected, in the accumulator. Notice that we do not need SEC here: CMP will set carry automatically before doing the subtraction.

(b) IF NUM1 >= 6 THEN GOTO 50

Without the CMP instruction we would need to subtract 6 and see if the result were greater than or equal to zero. Using CMP, we can do the subtraction and affect the appropriate flags without having the subtraction contaminate the accumulator. We have

```
            LDA    NUM1
            CMP    #6
            BCS    GTEQUAL
                    .
                    .
                    .
                    .
GTEQUAL             .
```

CMP #6 subtracts 6 from the accumulator, sets the relevant flags and then *throws away the result of the subtraction:* the contents of NUM1 are still in the accumulator, quite unaffected.

You may be wondering why we have not used BPL GTEQUAL here as we did in (d) of section 4.3. To understand this, suppose that (NUM1) = 135. We take away 6 and get 129, which is &81. The MSB is one and therefore the result is negative! BPL can be used to test only if bit 7 of some data is zero; in a few cases, like 4.3(d), this can be interpreted as testing if a result is positive, but in most cases it cannot be used like this. Generally speaking, *do not use BPL or BMI with the result of a CMP instruction: use BCS and BCC instead.*

To understand why BCS works here, recall what happens to the carry flag when we subtract. If no borrow has occurred, C will equal one (that is, carry will be set); if a borrow has occurred C will equal zero (that is, carry will be clear). In the former case, the number subtracted cannot be greater than the number it is subtracted from. So we have

BCS   Branch if result greater than or equal to zero

BCC   Branch if result less than zero.

This is not all that easy to remember, and the particular mnemonic I use for BCC is 'Branch if result of Comparison a Complement'. This reminds me that BCC branches only if the result is negative; by extension, BCS branches in all other cases.

(c) IF NUM < 35 THEN GOTO 50

```
        LDA     NUM
        CMP     #35
        BCC     LESS
                .
                .
                .
                .
LESS            .
```

Here the branch occurs if (NUM) − 35 is negative, that is, if NUM < 35. Equality will not give a branch.

(d) IF NUM >= −6 THEN GOTO 50

```
        LDA     NUM
        BPL     GTEQUAL
        CMP     #&FA
        BCS     GTEQUAL     (or BPL GTEQUAL)
                .
                .
                .
                .
GTEQUAL         .
```

We suppose here, of course, that NUM is to be interpreted as a signed byte. We check first if NUM is positive or zero with BPL. If not, then we make the comparison with −6, which is encoded of course as &FA (the BBC Micro's assembler will not allow CMP #−6). Hence &FF to &FA will give the branch (the result is 5 to 0) and &F9 to &80 will not (these give −1 to −122).

Notice that

```
        LDA     NUM
        CMP     #&FA
        BPL     GTEQUAL
```

will not work. Consider for example NUM = 122, which results in &80 or −128.

(e) IF NUM1 > NUM2 THEN GOTO 50

```
                    LDA   NUM1
                    CMP   NUM2
                    BEQ   EQUAL
                    BCS   GREATER
        EQUAL             .
                          .
                          .

                          .

        GREATER           .
```

The logic of this is similar to 4.3(e). Notice that we are not restricted to the immediate addressing mode with CMP (although it is often used like this in practice). In fact, CMP uses most of the addressing modes available (of which we have so far met Absolute and Zero Page—clearly Implied is not applicable). In the case here, the contents of NUM2 are subtracted from the accumulator, the result being thrown away.

It may help to summarise the cases following a CMP.

Branch if	Instruction	Suggested label	(followed by: Instruction	label)
Acc < memory	BCC	LESS		
Acc ≤ memory	BEQ	LESSEQ ;	BCC	LESSEQ
Acc = memory	BEQ	EQUAL		
Acc ≠ memory	BNE	NTEQUAL		
Acc ≥ memory	BCS	GTEQUAL		
Acc > memory	BEQ	EQUAL ;	BCS	GREATER

Exercise 4.2

Encode these BASIC statements into assembly language.

1. IF NUM > 15 THEN NUM = 0.

2. IF NUM <= −10 THEN INDIC = NUM ELSE NUM = 0: INDIC = 1.

3. IF NUM1 = NUM2 THEN NUM2 =NUM3 ELSE IF NUM4 > 16 THEN NUM2 = NUM4 ELSE NUM2 = 0: NUM4 = 0.

4.5 Comparing Numbers Greater Than 255

Consider first how we can test if (NUM1H; NUM1L) = (NUM2H; NUM2L). Here is the assembly code

```
              LDA   NUM1L
              CMP   NUM2L
              BNE   NTEQUAL
              LDA   NUM1H
              CMP   NUM2H
              BEQ   EQUAL
NTEQUAL             .
                    .
                    .
                    .
                    .
                    .
                    .
                    .
   EQUAL            .
```

The idea here is to establish first whether the lower bytes are equal: if they are not, then we can jump straight to NTEQUAL. If they are, we compare the higher bytes, and if they are equal, then both two-byte numbers are equal.

Consider now how we test for (NUM1H; NUM1L) ≥ (NUM2H; NUM2L). The easiest way to do this is to perform a subtraction and see if the result is non-negative. The coding for this is straightforward.

```
              LDA   NUM1L
              SEC
              SBC   NUM2L
              LDA   NUM1H
              SBC   NUM2H
              BCS   GTEQUAL
                    .
                    .
                    .
                    .
   GTEQUAL          .
```

The idea here is that if no borrow is required when subtracting the high bytes (that is, if C = 1 after this subtraction), then the first two-byte number must be at least as large as the second one. Notice that any borrow required from subtracting the low bytes is 'paid back' automatically in the second SBC instruction.

Now, an inspection of this code points to a way of shortening it. All we use from the first three lines is the carry flag: if set to one, there is no borrow, if zero, there is a borrow. We are not interested in the result of the subtraction. So we can replace the first three lines by two, involving CMP as follows

```
                    LDA    NUM1L
                    CMP    NUM2L
                    LDA    NUM1H
                    SBC    NUM2H
                    BCS    GTEQUAL
                             .
                             .
                             .
                             .
    GTEQUAL                  .
```

The carry flag is affected in just the same way, but we save a line since we do not need to set carry initially with SEC when using CMP.

Consider finally how to test for (NUM1H; NUM1L) > (NUM2H;NUM2L). This may seem identical to the previous case, but a little reflection will show you why it is not. In the last piece of coding we have no way of deciding whether the numbers are indeed equal. It does not suffice to know that the high byte difference is zero, since this would occur with, for example, &1A86–&1A52 and with &5C49–&5BA3.

Can we in some way combine the first two tests economically? Clearly if we compare the lower two bytes and they are not equal then we cannot have equality. So let us focus on the case when the lower bytes are equal. Consider (a) &149A–&139A and (b) &149A–&149A. Now in (a), if we pretended that there was a borrow from the lower byte subtraction, then the result of the higher byte subtraction would still be non-negative, whereas in (b) it would be negative. This provides the clue: if the lower bytes are equal we shall engineer a borrow before subtracting the higher bytes. Here is the coding

```
                    LDA    NUM1L
                    CMP    NUM2L
                    BNE    NTEQUAL
                    CLC
    NTEQUAL         LDA    NUM1H
                    SBC    NUM2H
```

              BCS   GREATER
                       .
                       .
                       .
                       .
    GREATER   .

CLC at line 4 engineers the borrow we require.

Exercise 4.3

Encode into assembly language, tests for

1. (NUM1H; NUM1L) < (NUM2H; NUM2L)

2. (NUM1H; NUM1L) ≤ :NUM2H; NUM2L).

3. (NUM1(3); NUM1(2); NUM1(1); NUM1(0)) ≥ (NUM2(3); NUM2(2); NUM2(1); NUM2(0)).

4. Can you find an economical way to test if (NUM(3); NUM(2); NUM(1); NUM(0)) = 0? (*Hint*: Use ORA).

4.6 Typing Assembly Language Programs with Labels into the BBC Micro

Listing 4.1 illustrates how to put labelled assembly programs into the BBC Micro. There are a number of new features here. First notice that the whole program from line 30 to 90 is assembled twice. On the first *pass*, as it is usually called, we use OPT0: this suppresses both listing and errors. On the second pass, we use OPT3 which gives both the listing and the errors. The reason why we suppress the errors on the first pass is because an error is bound to happen. When the assembler gets to line 50, it does not know what value to give to the label ZERO because it has not met it yet; ZERO does not appear until line 80. Therefore, it treats this as an undefined label error and leaves it unassigned. On the second pass, however, it has already met ZERO (in line 80 on the first pass) and can therefore assign a value to it. This two-pass idea must always be used if there are forward references in a program. A forward reference is the use of the label as an operand in a branch or jump instruction that has not yet been met: that is, the branch or jump is to a higher line number.

Listing 4.1

```
10 NUM=&70:DIM START 50
20 FOR I%=0 TO 3 STEP3:P%=START
30    [OPTI%
40    LDA NUM
50    BEQ ZERO
60    ADC #5
70    STA NUM
80    .ZERO
90    RTS:JNEXTI%
```

When we have to make two passes we need to change the way we allocate memory using the DIM statement. We cannot use DIM P% as before, because on the second pass a new set of memory locations will be allocated. What we require to happen is that the translation from the second pass goes into the same locations as those from the first pass. If this does not happen, the values of the labels from the first pass will not apply to the second. To ensure this, we give the address of the first location to the variable START using DIM START. Now, on both passes P% = START will put the start of the machine code in the same place. This method also dispenses with the need to use a label .START to mark the beginning of the program.

Listing 4.2 shows that two passes are not always required when using branches and jumps. Here, the branch at line 80 is defined on the first pass since BACK is defined in line 50. However, in more complex programs involving labels it is sometimes tedious to ascertain whether or not forward references are made. It does no harm, therefore, to use the two-pass method in listing 4.1 if in doubt, even if it turns out that two passes were not in fact necessary. You can discover if two passes are necessary by using FOR I% = 1 TO 3 STEP 2 and seeing if all labels are assigned on the first pass (OPT1 gives a listing but suppresses errors).

Listing 4.2

```
10 NUM=&70:DIM START 50
20 P%=START
30 [OPT3
40 LDA NUM
50 .BACK
60 ADC #5
70 CMP #200
80 BCC BACK
90 RTS:]
```

Notice that in both listings 4.1 and 4.2 the coding is not arranged in three columns. Thus if a label is used it is put in a line on its own, as in line 80 of 4.1. This is why a dot is required for column one labels on the BBC Micro, for otherwise the assembler could not differentiate between a label and a mnemonic. It is possible to put the label on the same line as the instruction (for example, .NOOVFLOW BPL NTNEG) but if we do this the column structure is destroyed and readability greatly impaired. We could preserve columns by indenting all the other lines by 10 spaces, but this would be exceptionally tedious. Hence, putting column one labels on single lines is the best solution, since it preserves columns two and three. This method is unique to the BBC Micro's assembler: other assemblers will allow simple formatting into three columns. But the advantage with the BBC Micro is that labels are of unrestricted length, a feature missing from most assemblers. Programs on paper should still be written in three columns, but when typed into the computer the two column format with column one labels on a single line should be used.

One final point. It is possible to use multi-line statements if required. For example, we could compress listing 4.1 into listing 4.3 if we liked. There are two problems with this: firstly, editing is more difficult; and secondly, the program is harder to read since the column structure is lost. It is a matter of preference, but in this book listings will use single line statements most of the time.

Listing 4.3

```
10 NUM=&70:DIM START 50
20 FOR I%=0 TO 3 STEP 3:P%=START
30   [OPTI%:LDA NUM:BEQ ZERO:ADC #5:STA NUM:.ZERO
     RTS:]NEXTI%
```

4.7 Relative Addressing

Look again at the assembly listing for listing 4.1, and focus in particular on the machine code translation of line 50. It is F0 04. F0 is the op code for BEQ, but what does the operand, 04, mean?

The mode of addressing used here is called *relative addressing*. The branch is made to an instruction located 4 bytes further on from that pointed to by the present contents of the program counter. That is, if Z = 1, four is added to the contents of the program counter, and this achieves the branch. Figure 4.2 shows this in more detail. The top location represents the beginning of the program, whose address is &0E93 the value of START, and so the PC is set initially to &0E93. The microprocessor thus loads the accumulator with the contents of location &70 and the PC is now set at &0E95. Now the next byte, F0, is fetched and decoded as a BEQ instruction; meanwhile the next byte is fetched, 04, and this is understood as the displacement if the branch occurs. At this stage the PC is at &0E97, the address of the next instruction (ADC). Hence, if the branch occurs, the displacement is added to the address of the next instruction. This is quite complicated to work out, and if we had to do it mistakes would

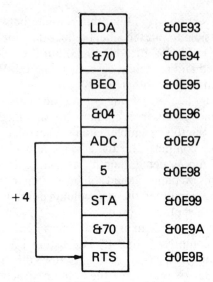

Figure 4.2: A forward branch

be common. Fortunately, the assembler allows us to use labels and it does the calculations for us.

Look now at the assembly listing for listing 4.2, and focus on line 80. The translation is 90 FA. 90 is the op code for BCC, and FA is interpreted as a signed integer, that is, as −6. So if the branch occurs (that is, if C = 0), 6 is taken from the contents of the PC. Figure 4.3 shows the details.

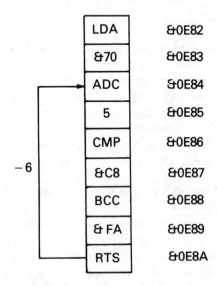

Figure 4.3: A backward branch

Hence the displacement to be added to the contents of the PC is always understood as a signed integer. This means that the maximum forward branch that can be made is +127 from the instruction after the branch, that is, +129 from the branch instruction itself. Similarly, the maximum backward branch is −128 from the instruction after the branch, that is, −126 from the branch instruction itself. Figure 4.4 shows this diagrammatically.

If we try to make a branch beyond this, the assembler will give us a 'branch out of range' error. Now most of our branches will be within this range, but what happens if we wish to go beyond it? Suppose that in line 50 of listing 4.1 the label ZERO refers to an address more than 129 from &0E95, the address of the BEQ instruction. We can recode it thus

```
          BNE    NOJUMP
          JMP    ZERO
NOJUMP
```

Similarly in line 70 of listing 4.2, if the branch is out of range we can recode

```
          8CS    NOJUMP
          JMP    BACK
```

Hence we solve the problem by *not* branching if the condition we require holds and then jumping to the desired place.

This solution is not ideal since it uses 5 bytes of storage instead of two, but it should not be required too often. We could in fact try to do it in four bytes by having as the original branch, BEQ PIVOT in listing 4.1, where

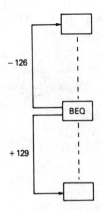

Figure 4.4: The maximum range for a branch

PIVOT is an intermediate point where a BEQ ZERO is located, ZERO being the final destination. This will work if the branch is within 256 bytes. The first solution, however, is universally applicable and does not require us to insert extra lines at points relatively isolated from the flow of the program. Hence, from a general point of view, the first solution is to be preferred. Nevertheless, the second solution has the merit of being relocatable, and for stand-alone machine code programs this might be important. Which solution we use depends on our needs at the particular time. (Relocatability is discussed in more detail in chapter 9.)

Relative addressing is justified because most branches *are* short and the two-byte instruction which relative addressing allows results in an improvement in speed and a reduction in program size. The reason for the term 'relative' should be obvious now. A branch is made x bytes relative to the present position of the program counter. Hence x is added to or subtracted from the PC. By contrast, the addressing mode of JMP is absolute: the contents of the PC are replaced by the operand of JMP. Notice again how the address is stored in the form low byte, high byte in the operand. This is not so confusing if you remember that the second storage location is higher than the first in memory. We are most fortunate though that we have an assembler that sorts all this out for us, relieving our memories of unnecessary burdens.

4.8 Using Branching in the Addition and Subtraction of Unsigned Numbers: INC and DEC

Let us first introduce two new instructions: INC and DEC. INC MEMLOC takes the contents of MEMLOC, adds one to it, and stores the result in MEMLOC. If (MEMLOC) = 255, INC MEMLOC produces 0 in MEMLOC. DEC MEMLOC takes the contents of MEMLOC, subtracts one from it and stores the result in MEMLOC. If (MEMLOC) = 0, DEC MEMLOC produces 255 in MEMLOC. The mnemonic INC stands for INCrement and DEC for DECrement.

Now armed with these two new instructions let us reconsider the coding that we used in listing 3.1 to add two single byte numbers together when the result may exceed 255. Here is an alternative using INC and a branch

```
            LDA    #0
            STA    SUMH
            LDA    NUM1
            CLC
            ADC    NUM2
            STA    SUML
            BCC    NOCARRY
            INC    SUMH
NOCARRY
```

The idea is that if there is no carry, C = 0 and a branch occurs to line NOCARRY. Otherwise SUMH is incremented by 1. Now a comparison of the assembled forms of these two programs will show that we have saved one byte (type this one in in the same way as listing 3.1 but with a two-pass assembly and check). But we do better still if we wish to encode the sum

$$(NUM1H; NUM1L) + (NUM2) \rightarrow NUM1H; NUM1L$$

Using the ideas in section 3.3 we obtain this program

```
LDA    NUM1L
CLC
ADC    NUM2
STA    NUM1L
LDA    #0
ADC    NUM1H
STA    NUM1H
```

Using the new ideas here, we have instead

```
         LDA    NUM1L
         CLC
         ADC    NUM2
         STA    NUM1L
         BCC    NOCARRY
         INC    NUM1H
NOCARRY  _____
```

a saving now of three bytes (type in both programs and check). We also, on average, save time in execution using this second method.

Exercise 4.4

Encode (NUM1H; NUM1L) − (NUM2) → NUM1H; NUM1L into assembly language (a) using similar ideas to section 3.6, and (b) using DEC and a branch. How many bytes are saved using (b)?

4.9 Monitoring Problems of Sign Using Branching
(this section can be omitted on first reading)

Consider the simple BASIC statement LET DIFF = NUM1 − NUM2 where NUM1 and NUM2 are positive integers less than 255. In assembly code we have, of course

```
            LDA   NUM1
            SEC
            SBC   NUM2
            STA   DIFF
```

But is this really correct? What happens if (NUM1) < (NUM2)? Clearly we should get a negative result, and to accommodate this we need to treat DIFF as a signed integer. We need to take remedial action, however, if the range falls outside −128 to 127. The first thing that we need to do is to assign two bytes for the difference, DIFFH, DIFFL, where (DIFFH; DIFFL) is considered a signed integer giving us a range now of −32768 to +32767, which is easily enough for our purposes.

Now there is no problem if NUM1 ⩾ NUM2; we store the result in &00; DIFFL, which is positive. What happens if NUM1 < NUM2? Let us consider an example: &83 − &C8. This gives &BB, which is to be interpreted as −69. −69 using two-byte signed integer precision is &FFBB (since &FFBB + &45 = (1)0000, and &45 is 69). It follows that the result is stored as &FF; DIFFL.

It should be clear now that the following coding will do the trick

```
            LDA   #0
            STA   DIFFH
            LDA   NUM1
            SEC
            SBC   NUM2
            STA   DIFFL
            BCS   NTNEG
            DEC   DIFFH
    NTNEG   _____
```

This is very similar to the coding of the answer to exercise 4.4. This sort of similarity is what makes the two's complement representation so useful.

Consider again the BASIC statement with which we began, but suppose now that NUM1 and NUM2 can be signed integers. If NUM1 and NUM2 have the same sign, then there is no overflow. If they were always the same sign we would, in fact, need only one byte to store the answer. This is not always the case if the signs do not agree, however. Consider 52 − (−92): here we will get overflow, since the answer will be &90 which is negative in single-byte precision signed integer.

We need something similar to the solution above. The flag that we need to monitor is the overflow flag. If this is not set, the sign of the answer is given by the MSB of the answer; if it is set, the sign of the answer is given by the opposite of the MSB of the answer.

Listing 4.4

```
 10 NUM1=&70:NUM2=&71:DIFFL=&72:DIFFH=&73:?&74=0:?&75=0
 20 DIM START 50
 30 FOR I%=0 TO 2 STEP 2:P%=START
 40    [OPTI%
 50    LDA #0
 60    STA DIFFH
 70    LDA NUM1
 80    SEC
 90    SBC NUM2
100    STA DIFFL
110    BVC NOOVFLOW
120    EOR #&80
130    .NOOVFLOW
140    BPL NTNEG
150    DEC DIFFH
160    .NTNEG
170    RTS:]NEXTI%
180 REPEAT
190    INPUT"First number",X:IFX<0 THEN X=256+X
200    INPUT"Second number",Y:IFY<0 THEN Y=256+Y
210    ?NUM1=X:?NUM2=Y:CALLSTART
220    PRINT~?DIFFH,~?DIFFL;
221    ANS%=!DIFFL
222    IFANS%>&7FFF THEN ANS%=ANS%-&10000
223    PRINTANS%
230    UNTIL FALSE
```

The coding is in listing 4.4. Notice that in line 30 we use I% = 0 and 2 giving us OPT0 and OPT2 in line 40. This suppresses the assembly translation listing completely and results in much quicker assembly. Unless we are specifically interested in seeing the translation, we should use this formulation, and we will do so from now on in this book.

EOR #&80 in line 120 reverses the MSB of the result if overflow has occurred. Notice here that we use BPL and not BCS: the carry flag has no meaning in single-byte precision signed arithmetic.

Put this program in your computer and test it with the following pairs of values for NUM1 and NUM2: -85, -18; -85, -110; -85, 30; -85, 60; 50, 20; 50, 80; 50, -30; 50, -80. Confirm that the results you get for (DIFFH) and (DIFFL) are correct.

Exercise 4.5

1. Encode the BASIC statement IF (NUM1 $-$ NUM2) > NUM3 THEN GOTO 50 where all are unsigned integers.

2. Write the assembly code to perform

(NUM1H; NUM1L) − (NUM2H; NUM2L) → DIFF2; DIFF1; DIFF0

where the first two numbers are to be considered as unsigned integers but where (DIFF2; DIFF1; DIFF0) is a triple-precision signed integer.

3. Write the assembly code equivalent to LET NUM = NUM1 + NUM2 where NUM1 and NUM2 are integers between −128 and 127.

4. Repeat question 2 if the first two numbers are to be considered as signed integers.

5. Write the assembly code to perform

(NUM1H; NUM1M; NUM1L) − (NUM2H; NUM2L) → NUM1H; NUM1M; NUM1L

where the first number is a negative integer but the second is not signed. Include a check for overflow.

6. Repeat question 3 if NUM1 and NUM2 are integers between −32768 and 32767 whose sum may lie outside this range without an error being signalled.

7. Write the coding to branch if NUM1 ≥ NUM2 where both are signed integers.

8. Repeat question 1 if NUM1 and NUM2 can be signed integers, but where NUM3 remains unsigned.

9. Repeat question 1 if all the numbers are signed integers.

10. Repeat question 7 if the numbers are each two-byte signed integers.

5 Loop Structure in Assembly Language

5.1 Loop Structures

BBC BASIC has two loop structures: the FOR...NEXT loop and the REPEAT...UNTIL loop. These structures are essential components of most realistic programs in BASIC, and the same is true of assembly language. However, in assembly language the structures do not come ready made as in BASIC, so we need to develop methods of building them up from the component instructions available. In doing this, we will also create a third important structure, regrettably missing in BBC BASIC: this structure we will term the REPEAT WHILE loop. The difference between REPEAT...UNTIL and REPEAT WHILE is that the former will always be executed at least once, since the exit is at the end; the latter need not be executed at all, since the exit is at the beginning.

The most important instructions needed to create loop structures in 6502 assembly language are connected with the X and Y registers, and to these we now turn.

5.2 Index Registers: Some New Instructions

There are two further registers in the 6502 microprocessor which can act as temporary storage locations of data: the X register and the Y register. Their relationship to the rest of the architecture can be seen in the diagram in appendix 2.

Data can be loaded into them from memory: the mnemonics are LDX and LDY. Data can be stored from them into memory: the mnemonics are STX and STY. There are also instructions identical in operation to CMP: CPX M compares the contents of X with (M) and sets the appropriate flags; similarly for CPY M.

A very important feature of the registers is that they can be incremented and decremented directly: the mnemonics are INX, INY, DEX and DEY. These are one-byte instructions utilising implied addressing and so they save space over a corresponding INC M or DEC M instruction (which is at least two bytes long). More importantly, they operate at least 2½ times as fast as the corresponding INC M and DEC M operations. This is very telling in loops, as we shall see.

59

No arithmetic or logical operations can take place on the X and Y registers: there is no equivalent to ADC, SBC, ORA, EOR or AND. Hence to add a number to X or Y we must first transfer X or Y to the accumulator, perform the addition or subtraction, and then transfer back. For this reason, there are special instructions allowing us to make these transfers: the mnemonics are TXA (transfer contents of X to A), TYA, TAX (transfer contents of A to X) and TAY. All are one-byte instructions.

5.3 The Assembly Language Equivalent of a FOR...NEXT Loop

(a) FOR X = 1 TO 40 .... NEXT

How can we implement this structure in assembly language? Here is the coding

```
               LDX   #1
     LOOP      .
               .
               .
               .
               .
               INX
               CPX   #41
               BNE   LOOP
```

We begin by setting the X register to 1. Then the first cycle of the loop is performed; that is, any instructions down to INX will be obeyed. On reaching INX, X is incremented and compared to 41; if the result is not zero the next cycle of the loop will be performed. Altogether there will be 40 cycles through the loop, and you should convince yourself of this.

(b) FOR X = 40 to 1 STEP −1. .... NEXT

This is more complicated in BASIC but easier in assembly language

```
               LDX   #40
     LOOP      .
               .
               .
               .
               .
               DEX
               BNE   LOOP
```

There is a saving of two bytes and a corresponding saving of time. This is because the decrement operation affects the Z flag (so too does the increment operation—as X or Y passes from 255 to 0 again—and both operations also affect the N flag). Hence there is no need for a CPX #0 after DEX.

Saving time is much more important in loops than in parts of a program that will be performed only once. If possible, then, we should try to organise our loops to count backward as here, rather than forward as in (a). And we should always use the X (or Y) register as the loop counter, since INX and DEX operate very much more quickly than INC and DEC.

(c) FOR X = 0 TO NUM.........NEXT

```
              LDX   #0
      LOOP    .
              .
              .
              .

              .
              INX
              BEQ   OUT
              CPX   NUM
              BCC   LOOP
              BEQ   LOOP
      OUT
```

Here X is compared with NUM, and the loop is performed if X is less than NUM (checked by BCC LOOP). This will give (NUM) cycles of the loop, and one more is gained when X equals (NUM) (checked by BEQ LOOP). Notice that we do not use BMI LOOP, tempting though it may be: if (NUM) is 130 or more, the loop would be performed only once! Finally, the purpose of BEQ OUT: without it, if (NUM) = 255, the loop would cycle indefinitely.

(d) FOR X = NUM TO 0 STEP −1.........NEXT

As before, this is more efficient than the forward loop, but for a different reason.

```
              LDX   NUM
      LOOP    .
              .
              .
              .

              .
              DEX
              CPX   #&FF
              BNE   LOOP
```

This time we still need a CPX, but we cannot use CPX #0: BCS LOOP since this will give us an infinite loop! Again, trying to do without the CPX and writing just BNE LOOP will miss out the last cycle of the loop (when X = 0). Hence we need to compare X to one less than zero, that is, &FF. But we save two bytes by needing only one test instead of two.

You might be wondering why we *cannot* write

```
          LDX   NUM
LOOP       .
           .
           .
           .
           .
          DEX
          BPL   LOOP
```

since DEX affects the N flag, and so save ourselves two more bytes. The problem is similar to that discussed in (c): if NUM is greater than 128, the loop will be performed only once.

Comparing the programs in (b) and (d) we see that it is more efficient to count down to 1 than to zero. Hence, if we can, we should try to organise our loop to count backward to 1 rather than to zero.

(e) FOR X = NUM1 to NUM2.........NEXT

If we assume NUM2 ⩾ NUM1 we can write

```
          LDX   NUM1
LOOP       .
           .
           .
           .
          INX
          BEQ   OUT
          CPX   NUM2
          BCC   LOOP
          BEQ   LOOP
OUT
```

What happens here if NUM1 < NUM2? Clearly, the loop is performed once. Most BASICs, including BBC BASIC, operate their FOR ... NEXT loops like this.

(f) FOR X = NUM1 to NUM2 STEP NUM3.........NEXT

```
                LDX    NUM1
LOOP            .
                .
                .
                .

                .

                TXA
                CLC
                ADC    NUM3
                TAX
                BCS    OUT
                CMP    NUM2
                BCC    LOOP
                BEQ    LOOP
OUT
```

To add on (NUM3) we need to transfer X to the accumulator (TXA), perform the addition and transfer back (TAX). We can now use CPX NUM2 or CMP NUM2, it does not matter. The statement BCS OUT guards against a case like FOR X = 6 TO 251 STEP 5, where X returns to zero before it can exceed 251.

Note that all of (a) to (f) will work equally well if Y replaces X.

Exercise 5.1

1. Will the programs in (e) and (f) need any amendment if we interpret the numbers as signed integers (that is, NUM1, NUM2 and NUM3 lie between -128 and 127)?

2. Assuming that we are dealing with unsigned integers write in assembly language

    (a) FOR X = NUM2 TO NUM1 STEP -1.........NEXT
    (b) FOR X = NUM2 TO NUM1 STEP $-$(NUM3).........NEXT

Take care if NUM1 = 0 in (a), and guard against something similar to 5.3(f) in (b).

3. Amend the program in 5.3(f) in line with the suggestions in the answer to question 1 if the numbers are signed integers.

5.4 FOR...NEXT Loops of More than 256 Cycles

(a) FOR N = 1 to 1000.........NEXT

To implement this in assembly language we need to use both the X and the Y counters. In general we choose for X the largest whole number less than 257 that will divide into the cycle count. Here we take 250 for X and 4 for Y as follows

```
                LDY   #0
LOOP1           LDX   #1
LOOP2            ·
                 ·
                 ·
                 ·
                 ·
                INX
                CPX   #251
                BNE   LOOP2
                INY
                CPY   #4
                BNE   LOOP1
```

The inner loop, LOOP2 to BNE LOOP2 is performed 250 times for each of the four values of Y (0, 1, 2 and 3).

To obtain the value of N, contained in two bytes of course, we would have to evaluate $250 * Y + X$. We will show how to do this in chapter 8.

(b) FOR N = 1000 TO 1 STEP -1.........NEXT

Once again, the backward loop is quicker

```
                LDY   #4
LOOP1           LDX   #250
LOOP2            ·
                 ·
                 ·
                 ·
                 ·
                DEX
                BNE   LOOP2
                DEY
                BNE   LOOP1
```

This time N is $250 * (Y - 1) + X$. It follows that if the value of N is required on each cycle of the loop, then there is less saving in moving backward through the loop. Having to subtract 1 from Y cancels out some of the time otherwise saved in the implementation of the loop. We can in this case alter the program so that N is $250 * Y + X$. Alter the first line to

LDY #3 and the last to BPL LOOP1. This is not a general solution but will work if the initial content of Y is less than 129.

(c) To generalise this for N = 0 TO (NUMH; NUML) we will need to use a different method. In any specific case we can examine the number of cycles and write the program as in (a) (or (b)). But, if we want to accommodate any number of cycles up to 65536, it is tricky to incorporate these factor-type calculations in the program. An easier method is to separate the loop into two parts: N = 0 TO {(NUMH) − 1)};FF and N = (NUMH);00 TO (NUMH; NUML).

The first loop is achieved by cycling on X 256 times for each value of Y = 0, 1, 2... (NUMH) − 1; the second by cycling on X for 0 to (NUML).

Here is the program

```
            LDX    #0
            LDY    #0
LOOP1        .
             .
             .
             .
             .
            INX
            BNE    LOOP1
            INY
            CPY    NUMH
            BNE    LOOP1
LOOP2        .
             .
             .
             .
             .
            INX
            BEQ    OUT
            CPX    NUML
            BCC    LOOP2
            BEQ    LOOP2
OUT
```

X in LOOP1 goes from zero back to zero, giving 256 cycles; Y goes from 0 to (NUMH) − 1, one for each complete loop of X. Then in LOOP2, X goes from zero to NUML. At any stage N = (Y; X).

It may seem rather wasteful to have two separate loops like this but, as we shall see in chapter 9, if a lot of code is required within the loop then a subroutine can be used. In this way, the memory overhead is not so great (though the subroutine solution will add a time cost).

This method is quite general: if we want to perform N = A TO B we use instead N = 0 TO (B − A), and compute N as (Y; X) + A.

Exercise 5.2

1. What happens to the program in (c) if NUMH is zero? Write some code to correct this.

2. Write the program in (c) using a 'backward' loop, N = (NUMH; NUML) TO 0 assuming (i) that N will not need to be computed (so that no strict order on N is necessary) and (ii) that N needs to be computed on every loop in the correct coding order. Are both programs an improvement over the forward loop?

5.5 The Equivalents of a REPEAT...UNTIL and a REPEAT WHILE...ENDWHILE Loop

(a) REPEAT.........UNTIL SUM > 200

There are two ways of coding this

(i)   REPUNTIL   .
                         .
                         .
                         .
                         .

```
           LDA   SUM
           CMP   #200
           BCC   REPUNTIL
           BEQ   REPUNTIL
```

(ii)   REPUNTIL   .
                         .
                         .
                         .
                         .

```
           LDA   #200
           CMP   SUM
           BCS   REPUNTIL
```

Clearly the second is more efficient, and illustrates a general principle: if possible, arrange the program so that a branch will occur when the value in the accumulator is greater than or equal to the value compared (or alternatively when the value in the accumulator is less than the value compared). Try to avoid branches on 'greater than's' or on 'less than or equal to's'. The same is true if we want to compare a value in the X or Y register with a value in memory or in immediate mode. Nevertheless, do not attempt to distort the flow of logic to achieve this, since you will end up with a less efficiently organised and hence slower program. Only if the choice of comparison can be made without any real alteration to the natural flow in the algorithm, should you contemplate it.

(b) REPEAT WHILE SUM < 200.........ENDWHILE

As mentioned this structure does not exist in BBC BASIC, but it should be clear what it does. ENDWHILE marks the end of the group of instructions to be repeated while the sum remains less than 200.

In assembly code

```
REPWHILE    LDA    #200
            CMP    SUM
            BCC    ENDWHILE
                    .
                    .
                    .
                    .
            JMP    REPWHILE
ENDWHILE
```

In practice it may be possible to use a branch rather than a jump here (see 5.7(c), for example). Notice the meaningful label names chosen. It is possibly good practice to stick to these names in all your programs, adding numbers if necessary to differentiate. So for example, you may have the labels REPUNTIL1, REPUNTIL2, REPWHILE1, ENDWHILE1, REPWHILE2, ENDWHILE2, LOOP1, LOOP2, LOOP3 in one program. Remember that the BBC Micro's assembler allows you to have label names of any length.

5.6 Arithmetic and Logical Operations Concerning the X and Y Registers

This section looks at some special techniques concerned with performing arithmetic on the X and Y registers. In all cases, where X is referred to, the same will hold for Y.

(a) $(M) + X \rightarrow M$

Recall that this means that the contents of the memory location whose address is M is added to the X register (X needs no brackets round it for its address is implicit and so X can unambiguously refer to the contents of the register). This result is to be put in the location with address M.

```
TXA
CLC
ADC   M
STA   M
```

We use TXA to economically transfer X to the accumulator where the arithmetic is performed.

(b) $(M) - X \rightarrow M$

We cannot use the last method for this, since it would produce $X - (M)$. It may seem that we need a temporary location to do this, thus

```
LDA   M
LDX   TEMP
SEC
SBC   TEMP
STA   M
```

but this is unnecessary, in fact.
   Instead we can write

```
LDA   M
STX   M
SEC
SBC   M
STA   M
```

Once we have put the original value of (M) into the accumulator the location M can be used as a temporary store for X.

(c) $A + X \rightarrow A$

Here it would seem that we have no alternative to a temporary location

```
STX   TEMP
CLC
ADC   TEMP
```

However, if the program is written in RAM, as all the BBC Micro's programs that you write will be, we can use the area of program itself as a temporary location, so economising on locations needed. The coding is

```
              STX    MEMLOC+1
              CLC
MEMLOC        ADC    #0
```

MEMLOC +1 is the address of the location where the value 0 is currently stored (this value of zero is a dummy value and could be any number between 0 and 255). Hence the value of X is stored as the operand of ADC 'immediate' as required. (Note that MEMLOC+2, MEMLOC+10 or even MEMLOC+I are possible too, if we need them: indeed any expression can be used as an operand and will be evaluated by the same arithmetic routines as the BASIC interpreter uses.) The main problem with this method is that it results in non-relocatable code (see chapter 9). So if you wish a particular stand-alone machine code program to be relocatable you will have to use a temporary location. A second problem is that we lose the benefits of zero page storage, and this gives a small time cost.

(d) $X - A \to A$

Using the idea in the last section, we can do without a temporary location external to the program

```
              STA    MEMLOC+1
              TXA
              SEC
MEMLOC        SBC    #0
```

The value in the accumulator becomes the operand of SBC#, since it is stored in location MEMLOC +1, the address of the value zero. Then X is transferred to the accumulator and the old value of A is subtracted from it.

(e) A : X?

This notation may be new to you. It means that A is to be compared to X, and a decision is to be made depending upon this comparison. In the context of assembly language, X is taken from A and the appropriate flags are set; the contents of A and X remain unchanged.

We can again use the ideas in (c)

```
              STX    MEMLOC+1
MEMLOC        CMP    #0
```

This compares the accumulator to the X register as required.

(f) Exchange X and Y without affecting A or any other external memory locations

Unfortunately there is no 6502 instruction to do this important task. Nevertheless, we can again use the ideas in (c) to produce a compact solution

```
              STX    MEMLOC2+1
              STY    MEMLOC1+1
MEMLOC1       LDX    #0
MEMLOC2       LDY    #0
```

Exercise 5.3

1. Write assembly code to perform the following operations as economically as possible

   (a) X − (M) → M
   (b) A − X → A
   (c) X − (M) → X
   (d) A − X → X
   (e) X + Y → A
   (f) X − Y → A
   (g) X : A?
   (h) X : Y?
   (i) exchange X and A

2. Write code to perform X + (M) → M which at the end of the operation leaves the contents of A and Y unchanged.

3. Rewrite (c) and (d) of question 1 leaving the contents of A and Y unchanged at the end.

4. Write code to perform X + Y → X, leaving A and Y unchanged at the end.

5.7 Some Example Programs Using Loop Structure

We consider now some examples utilising the foregoing ideas.

(a) To find the sum of the numbers from (NUM1) to (NUM2) inclusive (0 ⩽ (NUM1) < (NUM2) < 256)

We use the structure discussed in 5.3(e). The result of the addition is stored in SUMH; SUML (two bytes will be adequate since the sum must be less than 256^2). The program is in listing 5.1.

Listing 5.1

```
 10 NUM1=&70:NUM2=&71:SUML=&72:SUMH=&73:?&74=0:?&75=0
 20 DIM START 50
 30 FOR I%=0 TO 2 STEP 2:P%=START
 40    [OPTI%
 50    LDA #0
 60    STA SUML
 70    STA SUMH
 80    LDX NUM1
 90    .LOOP
100    TXA
110    CLC
120    ADC SUML
130    STA SUML
140    BCC NOCARRY
150    INC SUMH
160    .NOCARRY
170    INX
180    BEQ OUT
190    CPX NUM2
200    BCC LOOP
210    BEQ LOOP
220    .OUT
230    RTS:]NEXTI%
240 CLS:REPEAT
250    INPUT"Sum from",?NUM1
260    INPUT"To",?NUM2
270    CALLSTART
280    PRINT!SUML
290    UNTIL FALSE
```

(b) To find how many natural numbers from 1 must be added together for the sum to exceed (STOTAL) $(0 \leq (STOTAL) \leq 255)$

We use the structure in 5.5(a) and the program is given in listing 5.2. The number of numbers required will be contained in X, the interim result in SUM. Notice the importance of line 140: without this line, if (STOTAL) = 255, for example, there would never be an exit from the loop.

Listing 5.2

```
 10 SUM=&70:STOTAL=&71
 20 DIM START 50
 30 FOR I%=0 TO 2 STEP 2:P%=START
 40    [OPTI%
 50    LDA #0
 60    STA SUM
 70    TAX
 80    .REPUNTIL
```

```
 90     INX
100     TXA
110     CLC
120     ADC SUM
130     STA SUM
140     BCS OUT
150     CMP STOTAL
160     BCC REPUNTIL
170     BEQ REPUNTIL
180     .OUT
190     RTS:]NEXTI%
200 CLS:REPEAT
210     INPUT"Maximum total",?STOTAL
220     PRINT((USRSTART AND &OFFFFFFF)MOD &10000) DIV &100
230     UNTIL FALSE
```

Line 220 isolates the second byte from the left of USR(START), which is the contents of the X register. The purpose of AND is to make sure that the MSB is zero; if it is 1, the technique will not work. An alternative way of isolating bytes in the USR function is given in section 6.5.

Unlike CALL, USR always returns a value and must either be printed out or put equal to another variable. Its principal function is to return one or more of the registers' values. The value returned consists of four bytes in fact, PYXA, most significant to least significant, where P is the processor status register. We will have more to say about USR in chapter 6, but your *User Guide* contains full details on its syntax.

(c) To find the greatest number of natural numbers from 1 that can be added together with their sum not exceeding (STOTAL) $(0 \leq$ (STOTAL) $\leq 255)$

In this case, we need the structure in 5.5(b), since if (STOTAL) = 0 we do not want to perform the loop at all. Listing 5.3 contains the program.

Listing 5.3

```
 10 SUM=&70:STOTAL=&71
 20 DIM START 50
 30 FOR I%=0 TO 2 STEP 2:P%=START
 40     [OPTI%
 50     LDA #0
 60     STA SUM
 70     TAX
 80     .REPWHILE
 90     CMP STOTAL
100     BEQ ENDWHILE2
110     BCS ENDWHILE1
120     INX
130     TXA
140     CLC
150     ADC SUM
```

```
160     STA SUM
170     BCS ENDWHILE1
180     BCC REPWHILE
190     .ENDWHILE1
200     DEX
210     .ENDWHILE2
220     RTS:]NEXTI%
230 CLS:REPEAT
240     INPUT"Maximum total",?STOTAL
250     PRINT((USRSTART AND &OFFFFFFF)MOD &10000) DIV &100
260     UNTIL FALSE
```

Notice that there are two exits to the loop: ENDWHILE1 and ENDWHILE2. We exit to the former if (SUM) exceeds (STOTAL): in this case we must reduce X by 1, since we require the sum of the X's not to exceed (STOTAL). We exit to the latter if (SUM) equals (STOTAL): in this case, we have not exceeded (STOTAL) and so X does not need to be decremented.

Exercise 5.4

1. Write a program to obtain the sum of $1 + 2 + 4 + 7 + 11 + \ldots$ to NUM (≤ 256) terms. Put the result in SUM3; SUM2; SUM1. Store each term of the series in TERMH; TERML.

2. Write a program to find how many terms (< 256) of the series in question 1 must be added together for the sum to exceed STOTAL3; STOTAL2; STOTAL1.

3. Write a program to find the greatest number of the terms (< 256) of the series in question 1 that can be added together with their sum not exceeding STOTAL3; STOTAL2; STOTAL1.

6 Indexed Addressing

6.1 Moving a Section of Memory

Consider the following fragment of a BASIC program

```
100 FOR X = (NUMBER − 1) TO 0 STEP − 1
110 ? (NEWLOC + X) = ? (OLDLOC + X)
120 NEXT
```

Its purpose is to transfer a number of bytes from one section of memory to another. The starting location of the bytes to be moved is OLDLOC and the first location of the point to which they are to be moved is NEWLOC. Altogether, NUMBER bytes are transferred.

It would be very useful if we could write a program in assembly code to do this with the same structure as the BASIC program. Fortunately, an addressing mode exists which allows us to do this: it is called *indexed addressing*. Here is the assembly program

```
            LDX   NUMBER
            DEX
LOOP        LDA   OLDLOC,X
            STA   NEWLOC,X
            DEX
            CPX   #&FF
            BNE   LOOP
```

The new addressing mode is at lines 3 and 4: LDA OLDLOC, X and STA NEWLOC, X. The first loads the accumulator with the contents of the memory location whose address is OLDLOC + X; it is therefore equivalent to the right-hand side of line 110 in the BASIC program. The second stores the accumulator in NEWLOC + X, equivalent to the left-hand side of line 110.

The purpose of indexed addressing is to allow access to one of a series of up to 256 continuous bytes, the base address of which is known. Figure 6.1 illustrates this, where the base address is given the label BASMEM.

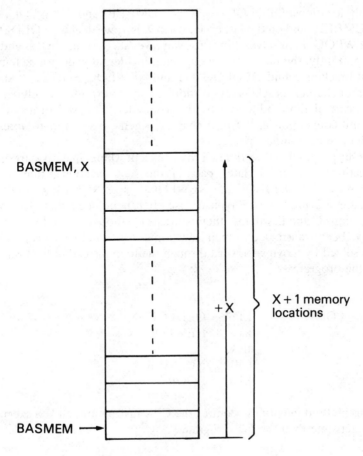

Figure 6.1: Indexed addressing

6.2 Improving the Program

The program in 6.1 can be improved upon. As it stands we need to compare X to &FF at each stage of the loop, which takes time. By rewriting the program, we can eliminate this step

```
          LDX   NUMBER
LOOP      LDA   OLDLOC – 1, X
          STA   NEWLOC – 1, X
          DEX
          BNE   LOOP
```

When this is assembled, 1 will be subtracted from the values of OLDLOC and NEWLOC. Hence on the first cycle of the loop, we deal with locations OLDLOC − 1 + NUMBER and NEWLOC − 1 + NUMBER; and on the last cycle, when X is 1, we deal with OLDLOC and NEWLOC themselves. In this way we save three bytes and, more importantly, significant processing time. Incidentally, do not be tempted to put brackets round OLDLOC − 1 and NEWLOC − 1. As we saw in an earlier chapter, brackets round addresses are interpreted as referring to the *contents* of those addresses by the assembler. This will turn out to be a useful convention in the next chapter, when we see how to access more than 256 continuous bytes.

Our program will work in all cases, except where an early part of the old locations overlaps a later part of the new locations, that is, where NEWLOC < OLDLOC but NEWLOC − 1 + NUMBER ≥ OLDLOC. Figure 6.2 illustrates a typical case. It can be seen that, for example, locations C and D will lose their contents (to those of A and B) before they have been transferred to their new homes (at E and F). This problem can be solved by moving forward through the loop instead of backward. Here is the program

```
             LDX    #0
   LOOP      LDA    OLDLOC, X
             STA    NEWLOC, X
             INX
             CPX    NUMBER
             BNE    LOOP
```

This method inevitably requires the CPX instruction, and so executes in a longer time than the first program.

Exercise 6.1

Under what circumstances will the 'moving forward' method not work?

6.3 The Range of Instructions for which Indexed Addressing is Available

All that we have said above applies equally to the Y register. but it turns out that the X-register indexed addressing mode has a much greater range of application than the Y-register indexed mode.

Some instructions allow both indexed-X and indexed-Y modes: ADC, AND, CMP, EOR, LDA, ERA, SBC and STA. But there are some that allow only indexed-X modes: INC, DEC, LDY and the new instructions to be covered in chapter 8. The byte- and time-saving aspects of zero page storage are available only with the X register: with indexed-Y, zero page must be treated as absolute; so, for example, LDA &70, Y will be translated as B9 70 00 by the assembler, whereas LDA &70, X will

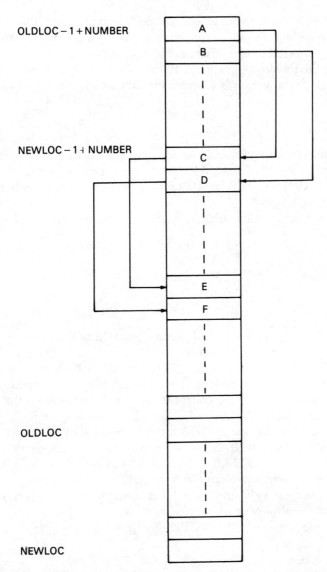

Figure 6.2: Where moving backward through a loop will not work

become B5 70. Moreover, zero-paged indexed-X operates circularly: for example, LDA &73, X when X is &FD will access location &70 (since &73 +&FD>&FF,&FD is treated as −3). This means that you can move forwards through a loop ending at X=0: for example LDX#&FD:.LOOP:LDA &73 ,X:INX:BNE LOOP, will load from locations &70 to &72 inclusive.

There are a few cases where zero page-Y is allowed: LDX and STX both allow this mode (and obviously do not allow indexed-X modes), and in the case of STX this is the only indexed mode available, absolute-Y not being permitted either (a similar constraint applies to STY where zero page-X is the only indexed mode). There are just three instructions that do not allow any indexed addressing: CPX, CPY and BIT (to be covered in chapter 9). All of this information is contained in tabular form in appendix 1.

6.4 Arrays

You will know that in BBC BASIC you can declare an integer array by writing simply, say, DIM ARRAY% (99). This produces 100 elements labelled ARRAY% (0) to ARRAY% (99), each one initially having the value zero.

Can we do a similar thing in assembly language? Here is the program

```
          LDX   #100
          LDA   #0
LOOP      STA   ARRAY − 1,  X
          DEX
          BNE   LOOP
```

ARRAY being the address of the first location of the memory.

Now, we have not, in fact, done exactly the same thing as in BASIC, since ARRAY% (99) allocates *four* bytes to each element of the array. These four bytes give a range of -2^{31} to $2^{31} - 1$, using signed arithmetic. Our program is in fact equivalent to the BASIC statement DIM ARRAY 99, which allocates 100 bytes, the first being at address ARRAY (which the interpreter will allocate as the first free location above TOP). To manipulate these bytes in BASIC, we would have to use statements like ?(ARRAY + X) = TEMP. This is a little clumsy in BASIC, but for our purposes it has the advantage of being very close to assembly language, so let us examine a very simple (and inefficient) sorting program, to sort the 100 bytes into numerical order, smallest first.

First the program in BASIC: see listing 6.1.

Listing 6.1

```
 10 DIM ARRAY 99
 20  FOR I%=0 TO 98 STEP4:!(ARRAY+I%)=RND:NEXT
 30 FLAG=0
 40 FOR I%= 0 TO 98
 50     IF ?(ARRAY+I%)<=?(ARRAY+I%+1)THEN100
 60     TEMP=?(ARRAY+I%)
 70     ?(ARRAY+I%)=?(ARRAY+I%+1)
 80     ?(ARRAY+I%+1)=TEMP
 90     FLAG=1
100    NEXTI%
110 IF FLAG=1 THEN30
120  FOR I%=0 TO 99: PRINT?(ARRAY+I%):NEXTI%
```

The idea is to scan through the 100 bytes and swap any contiguous pair of bytes where the lower byte is greater than the upper byte. Lines 60 to 80 perform the swap. The process is repeated until no swaps are necessary, when the sorting is complete: when this happens, FLAG will be zero on leaving the FOR...NEXT loop at 100. Lines 10 and 20 create an array of 100 random bytes, and line 120 prints out the results.

Thus we ran now construct an assembly language program to do this: listing 6.2.

Listing 6.2

```
10 DIM ARRAY 99 :DIM START 50
20  FOR I%=0 TO 98 STEP4:!(ARRAY+I%)=RND:NEXT
30 FLAG=&70:TEMP=&71
40 FORI%=0 TO 2 STEP 2:P%=START
50    [OPTI%
60    .BEGIN
70    LDX #0
80    STX FLAG
90    .LOOP
100   LDA ARRAY,X
110   CMP ARRAY+1,X
120   BCC OVER
130   BEQ OVER
140   STA TEMP
150   LDA ARRAY+1,X
160   STA ARRAY,X
170   LDA TEMP
180   STA ARRAY+1,X
190   LDA #1
200   STA FLAG
210   .OVER
220   INX
230   CPX #99
240   BNE LOOP
250   LDA FLAG
260   BNE BEGIN
270   RTS:]NEXTI%
280 CALL START
290  FOR I%=0 TO 99: PRINT?(ARRAY+I%),:NEXT
```

The details are

80	As line 30, listing 6.1
100–130	As line 50, listing 6.1
140	As line 60, listing 6.1
150–160	As line 70, listing 6.1
170–180	As line 80, listing 6.1
190–200	As line 90, listing 6.1
220–240	As line 100, listing 6.1
250–260	As line 110, listing 6.1

It is instructive to run both programs and compare the time taken! (Actually, the dice are weighted even more against BASIC since ARRAY is not an integer variable; changing this to ARRAY% speeds up the program a little.)

Now, while modelling our assembly program on a BASIC program makes it a little easier to write, it does not generally produce the most economical and efficient coding. In this case, a saving will be produced if we count backward from 99 to zero, and this is left as an exercise in exercise 6.2. (A saving also occurs if we use the stack for temporary storage, as we shall see in chapter 9.)

An analysis of the algorithm will point to an immediate improvement. On the first scan of the array, the largest value will end up in ARRAY + 99. We can therefore now ignore this and scan from ARRAY to ARRAY + 98: the next largest value will now be in ARRAY + 98. Now scan from ARRAY to ARRAY + 97, etc. The BASIC program for this is in listing 6.3.

Listing 6.3

```
 10 DIM ARRAY 99
 20   FOR I%=0 TO 98 STEP4:!(ARRAY+I%)=RND:NEXT
 30 FOR J%=1 TO 99
 40    FOR I%=0 TO 99-J%
 50       IF ?(ARRAY+I%)<=?(ARRAY+I%+1)THEN90
 60       TEMP=?(ARRAY+I%)
 70       ?(ARRAY+I%)=?(ARRAY+I%+1)
 80       ?(ARRAY+I%+1)=TEMP
 90     NEXTI%
100    NEXTJ%
110   FOR I%=0 TO 99: PRINT?(ARRAY+I%):NEXTI%
```

This method of sorting is called a bubble sort.

The assembly program is in listing 6.4.

Listing 6.4

```
 10 DIM ARRAY 99 :DIM START 50
 20   FOR I%=0 TO 98 STEP4:!(ARRAY+I%)=RND:NEXT
 30 TEMP=&70
 40 FORI%=0 TO 2 STEP 2:P%=START
 50    [OPTI%
 60    LDY #99
 70    .BEGIN
 80    LDX #0
 90    STY MEMLOC+1
100    .LOOP
110    LDA ARRAY,X
120    CMP ARRAY+1,X
130    BCC OVER
```

```
140      BEQ OVER
150      STA TEMP
160      LDA ARRAY+1,X
170      STA ARRAY,X
180      LDA TEMP
190      STA ARRAY+1,X
200      .OVER
210      INX
220      .MEMLOC
230      CPX #0    (Dummy operand)
240      BNE LOOP
250      DEY
260      BNE BEGIN
270      RTS:]NEXTI%
280 CALL START
290  FOR I%=0 TO 99: PRINT?(ARRAY+I%),:NEXT
```

We have used the Y register here to store the value $(99 - J\%) + 1$, which starts at 99 for the first FOR...NEXT loop and ends at one for the last. At each stage we compare X to the value of Y, using the device discussed in the previous chapter to do this.

The bubble sort is not the most efficient way of sorting (for example, a method called Shell–Metzner is better), but machine code is so quick that this is not really important here.

Exercise 6.2

1. Improve the first assembly program by counting backward, at the same time generalising it to allow the sorting of NUMBER bytes (NUMBER ≤ 256), making any other changes which improve economy. Explain why it is not necessary to treat NUMBER as an address in this case.

2. Repeat question 1 for the second assembly program. Notice that this time, the *smallest* value drops through to the *first* element of the scan, for example, after the first cycle, ARRAY will contain the smallest element. Is this design more or less efficient than the original design?

3. The following BASIC program is another type of sort (an insertion sort). Encode it into assembly language in the most economical way.

```
10 INPUT"HOW MANY BYTES",NUMBER
20 DIM ARRAY NUMBER-1
30 FORI%=0 TO NUMBER-2 STEP4:!(ARRAY+I%)=RND:NEXTI%
40 FOR J%=1 TO NUMBER-1
50   FOR I%=J% TO 1 STEP-1
60     IF ?(ARRAY+I%)>=?(ARRAY+I%-1)THEN110
70       TEMP=?(ARRAY+I%)
```

```
 80      ?(ARRAY+I%)=?(ARRAY+I%-1)
 90      ?(ARRAY+I%-1)=TEMP
100      NEXTI%
110   NEXTJ%
120 FOR I%=0 TO NUMBER-1: PRINT?(ARRAY+I%),:NEXT
```

6.5 A Fundamental Data Structure: The Queue

The queue is a familiar idea in everyday life: you go into a shop, but the shopkeeper is busy, so you form a queue. The person at the head of the queue, the person who has been there longest, gets served first. The principle is first in, first served.

Sometimes the microprocessor is very busy on important tasks, but data keeps arriving from some source. The microprocessor wants to store this data away until it has time to process it, and it wants to deal with it on a first come, first served principle. Thus it wants to form a queue of this data, and when it has the time it can deal with it. This is termed a first in, first out (FIFO) data structure, for obvious reasons.

Now it would seem very simple to deal with this. Just set 256 bytes of memory aside, and use an index register to point to the first free position in the queue as data arrives. When time allows, the microprocessor starts processing the data from the first item in memory upwards. Thus the situation is as in figure 6.3, where BASMEM is the lowest memory position and X points to the first free location in the queue. Then, STA BASMEM, X will put the next item of data in the memory, and INX will update the pointer to the free position. And when time permits, the microprocessor can access the data by performing the cycle LDA BASMEM, Y : INY, for Y taking values from 0 to X − 1.

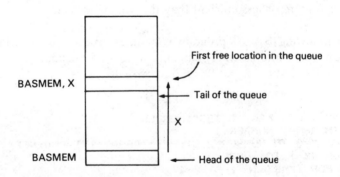

Figure 6.3: A very simple queue implementation

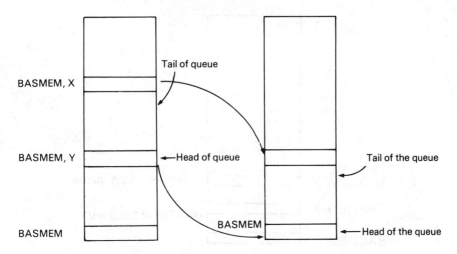

Figure 6.4: One solution to the memory wastage problem

A problem arises, however, if the microprocessor does not have enough time to access the whole queue. It may get half way through and have to go back to its more important tasks. But now more data may again arrive, and there is a danger that space will run out, even though the lower part of the memory allocation is actually free. One way round this is to move the remaining queue 'up', so that the head of the queue is again at BASMEM. Figure 6.4 illustrates this.

This idea is not very sensible, however. The microprocessor is not accessing the whole queue because it does not have time: it can hardly have time, then, to move up the entire queue! What is required is a way of always using all 256 locations without moving around memory; and this can be done by treating the memory as a circular and not linear series of 256 locations.

We need to use the X register to point to the first free location as before, and we use the Y register to point to the head of the queue. Thus STA BASMEM, X : INX will deposit a new item of data and adjust the tail pointer; and LDA BASMEM, Y : INY will withdraw the item at the head of the queue and adjust the head of queue pointer.

We begin with X = Y = 0. Data comes in and is put on the queue. The situation is now as in figure 6.3: Y is still 0, but X points to the next free location. The microprocessor gets some time and starts to access the queue, but before it finishes it has to go back to more important tasks. The situation is now as in the left-hand side of figure 6.4: Y points to the new head of the queue; and X points to the tail (which may be longer still, since data may have been entered on the queue while the microprocessor was accessing the head).

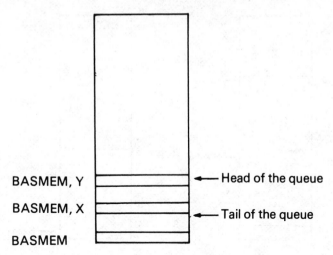

Figure 6.5: A better solution to the memory wastage problem

Suppose now that a large amount of data comes in so that X reaches 255. At this stage X resets to zero. More data still comes in, and the situation when the microprocessor is again ready to access the queue is as in figure 6.5. We see that Y is greater than X but this does not matter. The same instruction—LDA BASMEM,Y : INY—will withdraw the data one at a time; and this will continue to be so as Y increases through 255 to zero.

If at any stage X = Y then either the queue is empty or it is full. Which it is will depend on whether the last transaction was a withdrawal or a deposit. The microprocessor will need to keep track of this at each stage, and it will need to be permanently stored away in case the micro has to 'go off again'. We will use a zero page location, labelled INDIC, for this. We will set bit seven of INDIC to one if the last operation was a deposit, and set it to zero if it was a withdrawal. The reason for using bit 7 is that it is easily tested with a BPL or BMI test. So, if a deposit is required to be made but X = Y and (INDIC$_7$) = 1 (that is, bit 7 of INDIC is one), then the queue is full and an error condition is required. This is most easily done by setting carry before exiting. The micro will now inspect carry and take appropriate action to safeguard the data. Similarly if a withdrawal is demanded, but X = Y and (INDIC$_7$) = 0, the queue is empty.

Let us consolidate all this with a flowchart (see appendix 5 for flowcharting conventions). Figure 6.6 shows the flowchart for depositing an item.

Listing 6.5

```
10 DIM START 50:VDU14
20  DATUM=&70:INDIC=&71:DIM BASMEM 255
30 DIM TEST 256
40 X%=0:Y%=0:?INDIC=0
```

```
 50 FOR I%=0 TO 2 STEP2:P%=START
 60     [OPTI%
 70     STX MEMLOC+1
 80     .MEMLOC
 90     CPY #0 (Dummy operand)
100     BNE OK
110     LDA INDIC
120     BPL OK
130     SEC
140     RTS
150     .OK
160     LDA #&80
170     STA INDIC
180     LDA DATUM
190     STA BASMEM,X
200     INX
210     CLC
220      RTS:]NEXTI%
230 FOR I%=0 TO 256
240     ?DATUM=RND(256)-1:?(TEST+I%)=?DATUM
250     !&404=USR(START):X%=?&405:Y%=?&406
260     IF (?&407 AND 1) =1 THEN PRINT"ERROR AT
        "STR$(I%+1)"TH DEPOSIT":GOTO280
270       NEXTI%
280 PRINT'"        DEPOSIT    QUEUE"'
290 FOR I%=0 TO 255
300     PRINT ?(BASMEM+I%),?(TEST+I%):NEXTI%
310 VDU15
```

Listing 6.5 shows the program to deposit an item in the queue. Let us concentrate first on the assembly listing (lines 70 to 220). The table below gives the necessary documentation

Line(s)	Comment
70–90	Device to compare X and Y registers
100	If not equal, no need to check last transaction
110–120	Otherwise, check last transaction and if a withdrawal, OK
130–140	If deposit, indicate error condition and return
160–170	Store present transaction (a deposit) in indicator
180–190	Put datum in next free space in queue
200	and update pointer to next free space
210–220	Set non-error condition and return.

Before going on, it is worth making a few points about this style of documentation. Firstly, it is possible to document the program direct (line 90 is an example), but it is very wasteful of memory and tends to make the listing very cluttered unless TAB's are used. It is better, therefore, to keep documentation separate. The only exception is at line 90, where an instruction is not what it seems—then it is essential to include documenta-

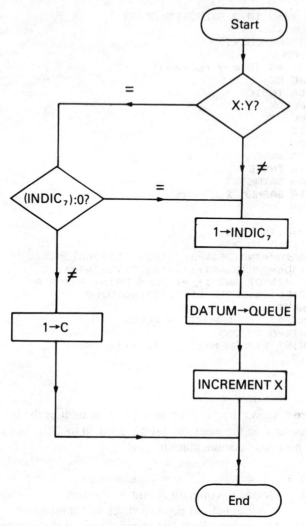

Figure 6.6: Flowchart for depositing an item in a queue

tion in the program itself. Secondly, documentation is essential, but overdocumentation is an obfuscation and is unfortunately much too common. Overdocumentation means stating the obvious. A typical example would be the following

70	Store X in the memory location MEMLOC + 1
80	Label for temporary storage
90	Compare Y to the values of X stored in this location
100	If they are not equal branch to OK
110–120	Otherwise set carry and return etc.

There is no merit in describing the meaning of the instructions: it is their *purpose* that is required when documenting. Sometimes the line between these styles is thin, but it is nevertheless important to keep on the right side of it.

Thirdly, a few words about flowcharting. Flowcharts are useful for small, self-enclosed algorithms, but become confusing and less useful for organising larger programs. One approach is to try to split the program into small parts, and flowchart each part, but this is not always feasible. Do not feel that every program you write has to be flowcharted: flowchart when and if you think it will be useful. And when you flowchart, do not try to pack too much into it.

Let us return to the rest of the program in listing 6.5, since there are a number of new ideas in it. The purpose of the program surrounding the assembly code is to test the working of that code. The code would never be *used* in a BASIC program like this: it would be part of a larger servicing routine, in all probability. Nevertheless, it has to be tested, and the approach used here is a simple way to do this.

There are a number of points to be made. Firstly, in line 40 we set X% and Y% to zero. The reason for this is that when a machine code routine is called from BASIC the X and Y registers are set to the least significant bytes of the variables X% and Y%. Usually, this is irrelevant to us since we set X and Y in the machine code program itself, but in this case, where we are testing a fragment of a program, X and Y are not set inside the program and so must be initialised before entering it. Note also that the least significant byte of A% is put into the accumulator on entry, though we do not need to exploit this here. Similarly, we set INDIC to represent a withdrawal, so that on first entry when X = Y, we do not get an error.

In line 240, we set DATUM to a random byte, and store it in a 'test area' for later recall. We then enter the machine code program in line 250 with the USR function. We recall from section 5.7 that the value returned consists of four bytes, PYXA, most significant to least significant, where P is the processor status register. By putting USR equal to !&404, we ensure that the least significant byte of A% equals the value of the accumulator on exit (the permanent address of A% is &404–&407). This is useful if we wish to return this value to the accumulator on the next entry to the machine code program and, although we do not require this for our present program, it is useful to follow this convention. In 250 we set X% and Y% to their values on leaving the machine code routine so that when re-entered the values of the X and Y registers are correctly updated.

Line 260 checks whether or not carry is set. Running the program shows that the queue correctly fills to the 256th deposit, but that on the 257th, an error condition is recorded since the queue is full.

Exercise 6.3

1. Draw the flowchart for the withdrawal of an item of data. Write a program to do this and test it in the same way as in listing 6.5. Fill the queue with 256 random bytes (as in listing 6.1). Put the withdrawals in a separate test area for later comparison, and do this by having the withdrawal in the accumulator on exit from the routine.

2. Combine the two routines into a single program (keeping the routines separate) that will accept a byte from the keyboard using BASIC and will go to the deposit routine (say at START1) if it is positive (that is, bit 7 = 0), otherwise go to the withdrawal routine (at START2). Start with the queue half-full (so that X% = 128, Y% = 0). At each stage print out the length of the queue, the item at its head and the item at its tail.

6.6 The Assembler Equivalent of PRINT

The writers of the BBC Micro's operating system have included a special subroutine for printing out characters to the screen. It is usually referred to as OSWRCH (for Operating System Write Character), and its address is &FFEE. It will print out the single character whose ASCII code is in the accumulator.

We will discuss subroutines at length in chapter 9, but for now we need know only that a subroutine is called with the instruction JSR (jump to subroutine) and that at the end of the subroutine an RTS instruction must be placed (return from subroutine). The idea is identical to GOSUB in BASIC: on return, the instruction directly following the JSR instruction is obeyed. As we will see in chapter 9, sometimes we wish to write our own subroutines, but there are certain very basic subroutines, like OSWRCH, which every computer manufacturer will include, so we would never need to write these ourselves.

You have probably met the idea of ASCII already. In BASIC, we can print out a character with the ASCII code CODE with the instruction PRINT CHR$(CODE). The assembly language equivalent of this is LDA #CODE: JSR OSWRCH (where OSWRCH has already been defined as &FFEE in the program). ASCII stands for American Standard Code for Information Interchange, and its function is to provide an agreed set of codes for every symbol commonly needed in computer communication. It was originally developed for exchange between a terminal and a computer, and for this reason the most significant bit was assigned a special function: it is called the parity bit, and it serves to check that the other 7 bits have been received correctly. Using odd parity, this bit is set to zero or one accordingly, so as to make the sum of the bits an odd number. There are therefore 128 codes available (from 0 to &7F) in ASCII. However, when used internally (as in the BBC Micro) no parity check is needed and so there are a full 256 codes available to the user; only the first 128 are accessible from the keyboard, though, these being the standard ASCII set.

It is, fortunately, not necessary to learn these codes, or indeed to have a table of them, since the BBC Micro will give any ASCII code; by typing PRINT ASC ("A"), for example, the number 65 will be returned, the ASCII code for A. The only symbols where one cannot do this are: carriage return (13), quote (34), delete (127) and escape (27). In any case, if one requires to print out text, no reference to ASCII needs to be made by the programmer. Let us see how to print out some text.

All text should be put at the end of a program if possible. To do this make the last statement the label .TEXT. Now when outside the assembly program, the text can be defined by writing $TEXT = "This is an example". The characters of this text will be encoded in ASCII, and the first will be put at the memory location TEXT, which we have defined as the first free location after the program. The very last character will be a carriage return (ASCII code 13).

It is also possible to allocate text from *within* an assembly language program. To do this we use the special instruction EQUS. We then write, for example

> .TEXT
> EQUS "This is an example"]

This will *not* have a carriage return at the end. If we wish to have a carriage return also, we write

> .TEXT
> EQUS "This is an example"
> EQUB 13]

EQUB 13 puts the single byte, value 13, into the next available position in memory (that is, after "e").

In some applications the EQUS method is easier than the $TEXT method, but in others (compare section 10.6) the latter is better. In the rest of this chapter we shall use both methods for illustration; thereafter, we choose the most appropriate method in each case.

Do not forget to allow for the text when allocating space using the DIM statement.

Now in order to print out this text, the following small routine is required

```
OUTPUT1    LDA    TEXT, X
           CMP    #13
           BEQ    ENDTEXT
           JSR    OSWRCH
           INX
           BNE    OUTPUT1
ENDTEXT    RTS
```

This will print out the text, without the carriage return. The BNE LOOP instruction will always result in a branch so long as the text does not exceed 255 characters, and saves space over the JMP as well as being intrinsically relocatable. Call it as a subroutine by writing LDX #0 : JSR OUTPUT1 (saving the old value of X beforehand, if necessary).

If we require to print out the carriage return also, we have to take a little care. Carriage return on its own does not generate a new line: it only returns the cursor to the beginning of the current line. To get a new line we must also output code 10, which moves the cursor down one line. Thus to get a new line we write

```
LDA    #10
JSR    OSWRCH
LDA    #13
JSR    OSWRCH
```

This is needed so often that the designers have included it as a separate subroutine, called OSNEWL at &FFE7. Hence to get a new line we need write only JSR OSNEWL (with OSNEWL defined at the beginning of the program, of course).

It would be useful if we had a subroutine that automatically jumped to OSNEWL if it encountered 13 in the accumulator, otherwise jumping to OSWRCH. There is such a subroutine and it is called OSASCI (at &FFE3). Hence, to print out text with a new line at the end, we use this routine

```
OUTPUT2    LDA    TEXT, X
           JSR    OSASCI
           INX
           CMP    #13
           BNE    OUTPUT2
           RTS
```

Call with LDX #0 : JSR OUTPUT2.

You may be wondering how we accommodate generally a whole series of print statements in a single program. This is a little more complicated and will be covered in full in section 10.6, although section 6.7 deals with two print statements in a less general way.

Finally, a word should be said about the VDU function in BASIC. You will have certainly used this function, and you will be pleased to know that it is available in assembler too. Actually this puts things the wrong way round: all that VDU does is to send a byte to OSWRCH, so that it is primarily an assembly code statement. You know that VDU 12 will clear the screen. Hence writing LDA #12: JSR OSWRCH will clear the screen. Similarly LDA #2 : JSR OSWRCH will turn on the printer. In ASCII, codes 0 to 31 are reserved as control codes: the BBC Micro gives these codes special functions which are specified in the VDU Driver section of your manual.

Moreover, this opens up all the colour and graphics facilities in a very simple way. COLOUR 2: VDU 19, 2, 9, 0, 0, 0 sets logical colour 2 to actual colour 9 (flashing red-cyan). In assembler we write

```
LDA   #17
JSR   OSWRCH
LDA   #2
JSR   OSWRCH
LDA   #19
JSR   OSWRCH
LDA   #2
JSR   OSWRCH
LDA   #9
JSR   OSWRCH
LDA   #0
JSR   OSWRCH
JSR   OSWRCH
JSR   OSWRCH
```

Again, PLOT 85, X, Y will draw a triangle from the two points last named to (X, Y). In assembler we have

```
LDA   #85
JSR   OSWRCH
LDA   # X MOD256
JSR   OSWRCH
LDA   # X DIV256
JSR   OSWRCH
LDA   # Y MOD256
JSR   OSWRCH
LDA   # Y DIV256
JSR   OSWRCH
```

X and Y are sent as two byte numbers, lower byte first in each case. The BASIC functions MOD and DIV make this easy to write in assembly language too.

And this means that it is not necessary, nor indeed is it desirable, to write complicated graphics handling programs in assembly language. We can maintain easy portability between languages and processors and make life easy for ourselves by using the same colour and graphics functions that we have in BASIC.

Nevertheless, you will have noticed that just a few VDU statements produce a huge number of assembly instructions (at least 2 and sometimes 4 for each number in the VDU statement). This can become very tedious to type in. In section 6.8 we will consider ways round this problem.

Exercise 6.4

Using OUTPUT1 and OUTPUT2 as subroutines, write programs to perform in assembly language the following BASIC statements (use both the $ and EQUS methods).

1. PRINT "This is question one"
2. PRINT "This is question two";
3. PRINT
4. PRINT "This is question "; : PRINT "four"

6.7 The Assembler Equivalent of GET$, INKEY$ and INPUT A$

A familiar construction in BASIC is

    10   A$ = GET$: IF A$ <> " " THEN 10

This waits until the space key is pressed before continuing. This is easy to do in assembler, using the operating system read character routine, OSRDCH (at &FFE0). This performs exactly the same function as GET$, putting the ASCII value of the character into the accumulator. So, here we have

```
LOOP        JSR    OSRDCH
            CMP    #ASC (" ")
            BNE    LOOP
```

There is one problem with this: if the escape key is pressed, the system will crash! To stop this happening, we must acknowledge escape using OSBYTE (at &FFF4), a general-purpose subroutine, putting &7E into the accumulator. If we wish otherwise to ignore the escape we can write

```
LOOP        JSR    OSRDCH
            CMP    #&1B        (the ASCII code for ESC)
            BNE    NTESC
            LDA    #&7E
            JSR    OSBYTE
NTESC       CMP    #ASC (" ")
            BNE    LOOP
```

Clearly, other responses to escape can be accommodated by appropriate coding after returning from OSBYTE.

Another construction is INKEY$. In BASIC we may have 10 ANSWER$ = INKEY$(500). This waits for 5 seconds before continuing, unless a key is pressed. This can be achieved by using OSBYTE again, with &82 in the accumulator. The time is contained in the X and Y registers (X the low byte); otherwise the function is as GET$ (and escape must be acknowledged in the same way). Here, since 500 = 256 + 244, we write

```
LDX    #244
LDY    #1
LDA    #&82
JSR    OSBYTE
```

On return, if no key has been pressed the accumulator will contain &80, and suitable action can be taken.

When using GET$ and INKEY$ in BASIC you will probably have used the statement *FX15, 1 to make sure that the keyboard buffer is empty before the keyboard is inspected: this is termed flushing the keyboard buffer. This is easily achieved in assembler using OSBYTE again, this time with 15 in the accumulator and one in the X register.

Thus we write

```
LDX    #1
LDA    #15
JSR    OSBYTE
```

In fact, all *FX commands are just the operating system mnemonics for OSBYTE. Hence, *FX5, 1 (which selects the Centronics printer port) is equivalent to putting 5 in the accumulator, 1 in the X register and jumping to the OSBYTE routine. It follows that any *FX command is easily translated into assembly code.

Finally 10 INPUT A$. This can be achieved by writing a subroutine using just GET$, but a system call exists that does everything required. This is OSWORD (at &FFF1), with zero in the accumulator. Unfortunately, its usage is a little complicated (we will discuss it in section 9.5). It is far easier to jump to part of the BASIC interpreter to perform this task. JSR &BC05 will read text into the direct command input buffer beginning at &0700. Pressing escape will automatically return the computer to direct command status (that is, out of the program) and pressing CTRLU will erase the entire line of text input. The text will end with carriage return (code 13). Here is an assembly program to produce the equivalent of the following BASIC statement

10   INPUT A$: IF LEFT$(A$,2) = "NO" THEN 100 ELSE IF LEFT$(A$,3) <> "YES" THEN 10

```
        START        JSR     &BC05
                      LDA     &700
                      CMP     #ASC("N")
                      BNE     NTNO
                      LDA     &701
                      CMP     #ASC("0")
                      BEQ     NO
        NTNO          LDA     &700
                      CMP     #ASC("Y")
                      BNE     START
                      LDA     &701
                      CMP     #ASC("E")
                      BNE     START
                      LDA     &702
                      CMP     #ASC("S")
                      BNE     START
        YES                   .
                              .
                              .
                              .
        NO                    .
                              .
                              .
                              .
```

It would not be difficult to combine this with the ideas of the previous section to produce a more friendly computer response. For example, in BASIC

10   INPUT "PLEASE ANSWER YES OR NO" A$: IF
          LEFT$(A$,2) = "NO" THEN 100 ELSE IF LEFT$(A$,3)
          <> "YES" THEN PRINT "I DON'T UNDERSTAND
          YOUR ANSWER": GOTO 10

As an exercise encode this into assembler, type it into the computer and see if it works. Put the statements to be printed into $TEXT and $(TEXT + 24) respectively (since the first statement is 24 characters long including the carriage return). Print out the first statement by using LDX #0 : JSR OUTPUT1 and the second with LDX #24 : JSR OUTPUT1. Produce a new line with JSR OSNEWL. Finally, recode this using EQUS. Which do you think is the easier approach?

If we wish to compare text to a longer string than "YES", then the above method is a little clumsy. Listing 6.6 is a program that will accept input from the keyboard and test whether it lies alphabetically between two strings. The two strings are input into the BASIC part of the program before the machine code routine is called, and put into zero page. Listing 6.6 contains the details.

Listing 6.6

```
 10 OSWRCH=&FFEE
 20 DIM START 50
 30 FOR I%=0 TO 2 STEP2
 40    P%=START
 50    [OPTI%
 60    LDA #ASC("?")
 70    JSR OSWRCH
 80    JSR &BC05
 90    LDX #&FF
100 .LOOP1
110    INX
120    LDA &700,X
130    CMP &70,X
140    BCC OUTSIDE
150    BEQ LOOP1
160    LDX #&FF
170 .LOOP2
180    INX
190    LDA &80,X
200    CMP &700,X
210    BCC OUTSIDE
220    BEQ LOOP2
230    CLC
240    RTS
250 .OUTSIDE
260    SEC
270    RTS:]NEXTI%
280 INPUT"Lower string limit",A$:IF LEN(A$)>15 THEN280
290 INPUT"Upper string limit",B$:IF LEN(B$)>15 THEN290
    ELSE IF A$>B$ THEN280
300 PROCASC(A$,&70)
310 PROCASC(B$,&80)
320 PRINT"Input your string":!&404=USR(START)
330 IF (?&407 AND 1)=0 THEN PRINT"Inside" ELSE PRINT
    "Outside"
340 PRINT'"Another?"
350 G$=GET$:IF G$="Y" THEN 320 ELSE IF G$<>"N" THEN 350
360 PRINT"New string limits?"
370 G$=GET$:IF G$="Y" THEN 280 ELSE IF G$<>"N" THEN 370
    ELSE END
380 DEF PROCASC(S$,M%)
390 S$=S$+CHR$(13):M%=M%-1
400 FOR I%=1 TO LEN(S$)
410    ?(M%+I%)=ASC(MID$(S$,I%,1))
420    NEXTI%
430 ENDPROC
```

Lines 60 and 70 print out a question mark prompt. Lines 110 to 150 compare the input string to the bottom string limit. Exit from this loop to line 160 will only occur if the input is higher alphabetically than the bottom limit. Thus if the bottom limit is MISTY and MIST is input, equality will occur for the first four letters, but then on the fifth we compare 13 (carriage return) to 89 (ASCII value of Y), obtain a negative result and branch to OUTSIDE. Equally, if the bottom limit is MIST and MISTY is input, then we compare 89 to 13, obtain a positive result and go through to line 160. In the same way lines 180 to 220 compare the input string to the upper limit. If the string is inside the limits, C is set to zero, otherwise it is set to 1. This is picked up at line 330 (as in listing 6.5, line 260), and the appropriate output delivered.

The procedure at lines 380 to 430, called at lines 300 and 310, is necessary since the $TEXT statement will not function if TEXT is in zero page. We use zero page here to save memory and gain speed with the zero page indexed addressing mode (lines 130 and 190). It is also possible to use EQUS thus

```
300     P%=&70
304     [OPT3
308     EQUS A$+CHR$13:]
312     P%=&80
316     [OPT3
319     EQUS B$+CHR$13:]
```

This is probably the easier approach, but the other is certainly more instructive.

Sometimes we may wish to use a different input buffer from &700 since &700 is of no use for anything other than temporary storage. Once outside the program all input will be lost. If we wish to store permanently the strings input, it would be more convenient to store them directly. We can do this as follows: put the lower byte of the address of the buffer in &37 and the higher byte in &38 and use JSR &BC0D. In addition, we can restrict the length of the string input by loading the accumulator with the length and using JSR &BC0F instead of &BC0D. The default length is 238 otherwise.

Listing 6.7 illustrates this with a program that stores a set of strings input in an array. No string is allowed to exceed 19 characters, since the strings are to be stored in fixed widths of 20 locations. In the next chapter, we will be able to relax these restrictions, and use variable width locations.

Listing 6.7

```
10 OSWRCH=&FFEE
20 DIM START 500
30 FOR I%=0 TO 2 STEP2
40    P%=START
```

```
 50      [OPTI%
 60      LDA #TEXT MOD 256
 70      STA &37
 80      LDA #TEXT DIV 256
 90      STA &38
100      .BEGIN
110      LDA #ASC("?")
120      JSR OSWRCH
130      LDA #19
140      JSR &BCOF
150      LDA &37
160      CLC
170      ADC #20
180      STA &37
190      BCC BEGIN
200      INC &38
210      BCS BEGIN
220      .TEXT:]NEXTI%
230 CALL START
```

Line 20 allows storage for at least 23 strings, starting at the location TEXT defined in 220. Lines 60 to 90 store the lower and higher bytes of TEXT in &37 and &38, and line 130 restricts the string input to 19 characters. Lines 150 to 210 increment the storage address by 20 for the next input. As it stands, we can exit from this program only by pressing ESCAPE; we will also improve on this in the next chapter.

Exercise 6.5

1. Write a program that will print out any string input in reverse. Use an infinite loop with exit by ESCAPE only.

2. Write a program that will print out any string input with all spaces removed. Loop until * alone is input, and then end.

3. Write a program to store a string starting in location TEXT (at the end of the program), with only the trailing spaces removed (that is, remove any spaces after the last 'visible' character input). Include a suitable test of your program.

6.8 Macros, Conditional Assembly and Tables: Simplifying VDU Statements

Consider the following set of instructions in BASIC.

```
MODE 4
VDU28,0,31,39,16        (set bottom half of screen for text)
VDU24,0;512;1273;1023;  (set top half of screen for graphics)
```

VDU29,0;512;	(move graphics origin to bottom left-hand corner of graphics screen)
VDU19,1,0;0;	(foreground black)
VDU19,0,3;0;	(background yellow)
MOVE 0,0	
DRAW 450,450	

The result of all this is to draw a line in the top half of the screen in black on a yellow background. We can in fact write this as one VDU statement, replacing MODE, MOVE and DRAW by their VDU equivalents (except that VDU22 will not reset HIMEM as MODE does).

VDU22,4,28,0,31,39,16,24,0;512;1273;1023;29,0;512;
19,1,0;0;19,0,3;0;25,4,0;0;25,5,450;450;

To encode this into assembly language would require us to type in 90 or so lines of code (there are 31 numbers, but 14 are double bytes, being followed by a semi-colon, for example 0; is &0000). There must be an easier way! Indeed, there are two such ways.

Listing 6.8 shows the first way. Lines 50–70 are included solely to show how the VDU statement can be put into the middle of an assembly program: they are quite arbitrary. Lines 80 and 90 contain the new ideas. Line 80 begins with an 'end assembly code' marker (]), and then a procedure is called. Line 90 contains the VDU numbers, with the small difference that 0; has been replaced by 0,0 and 3; by 3,0.

Listing 6.8

```
 10 OSWRCH=&FFEE
 20 DIM START 500
 30 FOR I%=0 TO 3 STEP 3:P%=START:RESTORE
 40   [OPTI%
 50   LDA #0
 60   STA &70
 70   STA &71
 80   ]PROCVDU(39)
 90   DATA 22,4,28,0,31,39,16,24,0,0,512,1273,1023,29,
      0,0,512,19,1,0,0,0,0,19, 0,3,0,0,0,25,4,0,0,0,0,
      25,5,450,450
100   [OPTI%
110   RTS:]NEXTI%
120 CALLSTART:END
130 DEF PROCVDU(N):LOCAL D,D$,H,L,J%
140 FOR J%=1 TO N:READ D$:D=EVAL(D$)
150   IF D>255 THEN H=D DIV 256: D= D MOD256 ELSE H=-1
160   IF D<>L THEN [OPTI%:LDA #D:]
170   [OPTI%:JSR OSWRCH:]
180   L=D:IF H=-1 THEN190 ELSE D=H:H=-1:GOTO160
190   NEXTJ%
200 ENDPROC
```

The procedure is in lines 130–200. Line 130 specifies the variables used as local so that they may be used again if required outside the procedure (the parameter N is automatically local). Line 140 reads the data from line 90 into the variable D. (It is read first into D$ and EVAL applied to it to accommodate hex numbers, for example, &1000 could be an item of data.) Line 150 checks whether D exceeds 255: if it does it splits it into two bytes, with H the higher and D the lower; otherwise it sets H to −1 as a flag.

Line 160 is an example of what is called *conditional assembly*. L contains the last byte output. If D is equal to L then we do not need an LDA statement because the accumulator will already contain this value. If D is not equal to L, the LDA statement is required. Notice the inclusion of OPTI% here: when we re-enter assembly mode (by using the marker [) OPT will be set to its default value 3 unless we re-specify it. I% is, of course, the current OPT value from the beginning of the program (that is, 0 or 3).

Again in 170 OPTI% is needed. Line 180 will set L (the last byte output) to D, and then will either read the next byte from the data, or if H contains a value will transfer that to D instead.

The parameter N contains the number of items in the data statement. Finally note the importance of RESTORE in line 30: there are two passes and the DATA statement must be restored after the first one.

If you run this with the page mode on (CTRL N) you will see all the LDA #D, JSR OSWRCH statements being assembled. Normally you would use it using I% = 0 TO 2, but we use I% = 3 here to demonstrate that all the VDU statements have been translated into assembly code.

This method of producing code is called *macro-assembly* and the procedure is an example of a *macro*. Macro-assemblers are usually only found on large expensive machines, but the facility is available to use because BASIC and assembly code can be mixed.

An alternative approach to line 80 is to use EQUS with a dummy null string and so remain within the assembler. Thus 80 becomes

```
80      EQUS FNVDU(39)
85      RTS:]NEXTI%
```

and lines 100 to 110 are not needed. The PROCVDU(N) in 130 becomes an FNVDU(N) and line 200 becomes

```
200     =" "
```

This is a particularly powerful way to implement macros on the BBC Micro, although it takes a little more getting used to. EQUS itself is doing nothing in this case except allowing us to access a function. And this function returns a null string: its real purpose is to perform our macro for us.

There is a second way of coding the VDU statement, and listing 6.9 shows it. Again lines 50–70 are arbitrary. Lines 80–140 perform a loop to load the accumulator with the next item of data from the table (stored at the address TABLE defined in line 160) and output it with OSWRCH. 45 is used as the comparison since there are 45 bytes (31 numbers but 14 are double bytes).

Listing 6.9

```
 10 OSWRCH=&FFEE
 20 DIM START 500
 30 FOR I%=0 TO 3 STEP 3:P%=START:RESTORE
 40    [OPTI%
 50    LDA #0
 60    STA &70
 70    STA &71
 80    LDX #0
 90    .LOOPVDU
100    LDA TABLE,X
110    JSR OSWRCH
120    INX
130    CPX #45
140    BNE LOOPVDU
150    BEQ OVERTABLE
160    .TABLE
170    ]PROCTABLE(39)
180    DATA 22,4,28,0,31,39,16,24,0,0,512,1273,1023,29,0,
       0,512,19,1,0,0,0,0,19, 0,3,0,0,0,25,4,0,0,0,0,25,5,
       450,450
190    [OPTI%
200    .OVERTABLE
210    RTS:]NEXTI%
220 CALLSTART:END
230 DEF PROCTABLE(N):LOCAL D,D$,H,J%
240 FOR J%=1 TO N:READ D$:D=EVAL(D$)
250    IF D>255 THEN H=D DIV 256: D= D MOD256 ELSE H=-1
260    ?P%=D: P%=P%+1
270    IF H=-1 THEN 280 ELSE D=H:H=-1: GOTO260
280    NEXTJ%
290 ENDPROC
```

The table of data values is set up using the procedure called in line 170. Using exactly the same data as in listing 6.8 (at line 180 here), line 260 puts each item of data into the current address pointed to by the program counter (stored automatically in P%) and increments the counter. When first entered P% = TABLE. On exit, P% will point to the first free location following the 45 bytes stored in the table. The table could have been stored at the end of the machine code program, but it is instructive to see here how it can be put in the middle when required.

Again, instead of line 170 we could have used EQUS. Also, instead of lines 250 to 270 we could have used EQUB and EQUW. EQUB puts a single byte into memory and EQUW a double byte (EQUD would put four bytes into memory). Note that EQUW and EQUD put the bytes into memory starting with the *lowest* first.

Thus we could replace line 170 with

```
170      EQUS FNTABLE(39)
175      RTS:]NEXTI%
```

and lines 190 to 210 are not needed. Line 250 becomes

```
250      IF D>255 THEN [OPTI%: EQUW D:]
         ELSE [OPTI%: EQUB B:]
```

and lines 260 and 270 are not needed. This is more economical than listing 6.9 but a comparison of the methods is very instructive.

Running listing 6.9 after a CTRL N points to the essential difference between the methods employed in listing 6.8 and listing 6.9. In the latter, the coding to perform the output to the VDU is written only once, but performed many times. In the former, the coding to perform the output is written many times but performed once. Thus the macro approach is an assembly time facility, whereas the table approach is a run-time facility.

In general, the table approach is much cheaper on memory than the macro approach, but it is slightly slower in execution time (since the table has to be read, X has to be incremented and compared to the limit, and a branch has to be made). As a rule, then, use tables unless speed is critical, when the macro approach can be used.

Exercise 6.6
Use a macro with conditional assembly to
   (a) Rewrite the coding to question 2 of exercise 3.2.
   (b) Combine the coding for question 2 of exercise 3.2 and question 2 of exercise 3.3 into a single assembly program, an index being set to A if exercise 3.2 is to be produced and to S if exercise 3.3 is to be produced.
In each case suppress the assembler listing, and in each case use the approach in listing 6.8 only (the EQUS method does not gain here).

7 Indirect Indexed Addressing

7.1 Moving a Section of Memory

Let us consider how we might move a section of memory which is more than 256 bytes long. In section 5.4(c) we saw a general method of performing a FOR...NEXT loop with more than 256 cycles. We can modify that idea for our present task. Listing 7.1 shows the program.

Listing 7.1

```
 10 NUML=&70:NUMH=&71
 20 INPUT"How many bytes will be moved",!NUML
 30 INPUT"Starting address of memory to be moved",A$:
    OLDLOC=EVAL(A$)
 40 INPUT"Starting address of new location",A$:NEWLOC
    =EVAL(A$)
 50 DIM START 100
 60 FOR I%=0 TO 2 STEP 2:P%=START
 70    [OPTI%
 80    LDX NUMH
 90    BEQ LOLOOP
100    LDY #0
110    .MEMLOC1
120    LDA OLDLOC,Y
130    .MEMLOC2
140    STA NEWLOC,Y
150    INY
160    BNE MEMLOC1
170    INC MEMLOC1+2
180    INC MEMLOC2+2
190    DEX
200    BNE MEMLOC1
210    .LOLOOP
220     LDX NUML
230    BEQ FINISH
240    .LOOP
250    LDA OLDLOC+256*?NUMH,Y
260    STA NEWLOC+256*?NUMH,Y
270    INY
280    DEX
290    BNE LOOP
300    .FINISH
```

```
310    RTS:JNEXTI%
320 CALL START
330 FOR I%=0 TO 256*?NUMH+?NUML-1
340    IF ?(OLDLOC+I%)<>?(NEWLOC+I%) PRINT "Error at
       move"I%+1:END
350    NEXTI%
```

As in chapter 6, the memory to be moved starts at OLDLOC and it is to be moved to a section of memory starting at NEWLOC. Altogether, (NUMH; NUML) bytes are to be moved. We move the (NUMH) sets of 256 bytes first. For reasons that will become clear in a moment, we use Y to index the move in each cycle and use X to count the number of sets of 256 cycles. X is initialised in line 80 (and if (NUMH) = 0, an immediate branch is taken to the move of the (NUML) bytes at 220). Then Y is initialised, and the 256 byte move occurs in lines 120–160.

In lines 170 and 180 we increment the high byte of the addresses OLDLOC and NEWLOC before repeating the 256 cycle move. For example, if OLDLOC is &8320 and NEWLOC is &4000, then at the end of the first 256 cycles we have moved the contents of locations &8320–&841F to locations &4000–&40FF. At the beginning of the next 256 cycles we want OLDLOC to begin at &8420 and NEWLOC to begin at &4100, and lines 170 and 180 achieve this. The process continues until we have moved all (NUMH) bits of 256 bytes. Then in lines 220–290 we move the residual number of bytes expressed in (NUML). Again, continuing the example, suppose we are moving &920 bytes; then (NUML) = &20. In lines 250 and 260 we begin the move from &8C20 (&8320 + 256 * 9), as required, and move it to &4900. The move ends at &491F, giving &920 bytes moved in all.

You may be wondering why in lines 220–290 we do not simply load Y with the contents of NUML and decrement Y as we go, so dispensing with X altogether. This would not work, however, since we would move a byte from &8C20 to &4920, and this should not happen. To make this work we would have to decrement Y before starting the move (so that Y contained (NUML) − 1), and check each stage of the loop with a CPY #&FF, since Y = 0 must be included. It turns out that all of this takes up more space and more time than using both the X and Y registers.

The reason we have used Y to index each cycle of the move rather than X is to accommodate the case where either OLDLOC or NEWLOC is a zero page location. If we used X in this case, the high byte of the address would not be available for incrementing (see section 6.3 to remind yourself of this). Using Y, zero page addresses are stored in two bytes; for example, if OLDLOC is &10

LDA OLDLOC, X is translated as B5 10 whereas
LDA OLDLOC, Y is B9 10 00.

There is one fundamental problem with this program. It works well, but it needs to be reassembled every time that we wish to change the number of bytes to be moved or the starting addresses OLDLOC or NEWLOC. This means that the program could never be a stand-alone machine code program; it would always have to be tied to the assembler. This is not good programming practice: in general, we should have to assemble a program only once; thereafter, any change in data should not require reassembly.

A solution to this problem is shown in listing 7.2. The address OLDLOC is put into two bytes OLDLOCL and OLDLOCH and passed as data. Similarly the address NEWLOC is put in NEWLOCL and NEWLOCH.

Listing 7.2

```
 10 NUML=&70:NUMH=&71:OLDLOCL=&72:OLDLOCH=&73:NEWLOCL
    =&74:NEWLOCH=&75
 20 INPUT"How many bytes will be moved",!NUML
 30 INPUT"Starting address of memory to be moved",A$:
    !OLDLOCL=EVAL(A$)
 40 INPUT"Starting address of new location",A$:!NEWLOCL
    =EVAL(A$)
 50 DIM START 100
 60 FOR I%=0 TO 2 STEP 2:P%=START
 70    [OPTI%
 80    LDA OLDLOCL
 90    STA MEMLOC1+1
100    STA MEMLOC3+1
110    LDA OLDLOCH
120    STA MEMLOC1+2
130    STA MEMLOC3+2
140    LDA NEWLOCL
150    STA MEMLOC2+1
160    STA MEMLOC4+1
170    LDA NEWLOCH
180    STA MEMLOC2+2
190    STA MEMLOC4+2
200    LDX NUMH
210    BEQ LOLOOP
220    LDY #0
230    .MEMLOC1
240    LDA &FFFF,Y Dummy operand
250    .MEMLOC2
260    STA &FFFF,Y Dummy operand
270    INY
280    BNE MEMLOC1
290    INC MEMLOC1+2
300    INC MEMLOC2+2
310    INC MEMLOC3+2
320    INC MEMLOC4+2
330    DEX
340    BNE MEMLOC1
350    .LOLOOP
360     LDX NUML
370    BEQ FINISH
```

```
380    .MEMLOC3
390    LDA &FFFF,Y Dummy operand
400    .MEMLOC4
410    STA &FFFF,Y Dummy operand
420    INY
430    DEX
440    BNE MEMLOC3
450    .FINISH
460    RTS:]NEXTI%
470 CALL START
480 FOR I%=0 TO 256*?NUMH+?NUML-1
490    IF ?(!OLDLOCL MOD65536+I%)<>?(!NEWLOCL+I%) PRINT
       "Error at move"I%+1:END
500    NEXTI%
```

Lines 80–190 take this data and store it into the relevant parts of the
program. Thus the address OLDLOC is put into lines 240 and 390; and the
address NEWLOC into lines 260 and 410. The program then operates
identically to listing 7.1, except that the addresses in 390 and 410 are also
incremented. Once this program has been assembled, we can reuse it with
any new data without reassembly.

7.2 A Better Method

The solution given in listing 7.2 works but is clumsy and long-winded.
Moreover, we could not use it if we wanted to put the program into a chip
in ROM. The designers of the 6502 microprocessor have provided us with a
better way of solving the problem.

The program is shown in listing 7.3, and the new ideas are in lines 100,
110, 220 and 230. LDA (OLDLOCL), Y means exactly the same as line
390 in listing 7.2 after the new contents have been assigned in lines 80–190.
It means load the accumulator with the contents of the location (OLD-
LOCH; OLDLOCL) + Y. Similarly STA (OLDLOCL), Y stores the
accumulator into memory location (OLDLOCH; OLDLOCL) + Y.
Figure 7.1 illustrates this.

Listing 7.3

```
 10 CLS
 20 NUML=&70:NUMH=&71:OLDLOCL=&72:OLDLOCH=&73:NEWLOCL
    =&74:NEWLOCH=&75
 30 DIM START 100
 40 FOR I%=0 TO 2 STEP 2:P%=START
 50    [OPTI%
 60    LDX NUMH
 70    BEQ LOLOOP
 80    LDY #0
 90    .LOOP1
100    LDA (OLDLOCL),Y
```

```
110      STA (NEWLOCL),Y
120      INY
130      BNE LOOP1
140      INC OLDLOCH
150      INC NEWLOCH
160      DEX
170      BNE LOOP1
180      .LOLOOP
190       LDX NUML
200       BEQ FINISH
210      .LOOP2
220      LDA (OLDLOCL),Y
230      STA (NEWLOCL),Y
240      INY
250      DEX
260      BNE LOOP2
270      .FINISH
280       RTS:]NEXTI%
290 INPUT"How many bytes will be moved",!NUML
300 INPUT"Startina address of memory to be moved",A$:
    !OLDLOCL=EVAL(A$)
310 INPUT"Starting address of new location",B$:!NEWLOCL
    =EVAL(B$)
320 CALL START:PRINT"Memory moved. Checking now."
330 A=EVAL(A$):B=EVAL(B$)
340 FOR I%=0 TO 256*?NUMH+?NUML-1
350    IF ?(A+I%)<>?(B+I%) PRINT "Error at move"I%+1:END
360    NEXTI%
370 PRINT"Check OK":GOTO290
```

This mode of addressing is called *indirect indexed* addressing, and it is very powerful. In listing 7.3, we are able to increment the addresses pointed to in lines 100 and 220 in one go by writing INC OLDLOCH in line 140. In listing 7.2 we had to do this twice, once for line 240 (at line 290) and once for line 390 (at line 310).

The mnemonic form used is actually very close to the one introduced in section 2.7 for our own use. Using that convention, we would be inclined to write LDA (OLDLOCH; OLDLOCL), Y. The 6502 can shorten this because it assumes that OLDLOCH is *always the next location up* from OLDLOCL, that is, OLDLOCH = OLDLOCL + 1. So we can write LDA (OLDLOCL), Y for short, since given OLDLOCL it knows OLD-LOCH.

The indirect indexed addressing mode is *always a two-byte instruction* because the operand, here OLDLOCL, *has to be a zero page address*. In practice, this is not a serious limitation, and it results in an increase in processor speed and a decrease in memory space used to store the program.

We cannot use the indirect indexed addressing mode with the X register: *it is available only with the Y register*. The X register has a special indirect mode of its own which we shall meet in appendix 3. Moreover, the indirect

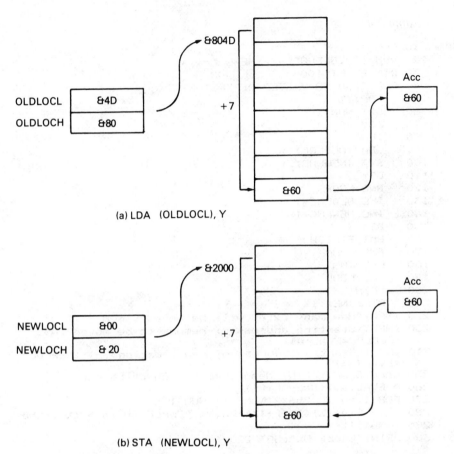

(a) LDA (OLDLOCL), Y

(b) STA (NEWLOCL), Y

Figure 7.1: An illustration of the indirect indexed addressing mode, where OLDLOC is &804D, NEWLOC is &2000, Y equals 7 and &8054 contains &60

indexed mode is not available with all instructions, as a glance at appendix 1 will demonstrate. It can be used only with ADC, AND, CMP, EOR, LDA, ORA, SBC and STA. But even with these restrictions, a great deal can be done with it as this and later chapters will show.

Since the high and low bytes of the address referenced indirectly in the indirect indexed mode must be stored in touching bytes, it is usual to dispense with the L and H suffixes on the labels. Thus instead of OLDLOCL we write simply OLDLOC; and if we wish to refer to OLDLOCH we do so by using OLDLOC + 1. This convention is illustrated in listing 7.4, which purports to be an improvement on listing 7.3. Notice that in line 20 NUM is put equal to &70, OLDLOC to &72 and NEWLOC to &74. This leaves &71 for NUM + 1, &73 for OLDLOCH and &75 for NEWLOC + 1.

Listing 7.4

```
10 CLS
20 NUM=&70:OLDLOC=&72:NEWLOC=&74
30 DIM START 100
40 FOR I%=0 TO 2 STEP 2:P%=START
50   [OPTI%
60   LDX NUM+1
70   LDY #0
80   .LOOP
90   LDA (OLDLOC),Y
100  STA (NEWLOC),Y
110  DEY
120  BNE LOOP
130  INC OLDLOC+1
140  INC NEWLOC+1
150  DEX
160  BMI FINISH
170  BNE LOOP
180  LDY NUM
190  BNE LOOP
200  .FINISH
210  RTS:]NEXTI%
220 INPUT"How many bytes will be moved",!NUM
230 INPUT"Starting address of memory to be moved",A$:
    !OLDLOC=EVAL(A$)
240 INPUT"Starting address of new location",B$:!NEWLOC
    =EVAL(B$)
250 CALL START:PRINT"Memory moved. Checking now."
260 A=EVAL(A$):B=EVAL(B$)
270 FOR I%=0 TO 256*?(NUM+1)+?NUM-1
280   IF ?(A+I%)<>?(B+I%) PRINT "Error at move"I%+1:END
290   NEXTI%
300 PRINT"Check OK":GOTO220
```

It is also conventional *in discussion* to refer to all the bytes associated with each label by just stating the label. Thus if we want to refer to OLDLOC and OLDLOC + 1 at the same time, and there is no ambiguity, we just say OLDLOC. Similarly, if a location NUMBER has associated with it four bytes, NUMBER, NUMBER + 1, NUMBER + 2, NUMBER + 3, then we could refer to these by just saying NUMBER. So, for example, the statements 'OLDLOC contains the address of the first location to be moved' and 'NUMBER contains the 32-bit signed integer' utilise this convention and are clearly unambiguous. In the rest of this book, we shall adopt this convention in our discussions where there is no danger of ambiguity.

Exercise 7.1

1. What relationship must hold between !OLDLOC and !NEWLOC for the program in listing 7.3 to work?

2. Write a program that will work in those cases where listing 7.3 does not. Use exactly the same data input as listing 7.3 (that is, the start of memory to be moved, the start of the new locations and the number of bytes to be moved). Which program is more efficient?

3. Listing 7.4 purports to be an improvement on listing 7.3. However, there are some faults in it. Correct what you can, and state which faults cannot be corrected.

7.3 Inputting a Series of Strings of Varying Lengths

In chapter 6, listing 6.7, we constructed a program to input a series of strings into an array. We had to restrict the length of strings to 19 and, regardless of the length input, 20 bytes had to be reserved for each string. Moreover, the only way we could indicate that we had finished input was by pressing the ESCAPE key which necessarily took us out of the program.

Listing 7.5

```
 10 OSWRCH=&FFEE
 20 DIM START 4000
 30 FOR I%=0 TO 2 STEP 2
 40    P%=START
 50    [OPTI%
 60    LDA #TEXT MOD 256
 70    STA &37
 80    LDA #TEXT DIV 256
 90    STA &38
100    LDA #12
110    JSR OSWRCH
120    .BEGIN
130    LDA #ASC("?")
140    JSR OSWRCH
150    JSR &BCOD
160    LDY #0
170    LDA (&37),Y
180    CMP #ASC("*")
190    BNE LOOP
200    INY
210    LDA (&37),Y
220    CMP #&0D
230    BNE LONG
240    RTS
250    .LONG
260    LDY #0
270    .LOOP
280    LDA (&37),Y
290    CMP #&0D
300    BEQ ENDSTRING
310    INY
```

```
320     BNE LOOP
330     .ENDSTRING
340     INY
350     TYA
360     CLC
370     ADC &37
380     STA &37
390     BCC BEGIN
400     INC &38
410     BCS BEGIN
420     .TEXT:JNEXTI%
430 CALLSTART
440 STRING=TEXT:VDU14:REPEAT
450     A$=$STRING :PRINTA$:STRING=STRING+LEN(A$)+1
460     UNTIL A$="*"
470 VDU15
```

Armed with our new addressing mode, we can improve on all of this.
Listing 7.5 allows a series of strings of any length to be input, stored in an
array at the end of the machine code. Exit is achieved by the input of a
single asterisk; **, for example, will not be interpreted as an exit signal.
The details are as follows

60–90	The low byte of the first free location at the end of the program (referenced by TEXT) is put in &37 and the high byte in &38. This is required for the routine at &BC0D (see section 6.7)
100–110	Clear the screen
130–150	Output the ? prompt, and accept input from the keyboard
160–190	Check if the first character is an asterisk. If not, go to line 280
200–260	Check if the second character is a carriage return. If so, the single asterisk exit signal has been input and so we return at 240. Otherwise reset the character index pointer (Y) to zero at 260
280–300	Get the next character. If it is a carriage return, the end of the string has been found, so go to 340
310–320	Otherwise increment the index pointer and branch back to 280. The branch always occurs since the string length cannot reach 256
340–380	Increment the base address of the buffer for input to the next free location in memory by adding the string length (Y + 1) to the old base address
390–410	If there is no carry branch immediately to 130 for the next string; otherwise, increment the high byte of the buffer address before branching to 130

As usual, we test the program using BASIC. Here, on exit from the machine code we print out the ASCII contents of the memory from TEXT onwards until a single asterisk is found.

Notice how the indirect indexed addressing mode solves our problems for us. We are able to accommodate variable length strings economically, because the buffer address can be set to the next free location by the simple expedient of adding the last string length to the last buffer address. We are also able to inspect each character of the string, which we could not do in listing 6.6, and so we can exit from the program without having to use ESCAPE. This would be important if the present program were part of a larger package, where the input strings were to be used.

7.4 Sorting a Series of Fixed Length Records

In some applications, it is practicable to use a storage method for records, where each field in the record is given a fixed amount of storage space. Thus the record is of a fixed length. An example of this might be wages data, where, say, 30 characters are given for the name, 5 for a payroll number, 3 for the hourly rate, etc. In such cases, it is usually required that we can sort the records, with respect to any of the fields. Thus we may want to sort according to name, or according to hourly rate or according to any other field that we choose. In this case, we have no need to mark the end of the records with a carriage return; rather we will require exact details of the whereabouts of the field upon which we will sort the records.

Listing 7.6 gives a program to achieve this. It will sort up to 256 records, each record being a fixed length up to 254 characters. The particular field is accessed by two indexes: one for the beginning of the field and one for the end. The indexes are relative to the beginning of the record: so, for example, the hourly rate above would be accessed with indexes 35 and 37, the payroll number with 30 and 34, and the name with 0 and 29.

Listing 7.6

```
  10 NUMBER=&70:FIRST=&71:SECOND=&73:TEMP=&75:RECLENGTH
     =&76:KEYSTART=&77:KEYEND =&78:BASE=&79
  20 DIM START 100
  30 FOR I%=0 TO 2 STEP 2:P%=START
  40    [OPTI%
  50    LDA BASE
  60    STA SECOND
  70    LDA BASE+1
  80    STA SECOND+1
  90    LDX #0
 100    .BEGIN
 110    LDY KEYSTART
 120    LDA SECOND+1
 130    STA FIRST+1
```

```
140     LDA SECOND
150     STA FIRST
160     CLC
170     ADC RECLENGTH
180     STA SECOND
190     BCC LOOP1
200     INC SECOND+1
210     .LOOP1
220     LDA (FIRST),Y
230     CMP (SECOND),Y
240     BCC NEWRECORD
250     BNE SWAP
260     INY
270     CPY KEYEND
280     BCC LOOP1
290     BEQ LOOP1
300     BCS NEWRECORD
310     .SWAP
320     LDY RECLENGTH
330     .LOOP2
340     DEY
350     LDA (FIRST),Y
360     STA TEMP
370     LDA (SECOND),Y
380     STA (FIRST),Y
390     LDA TEMP
400     STA (SECOND),Y
410     CPY #0
420     BNE LOOP2
430     .NEWRECORD
440     INX
450     CPX NUMBER
460     BNE BEGIN
470     DEC NUMBER
480     BNE START
490     RTS:]NEXT
500   CLS:INPUT"What is the record length",R:?RECLENGTH
      =R+1
510   INPUT'"What are the limits for the key",?KEYSTART,
      ?KEYEND
520   INPUT'"How many records",N:?NUMBER=N-1
530   DIM B ?(RECLENGTH)*N: !BASE=B
540   PRINT'"Setting up strings now"
550   FOR I%=0 TO N-1:FOR J%= 0 TO R-1:?(B+I%*(R+1)+J%)
      =RND(26)+64:NEXTJ%:?(B+I %*(R+1)+J%)=13 :NEXTI%
560   PRINT"Sorting now.":CALLSTART:PRINT"Checking."
570   FOR I%=0 TO (?RECLENGTH)*(N-2) STEP (?RECLENGTH):
      IF MID$($(B+I%),?(KEYSTART)+1,?KEYEND-?KEYSTART+1)
      >MID$($(B+I%+(?RECLENGTH)),?(KEYSTART)+1,
      ?KEYEND-?KEYSTART+1) THEN PRINT "ERROR AT"STR$(I%):END
580   NEXT:PRINT"O.K.":END
```

We use a bubble sort, as discussed in chapter 6. The program details are

50–80	Put the base address (of where the records are stored) initially in locations which will point to the second string in the bubble sort comparison
90	Set the record count to zero
110	Set the character index pointer to the lower limit for the field to be sorted upon
120–150	Put the old value of the pointer to the second string of the current pair into the pointer to the first string of the pair
160–200	Increment the second string pointer to the next record by adding the record length
220–230	Compare the relevant field of the first record of the current pair of records being considered in the bubble sort with that of the second record
240–250	If a character fails to match, either the records are correctly ordered (line 240) or they are not (line 250)
260–300	Otherwise, look at the next character. If we are past the limit for the field (that is, line 300 is entered), then the strings must be identical and need not be swapped
310–320	The routine to swap a pair of records. Y contains the record length
340–420	Swap characters one by one, starting at the end of the respective fields. TEMP is used as a storage intermediary
440–450	Continue until the current number of records has been examined
470–480	In that case, decrement the current number by one (the bubble principle) and continue until there are no records left to bubble through

Notice the use of the two sets of locations FIRST and SECOND here to point to the start of the current pair of records. By continually updating these on each cycle ((SECOND) → FIRST, (SECOND) + (RECLENGTH) → SECOND) we are able easily to move through the entire set of records, pair by pair, using indirect indexed addressing.

Again, we test the program using BASIC; here we set up the requisite number of random strings of the correct length, and after sorting, make sure that they are indeed in the correct order.

Exercise 7.2

Rewrite the program to deal with more than 256 records. Use LOOP-COUNTH to count the high byte of the loop and X for the low byte. Take particular care with the comparison: the problem is probably harder than you think.

7.5 Sorting a Series of 32-bit Signed Integers

In section 6.4 we saw how to sort a series of bytes into numerical order. Using indirect indexed addressing we are now able to go much further than this: we will write a program to sort a series of 32-bit integers into numerical order. You will recall that all integers in BASIC are stored in this format, so we will have a program that could sort BASIC integer variables (see section 10.2 for details of this).

Once again we will use the bubble sort. This is a fairly slow sorting method, and would be hopelessly inefficient in BASIC. However, in machine code the slowness is not a real drawback (1000 integers will be sorted in well under a minute) and there are compensating pedagogical features: the algorithm is easy to understand, and the program is short and generally economical in its use of storage locations.

Listing 7.7

```
  10 NUMBER=&70:FIRST=&71:SECOND=&73:TEMP=&75:BASE=&76:
     LOOPCOUNT=&78
  20 DIM START 100
  30 FOR I%=0 TO 2 STEP 2:P%=START
  40     [OPTI%
  50     LDA BASE
  60     STA SECOND
  70     LDA BASE+1
  80     STA SECOND+1
  90     LDA #0
 100     STA LOOPCOUNT
 110     .BEGIN
 120     LDY #0
 130     LDA SECOND+1
 140     STA FIRST+1
 150     LDA SECOND
 160     STA FIRST
 170     CLC
 180     ADC #4
 190     STA SECOND
 200     BCC NOCARRY
 210     INC SECOND+1
 220     .NOCARRY
 230     LDX #4
 240     SEC
 250     .LOOP1
 260     LDA (SECOND),Y
 270     SBC (FIRST),Y
 280     INY
 290     DEX
 300     BNE LOOP1
 310     BVC NOOVFLOW
 320     EOR #&80
 330     .NOOVFLOW
 340     EOR #0
```

```
350      BPL OVER
360      DEY
370      .LOOP2
380      LDA (FIRST),Y
390      STA TEMP
400      LDA (SECOND),Y
410      STA (FIRST),Y
420      LDA TEMP
430      STA (SECOND),Y
440      DEY
450      BPL LOOP2
460      .OVER
470      INC LOOPCOUNT
480      LDA LOOPCOUNT
490      CMP NUMBER
500      BNE BEGIN
510      DEC NUMBER
520      BNE START
530      RTS:JNEXT
540 CLS:INPUT"How many numbers",N:?NUMBER=N-1:
    DIM B 4*?NUMBER:!BASE=B
550 FOR I%=0 TO N-1:!(B+4*I%)=RND:NEXTI%
560 PRINT"Numbers assigned.  Sorting now":CALLSTART:
    PRINT"Done.  Checking now. "
570 FOR I%=0 TO N-2:IF  !(B+4*I%)>!(B+4+4*I%) THEN
    PRINT"ERROR AT "STR$(I%):EN
580   NEXTI% :PRINT"Checking O.K.":END
```

Listing 7.7 gives the program, the details of which are

50–80   Put the base address (of where the integers are stored)
        initially in locations which will be used subsequently to point
        to the second integer in the bubble sort comparison

90–100 Initialise the integer count. A location has to be used since
        the X and Y registers are used for other purposes

120   Set the byte pointer within an integer (Y) to zero

130–160 Put the old value of the pointer to the address of the second
        integer of the current pair into the pointer to the first integer
        of the pair

170–210 Increment the second integer pointer by 4 so it points to the
        next integer

230   Set the byte counter within an integer to four

240–300 Subtract the first integer from the second integer, 'throwing
        away' the result except for the most significant byte

310–320 If the overflow flag is set at the end of the subtraction,
        reverse the sign bit of the most significant byte (which is now
        in the accumulator)

340   This sets the negative flag to bit 7 of the contents of the
        accumulator. This is essential if no overflow has occurred,

	since 340 will be entered with the negative flag relating to DEX at 290. (ORA #0 or AND #&FF could have done equally well)
350	If the second integer is less than the first, there is no need to swap them. (If we had subtracted the second from the first in 260 and 270, we would have had to swap equal integers. BMI OVER would not pick up equality, and there is no simple test for equality in the absence of the four bytes of the result)
360–450	Swap the bytes of the integers one by one, starting with the most significant. Y already has the value 4 prior to line 360, so on entry to 380, Y = 3
470–500	Continue until the current number of integers has been examined. Notice that 470 and 480 are more efficient than LDA LOOPCOUNT : CLC : ADC #1 : STA LOOP-COUNT
510–520	Decrement the current number by one (the bubble principle) and continue until there are no integers left to bubble through

You may be wondering why we cannot in lines 260–300 use CPY #4 and dispense with using X altogether. The reason is that CPY #4 affects the carry flag, and we need to leave the carry flag alone so that it can register any borrowing that takes place. DEX does not affect the carry flag, so we are safe to use it. There is an alternative method which uses the stack, as we shall see in chapter 9, but it is still not as efficient as the one we use here.

Notice the similarity between this program and the one in the last section. Although one deals with fixed length strings and the other with fixed length integers, the indirect indexed mode allows a common structure.

As usual we test the program using BASIC. Here we create a set of random integers using the RND function.

Exercise 7.3

Rewrite the program to deal with more than 256 integers.

7.6 Sorting a Series of Variable Length Strings

We could try to use exactly the same structure as listing 7.6 to sort variable length strings, but we will come upon a large difficulty when we try to swap them. Since they take up different quantities of memory, we will need to keep opening up and closing up sections of memory to accommodate the swap. One solution would be to store the strings in fixed spaces of 255 bytes (the maximum permissible) but this would be exceptionally wasteful of memory if we are not dealing with record structures where fixed lengths are practicable.

There is another way which is much more efficient: create a list of pointers and swap those instead. That is, store separately a list of the addresses of each of the strings, and instead of swapping the strings swap the addresses. Then, at the end of the sort, the first address will point to the string earliest in the alphabet, the second address to the string next in the alphabet, and so on. The strings themselves remain fixed in memory; it is the pointers that are moved about.

Listing 7.8

```
 10 NUMBER=&70:FIRST=&71:SECOND=&73:TEMP=&75:ADDRESS=&76
    :STORE=&78:STORE1=&7A:STORE2=&7C
 20 DIM START 9000: DIM BASE 512
 30 FOR I%=0 TO 2 STEP 2:P%=START
 40     [OPTI%
 50     LDA BASE
 60     STA ADDRESS
 70     LDA BASE+1
 80     STA ADDRESS+1
 90     LDX NUMBER
100     .LOOP1
110      LDY #&FF
120     .LOOP2
130     INY
140     LDA (ADDRESS),Y
150     CMP #&0D
160     BNE LOOP2
170     INY
180     LDA STORE1
190     CLC
200     ADC #2
210     STA STORE1
220     BCC NOCARRY1
230     INC STORE1+1
240     .NOCARRY1
250     CLC
260     TYA
270     LDY #0
280     ADC ADDRESS
290     STA (STORE1),Y
300     STA ADDRESS
310     BCC NOCARRY2
320     INC ADDRESS+1
330     .NOCARRY2
340     LDA ADDRESS+1
350     INY
360     STA (STORE1),Y
370     DEX
380     BNE LOOP1
390     .LOOP3
```

```
400     LDA STORE
410     STA STORE2
420     LDA STORE+1
430     STA STORE2+1
440     LDX #0
450     .LOOP4
460     LDY #0
470     LDA STORE2+1
480     STA STORE1+1
490     LDA STORE2
500     STA STORE1
510     CLC
520     ADC #2
530     STA STORE2
540     BCC NOCARRY3
550     INC STORE2+1
560     .NOCARRY3
570     LDA (STORE1),Y
580     STA FIRST
590     LDA (STORE2),Y
600     STA SECOND
610     INY
620     LDA (STORE1),Y
630     STA FIRST+1
640     LDA (STORE2),Y
650     STA SECOND+1
660     LDY #0
670     .LOOP5
680     LDA (FIRST),Y
690     CMP (SECOND),Y
700     BCC NEWRECORD
710     BNE SWAP
720     INY
730     BNE LOOP5
740     .SWAP
750      LDY #1
760     .LOOP6
770     LDA (STORE1),Y
780     STA TEMP
790     LDA (STORE2),Y
800     STA (STORE1),Y
810     LDA TEMP
820     STA (STORE2),Y
830     DEY
840     BPL LOOP6
850     .NEWRECORD
860     INX
870     CPX NUMBER
880      BNE LOOP4
890     DEC NUMBER
900     BNE LOOP3
910     RTS
920     .TEXT:JNEXTI%
930 !BASE=TEXT:!STORE=BASE:!STORE1=BASE
940 INPUT'"How many records",N:?NUMBER=N-1
950 PRINT'"Setting up strings now"
```

```
960   S=0:FOR I%=0 TO N-1:R=RND(40):FOR J%= 0 TO R-1:
      ?(TEXT+S+J%)=RND(26)+64:NEXTJ%:?(TEXT+S+J%)=13 :
      S=S+R+1:NEXTI%
970 PRINT"Sorting now.":CALLSTART:PRINT"Checking."
980 FOR I%=0 TO N-2:IF $(!(BASE+2*I%)MOD &10000)
      >$(!(BASE+2*I%+2)MOD &10000) THEN PRINT"ERROR AT
      "STR$(I%):END
990   NEXT:PRINT"O.K.":END
```

The program is in listing 7.8, and the details are as follows

50–380   This section of the program sets up the list of pointers
50–80   Put the base address of where the strings are to be stored into
         locations which will be used to point to the current string
         found. The address of the location BASE is set above the
         machine code program and the strings in line 20. This will be
         the starting point of the list of pointers. The first pointer (to
         the first string) is passed as data in line 930
90   Initialise the string counter
110–160 Scan the current string, starting with the first character, until
         the end of the string is found
170   Set Y to the length of the string (including the carriage
         return). Recall that Y begins with zero, so the string length is
         Y + 1
180   STORE1 will contain the address of the next vacant space in
         the list of pointers. On entry, it is set to contain the address
         of BASE at line 930
190–230 Increment STORE1 by 2 so that it does now indeed point to
         the next vacant space in the pointer list
250–280 Compute the low byte of the address of the next string in the
         list of strings by adding the length of the last string to its base
         address
290   Store this low byte in the vacant space in the list of pointers,
         pointed to by STORE1 (set in lines 190–230). Y at this stage
         is zero
300   Also store this low byte in the location that we are using to
         point to the current string
310–320 Adjust the high byte of this pointer if carry has occurred
340–360 Set Y to 1 and store the high byte in the vacant space next
         door to the low byte stored in 290
370–380 Continue until all the strings have been accounted for

We shall pause at this point, because this is a fairly complicated piece of
coding. We have used indirect indexed addressing in two ways. Firstly,
using (ADDRESS), Y, we have been able to examine, character by

character, the contents of the current string being examined. Secondly, using (STORE1), Y, we have been able to access the next free location in the list of pointers. These are connected because we store the *contents* of ADDRESS in the memory location *pointed to* by the *contents* of STORE1. This idea will repay careful study, and you should not continue until you are confident you have fully grasped it. Symbolically, (ADDRESS) = ((STORE1), Y) when Y = 0 and (ADDRESS + 1) = ((STORE1), Y) when Y = 1.

The rest of the program does the sorting

400–430   STORE contains the address of the first pointer in the list of pointers (that is, it contains the value of BASE, *not* the contents of BASE). It is passed as data in line 930. It is a permanent record of this address: STORE1, which did contain the address, has lost it in lines 50–380; and it will do so again in this part of the program

440   Initialise the counter for the set of strings left to be sorted

460   Initialise the string character index pointer

470–500   Put the pointer to the location of the base address of the second string of the current pair being compared in the pointer to the first

510–550   Increment the pointer to the second string address by 2 so it points to the next string address in the list of pointers

570–650   Store the base addresses of the first and second strings of the current pair in locations on which indirect indexed addressing can be performed (in lines 680 and 690)

660–730   Compare the strings as in lines 220–300 of listing 7.6.

770–840   If strings need swapping, swap their addresses. Remember that STORE1 and STORE2 point to the *addresses* where the base addresses of the current strings are located, and not to the strings themselves

860–910   Continue with the bubble sort until there are no strings left to bubble through

Once again we check the program in BASIC. Here, random strings of random lengths up to 40 are used.

The ideas here are so important, and so tricky to grasp, that it is worthwhile finishing with a diagram to stress the relationship. Figure 7.2 considers a typical case. The current lower string of the pair begins at &2132. This address is contained in FIRST and FIRST + 1, whose contents were filled from the contents of &1682 and &1683. The first of these latter addresses is pointed to by the contents of STORE1 and STORE1 + 1. Illustrated is the flow of information required to access the sixth character (Y = 5) of the current lower string.

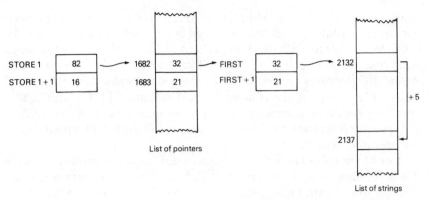

Figure 7.2: The relationship between locations in listing 7.8

Exercise 7.4

Rewrite the program to deal with more than 256 strings.

7.7 Indirect Jumps and Jump Tables

There is a non-indexed indirect addressing mode, available only with the JMP instruction. For example, the mnemonic JMP (&020E) will jump, not to &020E, but to the address *contained* in &020E and &020F (low byte first).

You are unlikely to want to use this in much of your programming. Its main use is in the structuring of operating system software, usually in conjunction with *jump tables.*

When you write JSR &FFEE for example (that is, OSWRCH) the microprocessor goes through what seems a tortuous path. It goes to &FFEE and encounters JMP(&020E). So it picks up an address from &020E and &020F and goes to the OSWRCH routine. Why this roundabout path? Surely it would be quicker to go straight to E0A4, the address of the write character routine?

When writing software, there are sometimes more important things than saving a few microseconds. There are two aspects to explain here: first the jump table, then the indirection. The BBC Micro has a series of operating system jumps stored from &FF00 onwards. These will either be straight jumps (that is, 4C XX XX) or indirect jumps (that is, 6C XX XX). In either case, there is a good reason for such a table of jumps. The jumps in this table represent most of the important operating system calls.

Now, later on Acorn, the BBC Micro's designers, may want to rewrite parts of the firmware (as software in ROM is often called). This may well involve changing some of the addresses for the important system calls.

Since a jump table has been used, however, all references to the call need not change. All that needs to be changed is the reference address. So, for example, all calls to OSWRCH remain as &FFEE; all that needs to change is the contents of &020E and &020F (which is set up on power on or reset). Again, all references to JSR &FFA1 (which is not indirected) remain; all we need to change is the contents of &FFA2 and &FFA3. This makes operating system management a much easier task. And it ensures that all your programs that use operating system calls will work with any change in the operating system.

Most of the important calls are indirected. One of the main reasons for this is to allow you to add pieces of code to the system software, while utilising the jump table idea. One example: suppose, when using OSRDCH, you always want to use the query prompt. Then you replace the contents of &0210 and &0211 (the indirection pointers for OSRDCH) by, say, &F8, &0D and write at &DF8 onwards

```
LDA    #ASC("?")
JSR    OSWRCH
JMP    &DEC5
```

Now all references to OSRDCH will indirect to &DF8.

The second reason for indirection is to allow you to intercept the operating system. As an example, suppose you wish to replace the prompt ">" by "?". If you type in and run the following program and then execute ?&20E = 1: ?&20F = &D, all occurrences of ">" will be replaced by "?".

```
10      FOR I% = 0 TO 2 STEP 2: P% = &D01
20      [OPT I%
30      CMP #ASC(">")
40      BNE OVER
50      LDA #ASC("?")
60      .OVER
70      JMP &E0A4 ]NEXT
```

To reset OSWRCH to its usual operation, execute ?&20E = &A4: ?&20F = &E0.

Used with care, this facility can be of considerable use in application programs. FINDCODE, one of the utilities on the cassettes available with this book, makes use of this to selectively list certain lines in a program.

The final reason for indirection is to allow different filing systems (namely *TAPE, *DISC, *ROM) to call different routines.

Exercise 7.5

1. Small letters are always &20 more than capitals in their ASCII values (that is, A is &41 and a is &61). Intercept OSWRCH to treat all small letters as capitals.

2. Use interception to give a query prompt to OSRDCH.

8 Multiplication and Division

8.1 A Simple Multiplying Algorithm for Decimal Numbers

Let us begin this chapter by reviewing the familiar algorithm for multiplying two base 10 numbers together.

Consider 1564×8401. We set out our working thus

$$
\begin{array}{rl}
1564 & \\
8401 & \times \\
\hline
1564 & (\times\ 1) \\
0000 & (\times\ 0) \\
6256 & (\times\ 400) \\
12512 & (\times\ 8000) \\
\hline
13139164 & \\
\end{array}
$$

We take each digit of the multiplier 8401 in turn, beginning with the least significant (the right-hand one), and multiply 1564 by it. As we move from right to left through the multiplier we move from right to left correspondingly through the columns. Thus each partial product is shifted one place to the left of the previous partial product. Then the partial products are added, column by column, to give the final result.

Each shift to the left is equivalent to multiplying by 10. Thus shifting twice and multiplying by 4 is equivalent to multiplying by 400; shifting three times and multiplying by 8 is equivalent to multiplying by 8000.

8.2 A Corresponding Algorithm for Binary Numbers

Consider now 1011×1101, both numbers being in binary. Our working is

```
   1011
     1101 ×
   ─────────
     1011
     0000
    1011
    1011
   ─────────
  10001111
  ─────────
```

The algorithm is identical, but very much simpler to perform since we only ever multiply by 1 or 0. Here, each shift to the left is equivalent to multiplying by 2.

8.3 Programming a 4-bit Microprocessor to Perform the Multiplication Algorithm

Imagine that instead of an 8-bit microprocessor (that is, with an 8-bit data bus and 8-bit registers) we have a 4-bit microprocessor (with 4-bit data bus and registers). How can we program it to perform the multiplication of 4-bit numbers? Once we have solved this problem for a 4-bit processor, it will be an easy matter to extend it to an 8-bit one.

Let us discover first what programming commands we have at our disposal. There are four.

(i) SHIFT RIGHT

This shuffles all the bits along one place to the right. The space created at the most significant end is filled with a zero. The bit that falls out at the right is put into the carry flag. Consider what happens to 1011. It becomes 0101 and 1 goes into the carry. Thus

(ii) SHIFT LEFT

Identical to shift right except all the bits are shuffled one place to the left, the least significant bit being filled with a zero, the most significant falling into the carry flag. Thus on 1011 we have

(iii) ROTATE RIGHT

This is just like shift right except that the space created at the most significant end is filled by whatever was in the carry. Thus, again considering 1011, if the carry contains a 1 we have

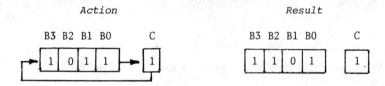

If the carry contains a zero we have

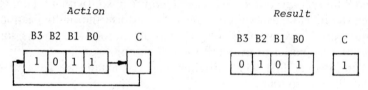

(iv) ROTATE LEFT

Identical to rotate right except that the movement is leftwards. The corresponding diagrams are

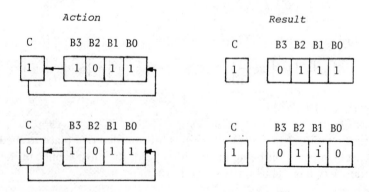

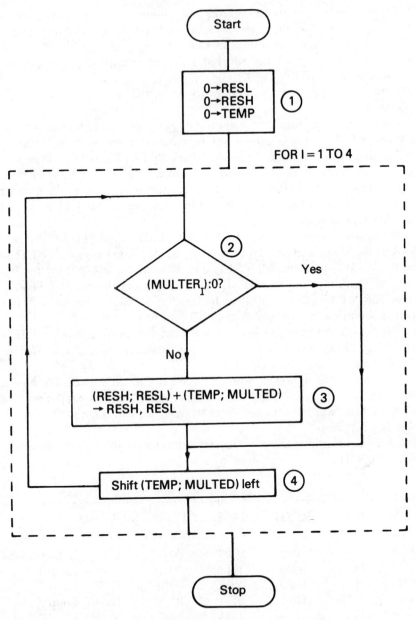

Figure 8.1

These four operations can act on any memory location, zero page or absolute. In addition, they can also act directly on the accumulator. This is something new, and constitutes an additional form of addressing, called, not surprisingly, *accumulator addressing*. In this case the operand is simply the accumulator itself.

Now, let us use these instructions to model the algorithm as closely as possible.

We will need two four-bit locations for our result: RESH for the top four bits and RESL for the bottom four bits (remember that at the moment we are assuming that memory locations hold only four bits). We will need a temporary location, TEMP; you will see why in a moment. Finally we need a place to store the multiplier, MULTER, and a place to store the number multiplied by this, MULTED. In our example above MULTER is 1101 and MULTED is 1011.

We begin by setting RESL, RESH and TEMP equal to zero. We now look at the least significant bit of MULTER. If it is one we add MULTED to RESL. We then shift MULTED one place to the left, putting the left next bit that drops out into TEMP. Look at the next bit of MULTER. If one, add MULTED to RESL and TEMP to RESH (together with any carry). Continue in this way through all four bits of MULTER.

·The flowchart of the process is in figure 8.1 (we assume that MULTER and MULTED already have their values assigned). Recall that (MULTER$_1$) refers to bit I of MULTER.

The only problem now concerns how we can test the successive bits of MULTER. This is most easily done by shifting right each time; the next bit of MULTER will fall into the carry flag and we can test this flag to see whether it is zero.

Since the ideas here are so important, let us follow through the flowchart for 1011 × 1101. The analysis is in table 8.1.

Table 8.1

MULTER	RESH	RESL	TEMP	MULTED	
1101	0000	0000	0000	1011	Initialisation
0110 [c=1]	0000	1011	0001	0110	Loop 1
0011 [c=0]	0000	1011	0010	1100	Loop 2
0001 [c=1]	0011	0111	0101	1000	Loop 3
0000 [c=1]	1000	1111	1011	0000	Loop4–End

8.4 A Program to Model the Multiplication Algorithm

Now we have understood the process using the simpler 4-bit microprocessor we can now write the program for our 8-bit microprocessor. The flowchart will be identical to figure 8.1 except that the loop is from 1 to 8.

Listing 8.1

```
10  TEMP=&70:MULTER=&71:MULTED=&72:RES=&73:?&75=0:?&76=0
20  DIM START 50
30  FOR I%=0 TO 2 STEP2:P%=START
40      [OPTI%
50      LDA #0
60      STA RES
70      STA RES+1
80      STA TEMP
90      LDX #8
100     .LOOP
110     LSR MULTER
120     BCC ZERO
130     LDA RES
140     CLC
150     ADC MULTED
160     STA RES
170     LDA RES+1
180     ADC TEMP
190     STA RES+1
200     .ZERO
210     ASL MULTED
220      ROL TEMP
230     DEX
240     BNE LOOP
250     RTS:]NEXTI%
260 CLS:REPEAT
270     INPUT"Numbers to be multiplied",A,B:
        ?MULTER=A:?MULTED=B
280     CALLSTART
290     PRINTA*B, !RES
300     UNTIL FALSE
```

The program is in listing 8.1. As usual we have used RES and RES + 1 for a two-byte label (instead of RESL and RESH). In this listing three of the mnemonics for the shifts and rotates are introduced. LSR is shift right; ASL is shift left; ROL is rotate left; and ROR, the one missing, is rotate right. Appendix 1 gives the symbolic diagrams and addressing modes. Note that LSR denotes *logical* shift right and ASL *arithmetic* shift left. These first words are of no consequence and are best ignored. So remember LSR as shift right and ASL as shift left; and to distinguish, think of shifting left as multiplying by 2 and so arithmetic.

The important thing to notice in listing 8.1 is the method of shifting TEMP; MULTED left. Shift MULTED left (ASL); then shift TEMP left rotating in the carry flag (ROL). Thus we use the carry flag as an intermediary in shifting the MSB of MULTED into the LSB of TEMP. This technique is used a great deal and should be thoroughly understood and committed to memory.

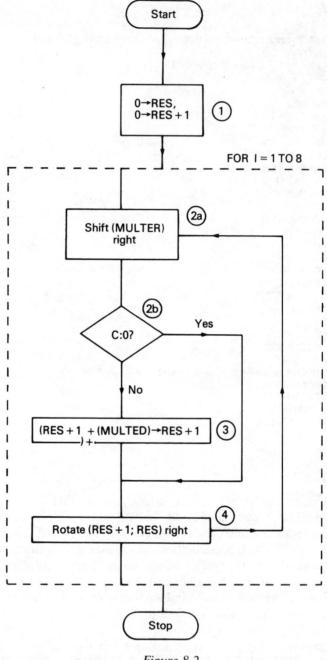

Figure 8.2

8.5 A More Efficient Algorithm for Multiplication

Our program in section 8.4 models very accurately the algorithm in section 8.2. But are we sure that this algorithm makes best use of the microprocessor's facilities? Let us return again to the 4-bit machine of section 8.3.

Consider the following method of performing 1011 × 1101

(1) Begin with 1011 0000 in RESH; RESL, since LSB of 1101 is 1. Shift right to 0101 1000.
(2) Since LSB of 0110 is 0 there is nothing to add on. Shift 0101 1000 right to 0010 1100.
(3) Since LSB of 0011 is 1 add 1011 0000 to 0010 1100, giving 1101 1100. Shift right to 0110 1110.
(4) Since LSB of 0001 is 1 add 1011 0000 to 0110 1110 giving 0001 1110 and 1 in carry. Rotate right to 1000 1111.

The great advantage here is that we do all our shifting in RESH and RESL and thus have no need for TEMP. As we move through the four stages of this process, the contents of RESH; RESL make the following changes

(1)	0101 1000	(2)	0010 1100
(3)	0010 1100	(4)	0110 1110
	1011 0000 +		1011 0000 +
	─────────		─────────
	1101 1100	1	0001 1110
→	0110 1110	→1000 1111	

The logic here is that we add on each partial product before shifting the partial result. In this way each partial product is shifted once less than the partial product immediately preceding it, and thus ends up in the correct column. The first partial product that we take is the one that will end up furthest to the right; the next one is the one that will end up one less column to the right; and so on.

Figure 8.2 gives the flowchart for an 8-bit processor, and listing 8.2 gives the program. Note the use of ROR RES+1 instead of LSR. This ensures that any 'ninth bit' is rotated in (a situation analogous to stage (4) in the 4-bit processor algorithm above).

Listing 8.2

```
10 MULTER=&70:MULTED=&71:RES=&72:?&74=0:?&75=0
20 DIM START 50
30 FOR I%=0 TO 2 STEP2:P%=START
40    [OPTI%
50    LDA #0
```

```
 60      STA RES
 70      STA RES+1
 80      LDX #8
 90      .LOOP
100      LSR MULTER
110      BCC ZERO
120      LDA RES+1
130      CLC
140      ADC MULTED
150      STA RES+1
160      .ZERO
170      ROR RES+1
180      ROR RES
190      DEX
200      BNE LOOP
210      RTS:]NEXTI%
220 CLS:REPEAT
230 INPUT"Numbers to be multiplied",A,B:?MULTER=A:
    ?MULTED=B
240      CALLSTART
250      PRINTA*B,!RES
260      UNTIL FALSE
```

8.6 More Efficiency Still: Accumulator Addressing

We met the idea of accumulator addressing in section 8.3. If you inspect listing 8.2 you will notice that after initialisation the accumulator is used only to load and store RES+1. We can therefore do without RES+1 until the end and perform the shifting on the accumulator instead. This has the bonus of being quicker too (2 cycles instead of 3).

Listing 8.3

```
 10 MULTER=&70:MULTED=&71:RES=&72:?&74=0:?&75=0
 20 DIM START 50
 30 FOR I%=0 TO 2 STEP2:P%=START
 40      [OPTI%
 50      LDA #0
 60      STA RES
 70      LDX #8
 80      .LOOP
 90      LSR MULTER
100      BCC ZERO
110      CLC
120      ADC MULTED
130      .ZERO
140      ROR A
150      ROR RES
```

```
160     DEX
170     BNE LOOP
180     STA RES+1
190     RTS:]NEXTI%
200 CLS:REPEAT
210     INPUT"Numbers to be multiplied",A,B:?MULTER=A:
        ?MULTED=B
220     CALLSTART
230     PRINTA*B,!RES
240     UNTIL FALSE
```

The new listing is in listing 8.3. Note that the mnemonic label for accumulator addressing is A—hence A cannot be used as a location name. As a final point, if we did not want to store the result, output it only to the screen (as we will do in the next section and in chapter 9) and then we could dispense with line 180 also.

Exercise 8.1

1. Adapt figure 8.2 to deal with the multiplication of two 16-bit numbers. You will need four locations for the result: RES+3, RES+2, RES+1, RES. Also two bytes for the multiplier, MULTER+1 and MULTER, and two for the multiplied number, MULTED+1 and MULTED.

Write the corresponding program. Can you make it more efficient by using the accumulator as a storage location for part of the result?

2. Adapt listing 8.3 to multiply two signed 8-bit numbers. You will need to check if either number is negative. If it is, you will need to form the two's complement. You will need to determine the sign of the final result also. This can be combined with the earlier checks by initially setting X to zero. Increment X if the first number is negative, decrement X if the second is negative. Now if X is zero the result is positive; otherwise it is negative (set Y to 1 in this case).

Now listing 8.3 can be used, and the sign of the result adjusted accordingly.

3. Write a program to compute 250 * Y + X (see section 5.4(b)).

8.7 An Interlude: Outputting Numbers Using Binary Coded Decimal

In chapter 6 we saw how to output characters to the screen, but we did not consider how we could output a number stored in a byte. For example, how can we output the byte &A3 to the screen as the decimal number 164?

We will consider a quite general way of doing this in the next chapter, but here we will combine some of the new instructions in the last few sections with a new way of storing data: binary coded decimal (or BCD).

Any byte consists of two sets of four bits, the four least significant and the four most significant. With their customary humour, computer scientists refer to these half-bytes as *nybbles*! We can conceive of the bottom nybble as representing a decimal digit, and the top nybble as another decimal digit. No problems will arise so long as we restrict the range of each nybble from binary 0000 to binary 1001 (that is, from 0 to 9). Thus we could understand 00110100 as decimal 34 in this approach. To put this another way, so long as each hex digit is restricted to between 0 and 9, we can interpret a hex byte as a two-digit decimal number. Then, a byte can now represent any of the decimal numbers from 0 to 99. This way of coding decimal numbers is called, for obvious reasons, *binary coded decimal* (BCD).

Now when we want to perform addition or subtraction using BCD numbers, we want the computer to behave in a special way. As an example, let us add 78 to 34 in BCD. We have

$$34 \qquad 0011\ 0100$$
$$78 \qquad 0111\ 1000$$

Without any special changes, the computer will produce 1010 1100 which is obviously rubbish in BCD. What we would like the computer to do is to generate a carry after it adds the lower two nybbles, correcting the result to BCD: thus

$$0100$$
$$1000$$
$$\overline{}$$
Carry 1 $\qquad 0010$

We want now to be able to add this carry with the addition of the higher two nybbles, and again generate a new carry correcting the result to BCD: thus

$$0011$$
$$0111$$
$$1$$
$$\overline{}$$
Carry 1 $\qquad 0001$

The final result will be [1] 12 in BCD (with the hundreds digit in the carry), which is correct.

There is a simple way to get the computer to behave like this: we just set a flag in the processor status register called the D flag. The instruction is SED.

While this flag remains set all occurrences of ADC and SBC are treated as BCD. Then an internal carry from the lower to the upper nybble will automatically occur as the lower nybble passes through 9, and it is automatically set back to 0. Similarly a carry to the carry flag is generated automatically as the upper nybble passes through 9, and this nybble also is set back to 0. Hence if we add 1 to itself 100 times we will obtain 00 with a carry of 1.

It is this idea that we exploit to convert our byte to a set of ASCII digits which we can output to the screen. The idea is to decrement the byte to be converted (using DEX, with the byte in X) and increment the accumulator by 1 in BCD (using ADC #1 with the D flag set). The highest digit can then be straightforwardly output (&30 + digit). The lower digits have to be separated: we use LSR A four times to shift the top nybble of the accumulator into the bottom nybble position, at the same time setting the top nybble to zero. Then again output in ASCII. Finally, we reclaim the accumulator, perform AND #&0F to set the top nybble to zero while leaving the bottom nybble unchanged; and then output in ASCII.

Listing 8.4

```
10 HIDIGIT=&70:NUMBER=&71:OSWRCH=&FFEE:OSNEWL=&FFE7
20 DIM START 100
30 FOR I%= 0 TO 2 STEP2: P%=START
40    [OPTI%
50    LDA #&30
60    STA HIDIGIT
70    LDA #0
80    LDX NUMBER
90    BEQ ZERO
100   SED
110   CLC
120   .BACK
130   ADC #1
140   BCC NOCARRY
150   INC HIDIGIT
160   CLC
170   .NOCARRY
180   DEX
190   BNE BACK
200   CLD
210   .ZERO
220   TAY
230   LDA HIDIGIT
240   JSR OSWRCH
250   TYA
260   LSR A
270   LSR A
```

```
280    LSR A
290    LSR A
300    CLC
310    ADC #&30
320    JSR OSWRCH
330    TYA
340    AND #&OF
350    ADC #&30
360    JSR OSWRCH
370    JSR OSNEWL
380    RTS:JNEXTI%
390 CLS:REPEAT
400    INPUT"Number to be output",?NUMBER
410    CALLSTART
420    UNTIL FALSE
```

The program is in listing 8.4, and the details are

50–60   Store in ASCII code for zero in the location for the highest digit

70–90   Initialise the accumulator and the X register. If the byte to be converted is zero, skip the BCD conversion

100–110   Set the relevant flags for the conversion

130–190   Add 1 in BCD to the accumulator and at the same time decrement the byte in X. If the accumulator passes from 99 to 00 increment the high digit. Continue until the byte reaches zero

200   Clear the D flag. It is most important to do this as soon as you are finished with BCD arithmetic, and also whenever you want to use a system subroutine like OSWRCH

220–250   Save a copy of the accumulator in Y, output the highest digit to the screen, and reclaim the accumulator (the copy is still in Y)

260–320   Set the top nybble into the bottom nybble position and set the top nybble to zero. Add the ASCII code and output to the screen

330–380   Get the accumulator back (stored in 220), set the top nybble to zero, add the ASCII code, output the digit to the screen, output a new line and return

This routine will always display three digits: 000 to 255. It can be adapted to output the contents of two or more bytes, but it is not really worth it since the next chapter contains a much more efficient routine. However, it is very straightforward to adapt it to count from 000 to 999 and this is left as an exercise.

You may be wondering why we do not use BCD to multiply, since we are so accustomed to base ten work. The problem is that BCD is very wasteful of space, and it is slow because many more byte movements are involved; for example, 193 × 253 will involve three instead of two bytes, and each multiplication by ten involves four shifts which multiplies by 16 in binary.

Exercise 8.2

What amendments to listing 8.4 are required to allow it to output numbers from 000 to 999?

8.8 A Second Interlude: A Pseudo-random Number Generator

Here is a relatively unknown, but very simple and very fast way to produce your own pseudo-random numbers.

We begin with a 32-bit shift register, which we seed initially when assembling the program with a 32-bit pseudo-random number from BASIC's generator (that is, we use RND).

Every time the program is called, this 32-bit register is 'specially' rotated left 8 bits, and the number remaining in the highest 8 bits is the random number. The 'special' aspect of the shifting lies in this: if the most significant bit of the register is 0 we simply rotate the register left one bit; if the most significant bit of the register is 1, we first exclusive-OR the bottom three bytes with a suitable constant before rotating left one bit. The constant we will use here is, highest byte first, &76, &B5, &53, but others are possible.

At the end of 8 rotations we have our random number, which we put into the accumulator. The program is given in listing 8.5. Lines 280 to 370 perform a chi-square test on some test data. When I ran this with 500 sets of 256, the null hypothesis of randomness could not be rejected even at a significance level of 25 per cent. This is strong evidence in favour of randomness. Permutation tests also show that there is no clustering. Moreover, it can be shown that repetition occurs only after 2^{29} bytes (that is, after 536,870,912 bytes). This is therefore a very good pseudo-random generator, especially given its simplicity and speed. By calling it four times, you can, if you wish, generate 32-bit signed integers equivalent to RND, with a repetition cycle of 134,217,728.

Listing 8.5

```
10 CONSTANT =&70:SHIFTREG=&73
20 DIM START 50
30 FOR I%= 0 TO 2 STEP 2:P%=START
40    [OPTI%
50    LDY #8
60    .BEGIN
70    CLC
80    LDA SHIFTREG+3
```

```
 90    BPL ZEROBIT
100    LDX #2
110    .LOOP
120    LDA SHIFTREG,X
130    EOR CONSTANT,X
140    STA SHIFTREG,X
150    DEX
160    BPL LOOP
170    SEC
180    .ZEROBIT
190    ROL SHIFTREG
200    ROL SHIFTREG+1
210    ROL SHIFTREG+2
220    ROL SHIFTREG+3
230    DEY
240    BNE BEGIN
250    LDA SHIFTREG+3
260    RTS:JNEXTI%
270 ?&70=&53:?&71=&B5:?&72=&76:!&73=RND:REM
    ***Initialisation***
280 VDU12:INPUT"How many sets of 256 for the test",T%
290 DIM N%(255):VDU12:FOR I%=1 TO T%
300   FOR J%=1 TO 256:A%=USRSTART:A%=?&404
310     N%(A%)=N%(A%)+1:NEXT
320   PRINTTAB(0,1)I%:NEXT
330 S%=0:FORI%=0 TO 255:S%=S%+N%(I%)^2:NEXT
340 PRINT"Chi-squared gives ";S%/T%-256*T%
350 PRINT"This compares with :"'FNCHI(1.64)" at
    5%"'FNCHI(1.28)" at 10%"'FNCHI(0.84)" at 20%
    and"'FNCHI(.675)" at 25%"
360 END
370 DEF FNCHI(X) = 0.5*(X + 22.56)^2
```

The program requires seven memory locations, all of which are initialised on assembly in line 270. Thereafter, no further initialisation is required. The details are

50	Initialise bit count
70	If most significant bit is zero, we require zero in the carry flag when rotating into the lowest byte of the shift-register at line 190
80–90	If MSB is zero, no need to exclusive-OR
100–160	Exclusive-OR bottom three bytes of shift-register with constant
170	Set carry to one for rotation in line 190
190–220	Rotate shift-register one bit to the left
230–260	Continue for 8 bits, load random number into the accumulator and return

Notice that we must initially load the carry flag with zero or one to perform the 32-bit rotation, since the rotation into the lowest bit will need to contain the contents of the highest bit.

8.9 A Third Interlude: Copying the High-resolution Screen to a Printer

As a third example involving our new instructions, we will consider how we can arrange to output the high-resolution screen to a printer. Specifically we shall focus on mode 4 and mode 0, since these are the two-colour modes where the maximum resolution is possible. The program is written for an Epson MX80 type II printer or any later version, but even if you lack any of these the ideas here will still be of use to you. From the programming point of view the techniques involved are of interest, and the information on how the BBC Micro organises its high-resolution graphics should be valuable too.

In mode 4 it is helpful to think of the screen as 32 rows, each row containing 320 bytes consisting of 8 rows and 40 columns. In mode 0, 32 rows again, but this time 640 bytes consisting of 8 rows and 80 columns.

As long as no scrolling has occurred since the last clear screen or mode change (this will typically be the case when we are plotting on the high-resolution screen) then the first byte of screen memory will be the first byte of the first row and first column of the screen. What happens if scrolling occurs (which will typically happen only in modes 0 and 4 if we are using user-defined characters textually) will be covered in chapter 9.

Thereafter, the memory is allocated as follows: we remain in row one, scan the first column of 8 bytes, then the second and so on to the eightieth (or fortieth) column. Then on to row two, and repeat the scan; then row three, etc. until we end at row 32. Figure 8.3 should make this clear. With no scrolling, the final byte at the bottom right-hand corner is &7FFF. In multi-colour modes, part of each byte contains the logical colour information but we are not concerned with this here.

Now in order to understand how we can copy the screen to the printer, we must understand how the Epson printer prints high-resolution graphics (other high-resolution printers operate similarly).

When the right control codes are passed to it (more on this in a moment) the Epson will treat each byte of data passed to it as specifying which of its 8 needles will fire (the ninth, bottom needle, will never fire in high-resolution mode). The top needle corresponds to the most significant bit of the byte of data, the eighth needle to the least significant. Thus &B3, which is 10110011 in binary, will fire the top needle, the third and fourth needles down, and the seventh and eighth needles down. The pattern produced is shown in figure 8.4: notice that it is a vertical pattern.

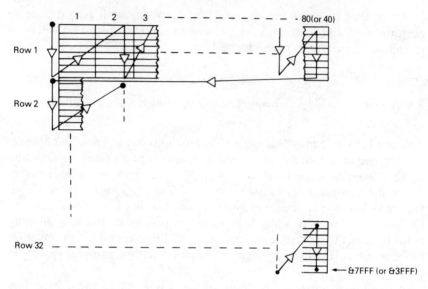

Figure 8.3: The organisation of screen memory on the high-resolution screen in mode 0 (or 4) when no scrolling has occurred since the last clear screen

Figure 8.4: The pattern produced on an Epson printer with the data &B3.
● *indicates a dot on the paper (i.e. needle fires)*
○ *indicates a space on the paper (i.e. needle does not fire)*

Now, in order to get the correct orientation on the paper it is necessary to output each of the 32 rows, column by column. That is, the first 8 × 8 bits must be output not in rows but in columns: figure 8.5 should make this clear. This is where our new instructions come in: we need to extract the column information from the 8 bytes that contain the row information.

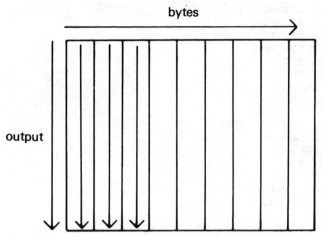

Figure 8.5: An 8 × 8 set of bits at the intersection of any row and column. The bytes relate to the rows of this grid, but the output must relate to the columns so that it matches the set-up in figure 8.4.

Listing 8.6

```
 10 COLUMNS=&70:ROWS=&71:COLCOPY=&72:LIMIT
    =&73:BEGINCONTROL=&74:LOCATION=&75:
    STORE=&77:OSWRCH=&FFEE:OSBYTE=&FFF4
 20 FORI%=0 TO 2 STEP 2:P%=&900:RESTORE
 30     [OPTI%
 40     LDA #3
 50     STA LIMIT
 60     LDX #0
 70     JSR CONTROL:LDA #2:JSR OSWRCH
 80     LDX #4
 90     LDA #&85
100     JSR OSBYTE
110     STY MEMLOC+1
120     LDA #&84
130     JSR OSBYTE
140     STX LOCATION
150     STY LOCATION+1
160     .MEMLOC
170     CPY #0 Dummy operand
180     BNE ZEROMODE
190     LDA #7
200     STA LIMIT
210     LDA #3
220     STA BEGINCONTROL
230     LDA #40
240     BNE FOURMODE
250     .ZEROMODE
260     LDA #11
270     STA LIMIT
280     LDA #7
```

```
290     STA BEGINCONTROL
300     LDA #80
310     .FOURMODE
320     STA COLUMNS
330     LDA #32
340     STA ROWS
350     .BEGIN
360     LDA COLUMNS
370     STA COLCOPY
380     LDX BEGINCONTROL
390     JSR CONTROL
400     .LOOP1
410     LDY #7
420     .LOOP2
430     LDA (LOCATION),Y
440     STA STORE,Y
450     DEY
460     BPL LOOP2
470     LDY #8
480     .LOOP3
490     LDX #7
500     LDA #1
510     JSR OSWRCH
520     .LOOP4
530     ASL STORE,X
540     ROR A
550     DEX
560     BPL LOOP4
570     JSR OSWRCH
580     DEY
590     BNE LOOP3
600     LDA LOCATION
610     CLC
620     ADC #8
630     STA LOCATION
640     BCC NOCARRY
650     INC LOCATION+1
660     .NOCARRY
670     DEC COLCOPY
680     BNE LOOP1
690     LDA #1
700     JSR OSWRCH
710     LDA #&0D
720     JSR OSWRCH
730     DEC ROWS
740     BNE BEGIN
750     LDA #13
760     STA LIMIT
770     LDX #11
780     JSR CONTROL:LDA #3:JSR OSWRCH
790     RTS
800     .CONTROL
810     LDA #1
820     JSR OSWRCH
830     LDA TABLE,X
840     JSR OSWRCH
```

```
850    INX
860    CPX LIMIT
870    BNE CONTROL
880    RTS
890    .TABLE:JNEXTI%
900 FOR I%=1 TO 13
910    READ ?P%
920    P%=P%+1:NEXTI%
930 DATA27,65,8,27,75,64,1,27,76,128,2,27,50
```

The program is shown in listing 8.6, and the details are

40–70   Output the first three bytes in the data statement (at 930) to the printer. This is ESCA 8 and it ensures that there will be no gaps between the lines output (that is, line feed is exactly 8 dots in depth)

80–110   Using OSBYTE with &85 in the accumulator returns the first memory location in screen memory with the mode number in the X register (here mode 4). The low byte goes into X and the high byte into Y. Here we store Y (at 170) for future comparison

120–150   OSBYTE with &84 in the accumulator returns the first memory location in screen memory for the current actual mode (low in X, high in Y). We store this address permanently into LOCATION

170–180   Since we assume the program will be used in either mode 0 or mode 4, if the comparison in 170 is not equal (that is, high byte of current screen memory is not the same as it would be in mode 4), we assume mode 0 operates

190–220   If mode 4, output ESCK 64 1 to the printer. ESCK is the normal-density high-resolution mode, which gives a maximum of 480 bits (that is, 60 columns of 8 bits/column) per line. This is adequate for mode 4. 64 1 is $64 + 1 \times 256$, that is, 320, and this tells the printer we will output 320 bits (that is, 40 columns of 8 bits/column) per line

230–240   Put the column count in the accumulator and always branch to 320

260–290   In mode 0, output ESCL 128 2 to the printer, which is double-density high-resolution (that is, maximum of 960 bits or 120 columns of 1 byte/column) per line. We inform the printer that we will output $128 + 2 \times 256 = 640$ bits (that is, 80 columns) per line

300   Put column count for mode 0 in the accumulator

320–340	Store the relevant column count in COLUMNS; ROWS is always 32 for either mode
360–370	COLUMNS will be required later, so store a copy in COLCOPY, which we can alter
380–390	BEGINCONTROL contains either 3 in mode 4 (from 220) or 7 in mode 0 (from 290). LIMIT is fixed from 200 or 270. Thus we output the same control information per line, that is, ESCK 64 1 or ESCL 128 2
410–460	Put the 8 bytes of the current column into STORE. Notice that in 440 we forgo the one byte saving available in zero page with STORE, X. However, there is only a small time penalty and it is overall much quicker to do this than to enlist X as well (we must use Y for line 430)
470	Initialise the byte counter (Y) for output to printer
490	Initialise the bit counter (X) for each byte output to printer
500–510	The next output will be to the printer only
530–570	Taking each byte in turn in STORE (moving backward) shift out a byte to the left and rotate it right into the accumulator. After the 8 bytes in store have been shifted once in this way the accumulator will contain 8 bits, the most significant relating to the top byte (that is, STORE, 0) and the least significant relating to the bottom byte (that is, STORE, 7). This accords with figures 8.4 and 8.5
580–590	Continue to shift until 8 bytes are output (that is, the 8 columns of figure 8.5)
600–650	Increment the screen memory location to the next column
670–680	Continue for the 80 (or 40) columns
690–720	Output to the printer a CR to mark the end of the line. (This assumes that your printer is set up so that CR generates an automatic LF)
730–740	Continue until all 32 rows are covered by returning to 360
750–790	Output some control characters which reset the line feed to its usual depth, and return
810–880	Outputs selected bytes from a data statement to the printer only

8.10 Division

Let us examine how we would divide 170 by 28 in binary. This is 10101010 ÷ 00011100. We shall use the familiar algorithm for long division, written a little more fully than usual.

```
Divisor    Dividend        Quotient
   11100)10101010        ( 0 1 1 0  (a)  Dividend < divisor so put
          ----------                       zero in quotient and do not
           11100000  (a)                   subtract divisor from
                                            dividend
Dividend  10101010
Divisor   01110000  (b)

          ----------
Dividend  00111010                    (b)  Dividend > divisor so put
Divisor   00111000  (b)                     one in quotient and sub-
                                            tract divisor from dividend
          ----------
Dividend  00000010
Divisor   00011100  (a)

          ----------
Dividend        10  remainder
```

The general idea here is to start at the most significant end of the dividend (the number into which we are dividing) and compare the five most significant bits with the five in the divisor. This is equivalent to attempting to subtract from the dividend the number 11100000 and seeing whether the result is positive. If it is, we put a one in the most significant bit of the quotient (the result); if not we put zero. If we put a one, we replace the quotient by the result of the subtraction; if we put a zero, we leave the quotient as it is.

We now shift the divisor one place right to give 01110000, and repeat the above process. We continue until we have shifted across to the original divisor, 00011100, and after we have performed the compare and subtraction process on that we stop. In order to know how many right shifts we must do before stopping, we start by shifting 11100 left until a one appears in bit 7. We store a count of the number of left shifts necessary and reverse this count when shifting right.

The flowchart for the process is in figure 8.6, where we use the X-register to count the shifts required. Notice how we ensure that the quotient has its digits in the correct place: we shift left for every shift right of the divisor, so that the digits automatically line up. The program is in listing 8.7. Notice that we have reversed the shift of (DVIS) and the incrementing of X in the REPEATWHILE loop: this is so that we can test the N flag as it relates it DVIS; if we put INX after this, the N flag would refer to X.

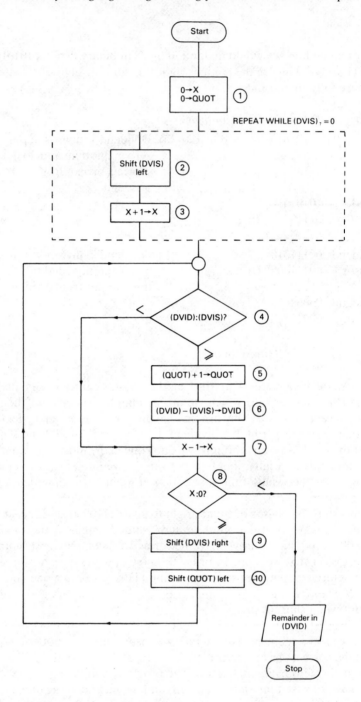

Figure 8.6

Listing 8.7

```
 10 DVID=&70:DVIS=&71:QUOT=&72
 20 DIM START 50
 30 FOR I%=0 TO 2 STEP 2:P%=START
 40   COPTI%
 50   LDX #0
 60   STX QUOT
 70   LDA DVIS
 80   .REPWHILE
 90   BMI LOOP
100   INX
110   ASL DVIS
120   BPL REPWHILE
130   .LOOP
140   LDA DVID
150   CMP DVIS
160   BCC LESS
170   INC QUOT
180   LDA DVID
190   SEC
200   SBC DVIS
210   STA DVID
220   .LESS
230   DEX
240   BMI FINISH
250   LSR DVIS
260   ASL QUOT
270   JMP LOOP
280   .FINISH
290     RTS:JNEXTI%
300 CLS:REPEAT
310   INPUT"Dividend",DD
320   INPUT"Divisor",DS
330   ?DVID=DD:?DVIS=DS
340   CALLSTART
350   PRINTDD DIV DS,DD MOD DS
360   PRINT?QUOT,?DVID
370   UNTIL FALSE
```

This program is very easy to extend to the division of a 16-bit dividend by a 16-bit divisor, that is, to any number from 0 to 32767 divided by any number from 1 to 32767. We need to assign two memory locations each to the divisor (DVIS+1; DVIS), the dividend (DVID+1; DVID) and the quotient (QUOT+1; QUOT). The program is left to you as an exercise in exercise 8.3.

Exercise 8.3

1. What happens in listing 8.7 if we try to divide by zero? Include a line that will stop this happening.

2. Write the 16-bit program referred to in the section above; indicate a check for division by zero.

3. Write the code that will round the quotient to the nearest whole number in the program of question 2. *Hint:* divide the divisor by 2 and round up if necessary; compare it with the remainder; unless the result is negative, add one to the quotient.

4. In a similar way to question 3 of exercise 8.1, write a program to divide two signed 8-bit numbers. Include a check for zero and a rounding operation, but do not output the remainder.

8.11 A Second Approach to Division

The programs developed in the previous section are modelled closely on the structure of the pen-and-paper algorithm for division. It is worth examining, however, whether an improvement can be made by deviating from this structure a little.

Rather than shift the divisor, let us see what we can achieve if instead we shift the dividend. Consider again dividing an 8-bit dividend by an 8-bit divisor. The idea is that we shift the dividend left one bit at a time into the accumulator and at each stage compare the accumulator with the divisor. If the divisor is greater than or equal to the accumulator we subtract it from the accumulator and put a one in the least significant bit of the quotient. On each shift of the dividend we need also to shift the quotient one bit left.

Using the last example, the first five shifts left into the accumulator result in zeros in the quotient. The next shift has 101010 in the accumulator, so we subtract 11100, obtain 1110 in the accumulator and put 1 in the quotient which is now 000001. We now shift across the seventh bit to get 11101 in the accumulator; we subtract 11100 to obtain 1 in the accumulator and put 1 in the quotient which is now 0000011. We now shift the eighth bit giving 10 in the accumulator, which is the remainder. The quotient is 00000110, the final answer.

An examination of this algorithm indicates that we can save significant time and storage space by depositing the quotient in the same place as the dividend. Then a shift of the dividend also shifts the quotient as required. Returning to the previous example, after the fifth shift the dividend will be 01000000. After the sixth we put a one in the least significant bit position to obtain 10000001; after the seventh we have 00000011; and after the eighth 00000110, as required.

A flowchart for the process is in figure 8.7 and the program is in listing 8.8. Notice how very much more concise it is than listing 8.7. The moral of this is that we must choose our algorithm with great care: mapping exactly on to an existing pen-and-paper algorithm is not always the best course.

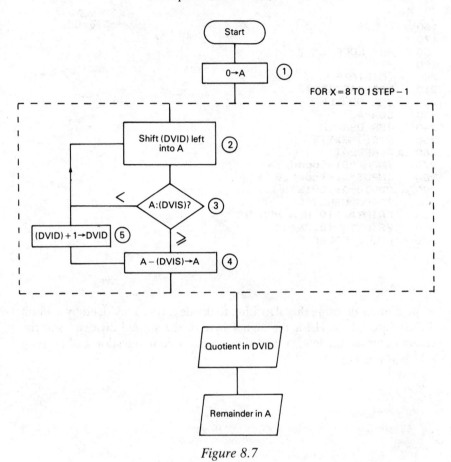

Figure 8.7

Listing 8.8

```
 10 DVID=&70:DVIS=&71:OSWRCH=&FFEE
 20 DIM START 50
 30 FOR I%=0 TO 2 STEP 2:P%=START
 40    [OPTI%
 50    LDA DVIS
 60    BEQ MISTAKE
 70    LDA #0
 80    LDX #8
 90    .LOOP
100    ASL DVID
110    ROL A
120    CMP DVIS
130    BCC LESS
140    SBC DVIS
150    INC DVID
```

```
160    .LESS
170    DEX
180    BNE LOOP
190    RTS
200    .MISTAKE
210    LDA #ASC("?")
220    JSR OSWRCH
230    LDA #7
240    JSR OSWRCH
250    RTS:JNEXTI%
260 CLS:REPEAT
270    INPUT"Dividend",A
280    INPUT"Divisor",B
290    ?DVID=A:?DVIS=B
300    !&403=USRSTART
310    PRINTA DIV B,A MOD B
320    PRINT?DVID,?&403
330    UNTIL FALSE
```

Exercise 8.4

Write a program using this algorithm to divide a 16-bit dividend by a 16-bit divisor (use QUOTH for the higher byte of the shifted dividend and the accumulator for the lower). Is it shorter than that in question 2 of exercise 8.3? Is it quicker?

9 The Stack: Subroutines and Interrupts

9.1 The Concept of a Stack

In section 6.5 we met the idea of a queue. This was described as a FIFO structure, in that the first item to enter the queue was the first to be taken from it. The contrasting structure to this is the *stack*, for this is a FILO data structure. Thus, the *first* item on the stack is the *last* to be taken from it; and conversely, the last item on the stack is the first to be taken from it.

Now this data structure is much easier to implement than is the queue. First of all, we need have no worries about memory wastage; secondly we need only one and not two pointers.

Figure 9.1 shows a section of memory to be used for a stack. Only two items of information are required: the base address of the stack (which is fixed) and the next free address in the stack.

Let us assume that there are 256 bytes available for the stack. The first item to arrive is put at BASE + &FF, so the next free address is at BASE + &FE. The pointer to this address is called a *stack pointer*, and its initial value is &FF. As an item comes into the stack this pointer will be decremented by one. So after one item arrives, the stack pointer is &FE.

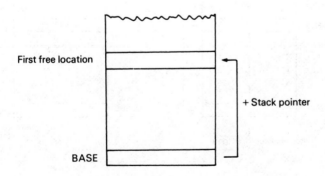

Figure 9.1: The memory set-up for a stack

Notice that we have started to fill up the stack from the top: this is conventional. To complete this imagery, it is usual to refer to the putting of an item on the stack as *pushing* an item on to the stack. The image is best conceived as pushing the next item up a kind of tube, the base of which is at location BASE. We keep going until we get to the first free location.

When we want to get an item from the stack we *pull* it off, pulling it down the tube as it were.

Now all of this would be very easy to program in software. Let us use X for the stack pointer. We initialise the stack by writing LDX #&FF. Now, to put an item on the stack we write

(a)   STA   BASE, X
                 DEX

assuming that the item was originally in the accumulator.

And to take an item from the stack we write

(b)   INX
                 LDA   BASE, X

Figure 9.2 shows the action of adding &10 to the stack when the pointer is &DA. Figure 9.3 shows the action of removing an item from the stack when the pointer is &E2.

Now the stack is such a useful device for temporarily storing information that the designers of the 6502 microprocessor have implemented the stack as part of its design. A special register, the stack pointer or SP, registers the next free location. And page one of memory, from &100 to &1FF, is

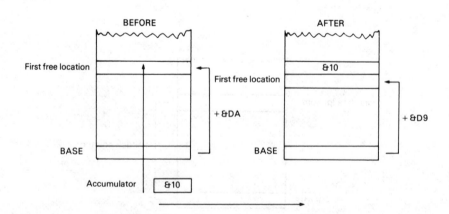

Figure 9.2: Adding the item &10 to the stack

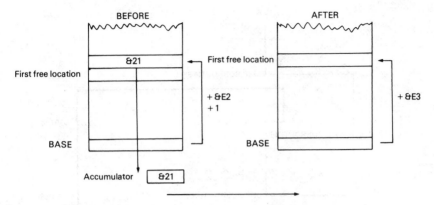

Figure 9.3: Taking the next item (&21) from the stack

reserved for the stack (that is, BASE = &100). Appendix 2 shows the SP register in relation to the rest of the architecture.

The useful thing about having this hardware stack (called a hardware stack because we do not have to write any special software to implement it) is that we do not tie up our X or Y registers in keeping track of it.

There are two special instructions to take the place of (a) and (b) above. Instead of (a) we write PHA: push the accumulator on the stack. The SP is automatically decremented. Instead of (b) we write PLA: pull the accumulator off the stack. The SP is automatically incremented.

When you turn the BBC Micro on, the SP is automatically initialised to &FF. It is possible to do this yourself, however; LDX #&FF : TXS is the coding. TXS transfers the contents of X to the stack pointer.

9.2 The Stack and Nested Subroutines

A particular program goes to a subroutine labelled SUBROUTINE1. While in this subroutine another subroutine SUBROUTINE2 is called; while in SUBROUTINE2, SUBROUTINE3 is called; and then, SUBROUTINE4! When RTS is met, how does the microprocessor remember where to go back to? The answer lies in the stack.

Figure 9.4 shows the situation that we have been discussing. The thin line shows the flow of logic as we call each subroutine in turn. The bold line shows the flow of logic as we return from each subroutine.

The first RTS (return from subroutine) that the microprocessor obeys is the one attached to SUBROUTINE4. At this stage the microprocessor needs to change the program counter to point to the next instruction after JSR SUBROUTINE4. The program counter increments uniformly, each new instruction being obeyed, until the next RTS is met. Now the

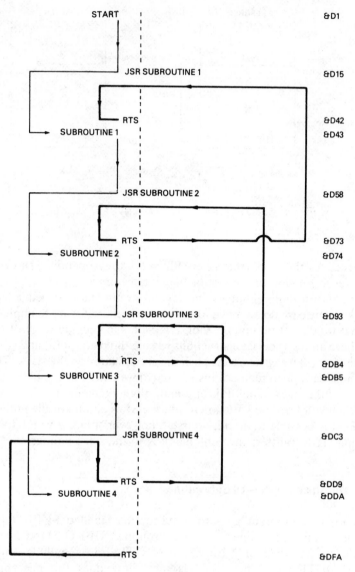

Figure 9.4: Nested subroutines

microprocessor needs to change the program counter to point to the instruction immediately after JSR SUBROUTINE3; and so on, back to the instruction immediately after the first call at JSR SUBROUTINE1. How does the microprocessor do it?

The algorithm it uses is a very simple one: when it meets a JSR instruction it puts the current contents of the program counter on to the stack (*high* byte then *low* byte) before going off to the subroutine. 'Going off to the subroutine' means that the program counter takes on the address referred to by the label attached to JSR. When it meets an RTS, the microprocessor restores the address to the program counter by taking it off the stack.

Actually, there is a slight anomaly in the way the 6502 does this. The address it puts on the stack when it meets a JSR is in fact *one less* than that of the next instruction. Hence, when it meets an RTS it automatically *adds one* to the restored program counter before continuing.

To understand the full operation let us follow through the contents of the PC, SP and stack on moving through figure 9.4. The memory locations are given on the right of that figure. Table 9.1 gives the details, where we assume (slightly unrealistically) that the stack begins empty.

When we get to &D15, we meet JSR SUBROUTINE1. 0D, 17 goes on to the stack (first in is 0D so it is last out). Notice that &D17 is one less than the return address. The program counter now contains the address of SUBROUTINE1. At each new JSR the same thing occurs: on to the stack with the return address (less one); into the program counter with the address of the subroutine.

Then the first RTS is met at &DFA. The first byte off the stack goes into the low byte of the PC; the next into the high byte. Then the PC is incremented by one, and the execution of the program continues from &DC6, the next instruction after JSR SUBROUTINE4. And so it continues until we ultimately return to &D18.

You will notice a final RTS at &D42, but in table 9.1 there is nothing left on the stack. In fact, there will be two more bytes: these point back into ROM, returning to the interpreter routine for CALL (USR is a little more complicated, but we need not consider it now). Thus, when we execute CALL&D01, a return address from the CALL routine is put on the stack, and the final RTS picks this up.

Apart from the CALL then, there is room for 126 nested subroutines in the 6502 (fewer with USR), far more than you are likely to need (unless you use a lot of recursion, that is, subroutines calling themselves).

Table 9.1 The contents of PC, SP and stack during the operation of the program in figure 9.4

Present contents of program counter	New contents of program counter	Stack Pointer	Stack (first out on extreme left)
0D01		FF	
0D15	0D43	FD	17, 0D
0D58	0D74	FB	5A, 0D, 17, 0D
0D93	0DB5	F9	95, 0D, 5A, 0D, 17, 0D
0DC3	0DDA	F7	C5, 0D, 95, 0D, 5A, 0D, 17, 0D
0DFA	0DC6	F9	95, 0D, 5A, 0D, 17, 0D
0DD9	0D96	FB	5A, 0D, 17, 0D
0D B4	0D5B	FD	17, 0D
0D 73	0D18	FF	

However, as we shall see later, the stack is also often used to store data using PHA and PLA.

The main purpose of using subroutines is to economise on program space. When using a high-level language, it is often advisable to use subroutines and procedures anyway, to make the program easier to follow. However, there are two disadvantages with subroutines which must be borne in mind if you wish to do this in assembly programming.

The first is that there is a time overhead to be paid. JSR takes 6 machine cycles to perform, and so does RTS, so there are at least 12 cycles in excess. Moreover, there may be a little more time taken up with passing parameters (see section 9.4). On the BBC Micro, 12 cycles is only 6 microseconds (6×10^{-6} s) — this is actually the 'best case' timing — which may not seem very much. Indeed it is not, but if your subroutine call is in a loop that executes a hundred thousand times (this is not untypical), then the subroutine call alone costs 0.6 s, which is more substantial. An important principle, then, is not to use subroutines in large loops if time is critical.

The second disadvantage is that subroutines do not allow a program to be relocatable. By *relocatable*, we mean that the machine code translation can go into any part of memory and work, without having to be reassembled. This means that there must be no JMPs (except for indirect jumps) and no JSRs (unless the subroutine goes to a fixed location like JSR OSWRCH). Branching is allowed, since it uses relative addressing, and in principle it is always possible to replace JMPs by branches, though it can sometimes be a little complicated. Relocatability is a desirable property, but not at the expense of program compactness or simplicity. Some programs are easy to make relocatable (an example is the REPLACE program, available on the cassette which can be purchased with this book; others are STRINGSORT and RETRIEVE in the next chapter). But in general, do not waste time and energy trying to do without subroutines just to achieve relocatability. With an assembler as fast as the BBC Micro's, reassembly takes only a moment anyway. However, there are sometimes useful tricks which can allow subroutines while retaining relocatable code: see section 10.5 for an example of this.

9.3 Interrupts

You are working at some fairly complex problem when the telephone rings. You make a brief note of where you are up to, put aside your work and answer the 'phone. When you have finished, you get your work back, read the note that you left yourself to remind you exactly where you were, and continue. The 'phone call represented an interruption, one too intrusive to ignore.

The microprocessor can be interrupted in a very similar way. One of its pins is connected to special circuitry such that, when this pin is grounded,

&D32   AD ←Interrupt happens while microprocessor here

&D33   03

&D34   04 ←The instruction (LDA &0403) is finished.

At this point, PC = &D35 and SR is, say, &81. Then,

&0D→stack

&35→stack

&81→stack

Address of interrupt service routine→PC.

Figure 9.5: Program sequencing during an interrupt request

an interrupt request passes to the microprocessor. The microprocessor finishes the instruction that it is doing, saves some relevant information on the stack and goes off to an interrupt service routine. Figure 9.5 shows an example of this.

Now, sometimes you do not want the microprocessor to be disturbed in this way. You want to do something similar to taking the phone off the hook. You can do this by setting a flag in the processor status register, by writing SEI. This sets the interrupt disable flag. When you want the microprocessor to answer interrupts again, you enable interrupts by clearing the disable flag with CLI.

It is possible that some interrupts are just too important to ignore. For this reason, the 6502 has two separate interrupt lines: NMI for Non-Maskable Interrupt and IRQ for Interrupt Request. The former cannot be ignored, whether or not I is set; the latter will be ignored if I is set, but not if I is clear.

The NMI interrupt is used by the disc and Econet systems if you have them. Even if you do not, the NMI vector will always point to &D00, and it is for this reason that &D00 always contains 64, the code for RTI (which we shall meet in a moment): it is just possible for stray NMI interrupts to occur! In this book we shall concentrate on IRQ since this is the interrupt most likely to be implemented by users.

When the microprocessor is interrupted on IRQ, how does it know where the interrupt service routine is? The answer is that it always looks for the address of the routine in &FFFE and &FFFF. This happens automatically; it is part of the internal make-up of the 6502 and has nothing to do with the BBC Micro. However, the address contained in &FFFE and

&FFFF is at the disposal of the BBC Micro's designers, and the code at that address must be provided by them. The address of the service routine is at &DC1C.

Now, there are a number of devices that could interrupt the microprocessor in the BBC Micro: for example, the printer or the user port, if available, and the cassette system. However, the most usual interrupt comes from an internal timer which is part of a VIA (a complex interface chip), memory mapped from &FE40 to &FE4F. You can disable interrupts from this timer only, by writing LDA #&40: STA &FE4E; but then no keyboard interruptions are possible, so JSR OSRDCH will not work, and neither will the input routines.

To re-enable interrupts from the timer, write LDA #&C0; STA &FE4E. You can disable *all* the interrupts with SEI; OSRDCH will still not work but entering the input routines will clear the flag.

Assuming that no interrupts have been disabled, how can the microprocessor decide which device has caused the interrupt? The answer is that a number of memory locations need to be used to reflect which device is calling for service. For example, if bit 7 of &FE4D is 1, then it is the timer in the keyboard VIA that is asking for service. In this latter case, after the system clock has been updated, the routine will need to ascertain whether a key has been pressed on the keyboard too. The interrupt service routine must interrogate each of these status memory locations in a fixed order, and when it finds the cause of the interrupt it must service it.

It is conceivable that more than one device interrupts at the same time. In this case, more than one of the status locations will be set. The fixed order that the service routine uses to interrogate the status locations reflects the priority of the devices to be served. The VIA timer gets a lower priority for example. Moreover, while one device is being serviced, it is essential that no other device can interrupt, otherwise some devices are in danger of never being serviced adequately. Because of this, the interrupt disable flag is automatically set when the calling device is being serviced. When the microprocessor returns from the interrupt, the status register is taken off the stack, as we shall see in a moment, and the interrupt disable flag will automatically be cleared again and new devices can interrupt. In general, it is unwise to clear the interrupt flag inside an interrupt handling routine.

When the microprocessor is interrupted, it automatically puts the return address on the stack (not less one as with a JSR). But in addition it puts the processor status register on the stack, because this register is very volatile (see figure 9.5). Since there are three bytes to remove from the stack and not two, and since there need be no correction to the return address on the stack, RTS cannot terminate the interrupt. Instead, a new instruction RTI is used: this restores the processor status register, and then restores the return address (not incrementing it by one as in RTS).

Any service routine worthy of the name will certainly use the accumulator, and most will use the X and Y registers also. It is essential to preserve these registers, therefore, and very early in the service routine this must be done. We can save them on the stack by using PHA: TXA: PHA: TYA: PHA. At the end of the routine, just before the RTI, we restore the registers with PLA: TAY: PLA: TAX: PLA. Notice the reversal of order here when regaining the registers, having stored them in the order A, X, Y.

There are three main ways to interrupt the BBC Micro.

(a) *Events*

This is the easiest way to handle interrupts on the BBC Micro, and is generally recommended. There are a number of 'events' that can be used to interrupt the BBC Micro: the following table shows them.

Accumulator	Event	Enable	Disable
0	Output buffer empty	*FX14,0	*FX13,0
1	Input buffer full	*FX14,1	*FX13,1
2	Character entering input buffer	*FX14,2	*FX13,2
3	ADC conversion complete (only if interface fitted)	*FX14,3	*FX13,3
4	Start of vertical sync.	*FX14,4	*FX13,4
5	Interval timer crossing zero	*FX14,5	*FX13,5
6	Escape pressed	*FX14,6	*FX13,6
7	RS423 error detected	*FX14,7	*FX13,7

Normally events are just ignored by the BBC Micro. However, you can force the BBC Micro to take notice by using the appropriate *FX command as shown in the table. Thus, *FX14,5 will activate the timer event; typing *FX14,6 in addition will also activate the ESCAPE event, and so on.

When an event occurs and is activated, the BBC Micro saves the return address and indirects through &220 and &221 (referred to as the EVNTV vector) to a routine supplied by you. The first thing that you should do in that routine is save all the registers, *including* the status register. However, you will need to test the value of the accumulator to see which event has occurred (see the table above). This is most easily done by storing the accumulator temporarily in &FC (a location reserved for this purpose on the BBC Micro), saving the registers and then loading &FC into the accumulator and making the comparison. The only other points to bear in mind are that your routine should not be too long, you should restore the registers before exiting, and, most important, you should end with RTS, *not* RTI. This is because the interrupt software is already included in the BBC Micro, and the system designers have implemented event handling as a standard subroutine.

Listing 9.1

```
 10 OSWRCH=&FFEE
 20 DIM START 50
 30 FOR I%=0 TO 3 STEP 3:P%=START
 40   [OPTI%
 50   STA &FC
 60   PHA:TXA:PHA:TYA:PHA:PHP
 70   LDA &FC
 80   CMP #2
 90   BNE FINISH
100   LDA #7
110   JSR OSWRCH
120   .FINISH
130   PLP:PLA:TAY:PLA:TAX:PLA
140   RTS:]NEXT
150 ?&220=START MOD 256:?&221=START DIV 256
160 *FX14,2
```

Listing 9.1 gives a simple example. Every time that a key is pressed we want a beep to occur automatically. Hence we use event 2. These are the details

50–60	Save accumulator temporarily and save registers on the stack
70–80	Restore accumulator and check if event 2 has occurred
90	If not end
100–110	Otherwise output a beep
130–140	Restore registers and end
150	Set event vector to point to new routine (note that this is done *after* assembling the routine)
160	Activate the event (note that this is done *after* setting the event vector)

We will return to events again in section 9.4, where there will be an exercise for you to try.

(b) *Using the IRQ vector*

When an IRQ interrupt occurs, the microprocessor will ultimately indirect through &204 and &205 (called IRQ1). It is possible to intercept this by putting the address of one's own routine here. In this case, one should save A, X and Y (not P), perform whatever functions one requires, restore A, X and Y and *jump to the routine originally pointed to in &204 and &205*.

Since many other devices are interrupting the microprocessor, if you are putting your own routine in IRQ1 it is essential that you have a means of deciding whether it is 'your' interrupt rather than some other device's. This requires the automatic setting of a flag and cannot be done in software: an additional piece of hardware (like a VIA) is required, which will automatically set a flag when interrupting.

In general, the use of IRQ1 is not to be recommended; use events instead where possible.

As you will see in appendix 7, the user port on the BBC Micro generates interrupts with automatic flagging. However, it should not be necessary to use IRQ1 for this, for if you do you will be giving the user port top priority when it does not merit it. Instead, you can use &206 and &207 (IRQ2). This has the lowest priority and the system will indirect through here only after all the standard system interrupts have been satisfied. See appendix 7 for further details.

(c) *BRK: a software interrupt*

There is a software interrupt, called BRK, which you might sometimes want to use. The term 'software interrupt' needs to be explained first. The IRQ interrupt is a hardware interrupt, since it is produced by altering the voltage of a pin on the microprocessor. Sometimes, however, especially when debugging, one wishes to interrupt the flow of a program to go to some other routine. One way of doing this is to use BRK. This is a one-byte instruction, and when working in machine code it makes it easy to patch in a software interrupt. At the place where we wish to stop we replace the next byte by &00, the op code for BRK. When the microprocessor encounters this, it puts on to the stack the return address *plus* one and the processor status register; and then goes to the software interrupt routine. Later, when we have completed the debugging, we can restore the old byte again.

The choice of zero as the op code for BRK is quite deliberate. When memory locations develop faults, they often give the impression of containing zero. Hence, by using a software interrupt routine in conjunction with BRK, faults of this type need not be catastrophic. But, the question arises: what is the address of the software interrupt routine? Where does the microprocessor get this information?

The answer is that it gets it from the same address as with IRQ; namely at &FFFE and &FFFF. This means that when it enters the interrupt routine, it must check first to see if it is via BRK or IRQ. To enable it to do this, a special flag is reserved in the processor status register, the B flag. This is automatically set to 1 if a BRK is encountered. Hence, every service routine must start as follows

```
STA    TEMP
PLA
PHA
AND    #&10
BNE    BREAK
```

The accumulator is first saved temporarily. Then the processor status register is removed from the stack, and copied back to the stack. Then (line 4) bit 4 of the status register (the B flag) is isolated, so that the result will be zero if B = 0 and non-zero if B = 1. Hence, if the result is non-zero, we branch to the BRK servicing routine. Otherwise, we save all the registers on the stack, as mentioned earlier, and continue with the IRQ service routine.

Now the BRK command is used in a very special way by the BBC Micro. Most error messages are handled through the BRK command. What happens is that following BRK is put the error number. The address of this location is stored in &FD and &FE. The contents of the accumulator are put in &FC. A jump is then made to an address located at &0202, using the indirect jump instruction, JMP (&0202), which prints out the message located after BRK and the error number. Figure 9.6 shows the set-up for ESCAPE.

It is very easy to use this facility oneself. For example

BRK : EQUB 102 : EQUS "VERY SILLY" : EQUB 0

will, if called, print what might be a suitable message! (We will see another example of this in section 9.5 below.)

Since &0202 is in RAM it is possible to create routines for oneself for BRK, but there is a problem here. Unless you incorporate a way of deciding whether BRK was encountered while checking your own assembly program rather than in the course of normal error processing in a BASIC program, you will lose all the error messages when using BASIC. For example, if you press ESCAPE (which is error number 17) and &0202 points to your own routine, you will jump into that routine. However, it is easy to solve this. All system uses of BRK will initiate from memory locations at &8000 and above. It is therefore necessary only to test the top bit of &FE: if it is 1 we use the system's BRK routine; if 0, we can use our

0	BRK
17	Error number
69	E
83	S
67	C
65	A
80	P
69	E
0	Terminating sign (always zero).

Figure 9.6

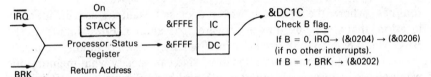

Figure 9.7: Interrupts on the BBC Micro. ($\overline{IRQ}$ means that the IRQ pin on the microprocessor has been pulled low. BRK means that the opcode zero has been encountered in a program.)

own. Thus we should store the original contents of &202, &203 in a variable called BREAK, say. Our own routine's address is now put in &202 and &203, and the first thing that that routine should do is to test the sign of &FE

```
        LDA     &FE
        BPL     OVER
        JMP     BREAK
        .OVER
```

Our routine proper will start at OVER onwards. Note that the status register is still on the stack and the original contents of the accumulator are at &FC.

Actually with a fast resident assembler like the BBC Micro's, BRK is not really necessary for debugging purposes. As we will see in section 10.6, JSR is just as good and much easier to use.

Figure 9.7 acts as a summary to this section on interrupts, which has been fairly complicated.

9.4 Passing Parameters to and from Subroutines

There are three ways of passing information to and from subroutines, and we shall examine their merits here.

(a) *Through registers*

This is the simplest way to convey information between the main program and the subroutine. If only one 8-bit parameter needs to be passed then the accumulator is the natural place: OSRDCH and OSWRCH use this method. If a second or third parameter is needed, X and Y can be used: OSBYTE uses this method.

If more than three parameters are to be passed, the registers can still be used as a pointer. A common convention is to put the low byte in X and the high byte in Y: OSWORD uses this method. Then the subroutine can store these in zero page locations of its choice and use indirect indexed addressing. This method is commonly used in operating system subroutines, where the firmware writer does not want to use up memory locations that will be used by a software programmer. For example, in the BBC Micro &70 to &8F are kept free: when one uses certain system calls that refer to a large memory allocation, one can specify what memory one wants to use by passing the pointer in X and Y. In this way, one can be free to partition one's own memory requirements and still have the advantage of using powerful system routines.

The disadvantage of using registers for passing parameters is that they might well contain important information which needs to be kept. The remedy here is to save the registers on the stack and recall them on return. It is good programming practice to save any registers used in the body of the subroutine, but not being used to pass parameters, in the subroutine itself. So, for example, if X and A are used to pass parameters, write PHA: TXA: PHA prior to loading X and A with the parameters and going to the subroutine. Y should be automatically preserved, for if the subroutine uses Y it will use TAY: PHA and recover Y with PLA: TYA at the end.

(b) *Through the stack*

Returning results from a subroutine on the stack or passing parameters to the subroutine using the stack needs care, since the return address is put on the stack just before entry and taken off just prior to exit. This means that the address needs to be saved in the subroutine itself. This is not generally used in firmware programs, but in your own programs it might be a possibility if you need to keep zero page free for some reason.

The first lines in the subroutine will be

```
        PLA
        STA    MEMLOC1 + 1
        PLA
        STA    MEMLOC2 + 1
```

and the last lines will be

```
MEMLOC2    LDA    #0            Dummy operand
           PHA
MEMLOC1    LDA    #0            Dummy operand
           PHA
           RTS
```

Notice the order of replacement: FILO dictates that the first item taken off be the last put on the stack.

Once this is done, items can be passed on the stack with complete freedom. If a lot of data is to be passed, this method could actually result in a saving of memory since PHA and PLA take up only one byte. The 14 bytes used up in storing and restoring the return address are a large overhead in most cases, however; and there is also a large time penalty attached.

I mentioned above that such techniques are not usually used in firmware. There is one exception to this, and this involves subroutines that may be called by the interrupt service routine, but that may be used also by the program being interrupted. In this case, it is conceivable that a section of program is interrupted, and then the interrupt routine uses just that section of program. In such a case, it is essential that the subroutines be capable of re-entry without destroying what has gone before. Such subroutines are called *re-entrant*. The fundamental consideration is that no fixed memory locations be used: this confines the subroutine to using registers (which are saved at the beginning of the interrupt routine) and the stack. If the stack is used, the X register will carry a zero pointer to where the return address can be stored. A small section of zero page memory will be set aside for interrupt routine use, and its use will not corrupt any other program. The X register is used because it simplifies the coding. The subroutine will begin

```
PLA
STA    0, X
PLA
STA    1, X
```

It is necessary that the X register is not otherwise used in the routine, since its contents will be required at the end when the return address is restored (unless there is room in zero page for this information also)

```
LDA    1, X
PHA
LDA    0, X
PHA
```

X is used in preference to Y here, since zero page addressing is not available with Y.

There is one other way the stack can be used to pass data. Look at the following coding

```
JSR    EXAMPLE
M
E
S
S
A
G
E
0
0D
54
```

The word MESSAGE is encoded in ASCII following the JSR, and ends with zero. Following this is the address to which the subroutine should return (minus *one*). The subroutine picks this up as follows

```
EXAMPLE    CLC
           PLA
           ADC   #1
           STA   ADDRESS
           PLA
           ADC   #0
           STA   ADDRESS+1
```

where ADDRESS is a zero page location. Now, indirect indexed addressing can be used to pick up the message, that is, LDA (ADDRESS), Y. When zero is encountered, the message is over and the subroutine returns as follows

```
           LDA   (ADDRESS), Y
           PHA
           INY
           LDA   (ADDRESS), Y
           PHA
           RTS
```

This method is not re-entrant, and so is not used in interrupts, but messages are not usually needed in interrupts in any case. The BBC Micro uses this method in cases where a message is required but the BRK method, discussed earlier, is not suitable.

(c) *Through fixed memory locations*

This is the method that you will use most often when you write your own subroutines. It is generally frowned upon by many authorities on programming because it makes it difficult to establish a library of subroutines. This is because a subroutine may use memory that interferes with the main program.

This is not a problem on the BBC Micro, however, so long as you store a copy of your program in its unassembled (source code) form. It can then be combined with other subroutines and the main program, and memory allocated at the end.

The only problem with this method is that labels may interfere with each other. For example, we may have OVER in the main program and the subroutine. It should not be difficult, however, to check a program for this. A utility program on the cassette (FINDCODE) will be of assistance in this.

9.5 Three Examples of Using Registers to Pass Parameters

To illustrate the above ideas, let us look at three commands on the Electron which use the A, X and Y to pass information.

(a) *CODE U, V

This command puts the value U in the X register, the value V in the Y register and 0 in the accumulator (in practice, U and V must be replaced by constants, or OSCLI must be used). An indirect jump is then made to the contents of &200 and &201, referred to as the user vector or USERV (see section 7.7 to remind yourself about indirection). Normally, the contents of these locations point to a routine which prints out the message 'Bad Command'. However, by changing the contents to point to your own routines, you can pass to that routine the values U and V in the X and Y registers. This may not seem particularly useful, but its main purpose will become apparent when we look at the next command.

(b) *LINE s

Here, s stands for a string of any characters, which should *not* be enclosed in quotes unless you also wish to pass quotes to your routine. Again, a jump is made to the contents of USERV, but this time the contents of X and Y point to the starting address of the string (low byte in X, high byte in Y) and the accumulator contains 1. Thus, by inspecting the accumulator one can decide whether the indirection has come from a *CODE command or a *LINE command and act accordingly.

The main purpose of *LINE is to enable a variety of new commands to be used in BASIC programs. For example, *LINE GRAPH can be decoded accordingly and the appropriate routine used. A disadvantage of this approach, though, is that no values can be passed to the subroutine GRAPH without some fairly complex coding. In such a case the use of CALL with parameters is easier (see section 10.2), although it does have disadvantages that we shall mention in a moment.

However, if you want to pass no more than two values, both within the range 0 to 255, then you can use *CODE as well. So, for example, you might write

*LINE GRAPH
*CODE 52,200

to pass 52 and 200 to the routine GRAPH. The advantage of this over CALL is that to write CALL GRAPH you would need to equate GRAPH to some specific location within whatever program you were using it. This makes the use of a library of extra commands a little fiddly. With *LINE one can simply load in the code for the extra commands and set up &200 and &201 accordingly. From then on, one can refer to the newly defined commands simply by using *LINE and *CODE.

Listing 9.2

```
  10 DIM START 200
  20 OSWRCH=&FFEE
  30 MISTAKE=&E310
  40 ?&200=START MOD 256:?&201=START DIV 256
  50 FOR I%=0 TO 2 STEP 2:P%=START
  60    [OPT I%
  70    CMP #0
  80    BEQ CODE
  90    STX &71
 100    STY &72
 110    LDX #255
 120    .LOOP1
 130    LDY #255
 140    .LOOP2
 150    INX
 160    INY
 170    LDA TEXT,X
 180    BEQ Error
 190    CMP #13
 200    BEQ MATCH
 210    CMP (&71),Y
 220    BEQ LOOP2
 230    .LOOP3
 240    INX
 250    LDA TEXT,X
 260    CMP #13
 270    BNE LOOP3
 280    INX
 290    JMP LOOP1
 300    .Error
 310    JMP MISTAKE
 320    .MATCH
 330    LDA TEXT+1,X
 340    STA &70
 350    RTS
 360    .CODE
 370    LDA &70
 380    CMP #1
 390    BEQ One
 400    CMP #2
 410    BEQ TWO
 420    CMP #3
 430    BEQ THREE
 440    JMP NOLINE
 450    .One
 460    JMP GRAPH
 470    .TWO
 480    JMP GRID
 490    .THREE
```

```
500     JMP STAR
510     .GRAPH
520     LDA #ASC("A")
530     JSR OSWRCH
540     JMP FINISH
550     .GRID
560     LDA #ASC("B")
570     JSR OSWRCH
580     JMP FINISH
590     .STAR
600     LDA #ASC("C")
610     JSR OSWRCH
620     JMP FINISH
630     .FINISH
640     STX &73
650     STY &74
660     RTS
670     .NOLINE
680     BRK
690     EQUB 100
700     EQUS "No *LINE"
710     EQUB 0
720     .TEXT
730     EQUS "GRAPH"
740     EQUW &10D
750     EQUS "GRID"
760     EQUW &20D
770     EQUS "STAR"
780     EQUW &30D
790     EQUB 0:]NEXT
800     *KEY0 ?&70=0:*CODE5,6¦M
810     *LINE GRAPH
820     *CODE15,200
830     PRINT?&73,?&74
840     *LINE GRID
850     *CODE20
860     PRINT?&73,?&74
870     *LINE STAR
880     *CODE36,39
890     PRINT?&73,?&74
900     *LINE GRAP
```

Listing 9.2 shows how you can set this up for three commands GRAPH, GRID and STAR. The idea is that *LINE goes to a routine that checks the following string—it must be exactly correct or 'Bad Command' will be printed. If the command is GRAPH, 1 is put in &70; if GRID, 2 is put in &70; if STAR, 3 is put in &70. (Thus the method will accommodate up to 256 commands.)

*CODE then transfers parameters in X and Y to the appropriate routine. In listing 9.1 these routines just output the letter A, B or C and store X and Y simply to test that the method is working. Obviously, in real applications these routines would do rather more!

Let us look at the details of the program now.

30	The contents of USERV originally point to 'Bad Command', and this is &E07E
40	Put the start of the routine in USERV
70–80	If *CODE, jump to 370
90–100	Low byte of string in &71, high byte in &72, to be used with indirect indexed addressing later
110–140	Initialise X and Y. X will point to the stored text in the table at 720 onwards; Y will point to the characters in the string in *LINE
170–180	If the zero end byte is not in the stored text, no match of *LINE string can be found, and the error routine at 310 is entered
190–200	If carriage return in stored text is reached, match has been achieved so go to 330
210–220	Continue looping if next characters compare
240–290	If not, search for next carriage return in stored text (this marks the end of the current command being searched). When found, increment pointer to step over number code and return to 130
300–310	Output 'Bad Command'
320–350	Put number code into &70 and return
360–440	*CODE enters here. Check the contents of &70 and go to the appropriate routine. If contents of &70 are inappropriate, go to error routine at 680
450–660	Sample output routines to test that method works
680–710	Use of BBC Micro's BRK handler to print out error message. 100 is a dummy error number; the message must always end with 0
730–790	Look-up table
800–890	Test lines

Run the program and note the output: line 890 should give 'Bad Command'. Now press f_0 and you should get 'No *LINE'.

You should now be in a position to implement your own new commands using *LINE and *CODE if you wish.

(c) *OSWORD*

OSWORD (at FFF1) is a general-purpose subroutine which uses a parameter block to pass information to and fro. The first address of this block is pointed to by the contents of X and Y (X low byte, Y high byte).

Hence, if you wanted the block to begin at &80 you would put 0 in Y and &80 in X. The value in A determines which particular use of OSWORD is required.

One use of OSWORD is to set the internal interval timer for use with events: the accumulator should be set to 4 on entry. X and Y point to a block of five bytes which represents the point from which the internal clock will count in units of 1/100 second. When the timer crosses zero an event will be generated and, if it is enabled (*FX14,5), an entry will be made to your handling routine (compare section 9.3). So, for example, we may want to initiate an event every second: we therefore need to set the timer to &FFFFFFFF9C, whereby &64 (100) pulses later an event is generated. If we decide to store this time in &80 to &84, we put &FC in &80 and &FF in &81 to &84, and set X to &80 and Y to 0 before entering OSWORD with A set to 4. In the handling routine itself, having saved the registers, we would reset the timer prior to performing whatever task we wanted the handling routine to do. In this way, the event will continue to occur every second. Achieving this is left as an exercise for you below.

As a second example, let us consider how to use OSWORD to achieve the equivalent of INPUT (recall our initial discussion of this in section 6.7). This requires 0 in A. The block required is 5 bytes, and we shall use &80 to &84: hence 0 in Y and &80 in X. In &80 and &81 we put the address of the buffer that we shall use for the input line; in &82 we put the maximum length of the line; and in &83 and &84 the minimum and maximum ASCII values allowed for each character (in these latter two, any character will be accepted from the keyboard, but only characters in the range will be entered into the buffer).

Implementing all of the above is left to you as exercise 9.1, but before moving on to that let us summarise the three main uses of the X and Y registers in this section.

In (a), we use X and Y simply to pass values; in (b) we use X and Y to pass the start address of our data; in (c) we use X and Y to pass the start address of a block which may contain data, but which may also contain an address of where the data is to be found. (It is worth adding that we could use the ideas in (c) with *CODE to pass a parameter block to *LINE. But now, it may well be that the advantages over CALL are lost.)

Exercise 9.1

1. Generate an event every second and, in response to that event, output a beep.

2. Rewrite listing 6.7, using OSWORD instead of the jump to the BASIC interpreter, and restrict input to capital letters only. Note that on return from OSWORD the carry flag is set to 0 if carriage return has been pressed, and to 1 if ESCAPE has been pressed (in both cases Y is set to the length of the string input, including the carriage return, if relevant). You should arrange for the routine to end if ESCAPE has been pressed.

Why is the OSWORD method to be preferred in general?

9.6 Two Important Subroutines

In order to illustrate the ideas considered in section 9.4, especially those in (c), let us examine two very useful subroutines. The first accepts numerical input in decimal from the keyboard and converts it into a signed four-byte hex number. It therefore fulfils the function of INPUT N as opposed to INPUT N$, which we covered in chapter 6. The second outputs in decimal a signed four-byte hex number: it fulfils the function of PRINT N.

Listing 9.3: A subroutine to convert from decimal to hex

```
 10  LOOPCOUNT=&70:INDIC=&71:BUFFER=&73:SPOINT=&75:NUMBER
     =&76:OSWRCH=&FFEE
 20  DIM START 200
 30  FOR I%=0 TO 2 STEP 2:P%=START
 40     [OPTI%
 50     PHA
 60     TXA
 70     PHA
 80     TYA
 90     PHA
100     TSX
110     STX SPOINT
120     LDA #ASC("?")
130     JSR OSWRCH
140     JSR &BC05
150     LDY #0
160     LDX #3
170     .INITIALISE
180     STY NUMBER,X
190     DEX
200     BPL INITIALISE
210     STY INDIC
220     STY BUFFER
230     LDA #7
240     STA BUFFER+1
250     LDA (BUFFER),Y
260     CMP #ASC("-")
270     BNE NTMINUS
280     LDA #&80
290     STA INDIC
300     BNE OVER
310     .NTMINUS
320     CMP #ASC("+")
330     BNE CHARGET
340     .OVER
```

```
350     INC BUFFER
360     .CHARGET
370     LDA (BUFFER),Y
380     CMP #&0D
390     BEQ CHECKSIGN
400     JSR MULTTWO
410     LDX #3
420     .STACK
430     LDA NUMBER,X
440     PHA
450     DEX
460     BPL STACK
470     JSR MULTTWO
480     JSR MULTTWO
490     LDX #0
500     LDA #4
510     STA LOOPCOUNT
520     CLC
530     .XTEN
540     PLA
550     ADC NUMBER,X
560     STA NUMBER,X
570     INX
580     DEC LOOPCOUNT
590     BNE XTEN
600     BVS OVERFLOW
610     LDA (BUFFER),Y
620     SEC
630     SBC #&30
640     BCC MISTAKE
650     CMP #10
660     BCS MISTAKE
670     ADC NUMBER
680     STA NUMBER
690     BCC NOCARRY
700     INC NUMBER+1
710     BCC NOCARRY
720     INC NUMBER+2
730     BCC NOCARRY
740     INC NUMBER+3
750     BMI OVERFLOW
760     .NOCARRY
770     INY
780     BNE CHARGET
790     .CHECKSIGN
800     LDA INDIC
810     BPL PLUS
820     JSR FLIPSIGN
830     .PLUS
840     CLC
850     BCC REGS
860     .OVERFLOW
870     LDA INDIC
880     ORA #&40
890     STA INDIC
900     .MISTAKE
```

```
910    LDX SPOINT
920    TXS
930    SEC
940    .REGS
950    PLA
960    TAY
970    PLA
980    TAX
990    PLA
1000   RTS
1010   .MULTTWO
1020   ASL NUMBER
1030   ROL NUMBER+1
1040   ROL NUMBER+2
1050   ROL NUMBER+3
1060   BMI OVERFLOW
1070   RTS
1080   .FLIPSIGN
1090   LDY #4
1100   LDX #0
1110   SEC
1120   .FLIP
1130   LDA #0
1140   SBC NUMBER,X
1150   STA NUMBER,X
1160   INX
1170   DEY
1180   BNE FLIP
1190   RTS:]NEXTI%
1200 REPEAT
1210    !&404=USRSTART
1220    IF (?&407 AND 1) = 0 THEN PRINT!NUMBER ELSE IF
       (?INDIC AND &40) = 0 PRINT"Not a valid number"
       ELSE IF (?INDIC AND &80) = 0 PRINT"Number too
       large" ELSE PRINT"Number too small"
1230   UNTIL FALSE
```

Listing 9.3 contains the program and the details are

50–90	Saves registers on the stack
100–110	Save stack pointer in case exit from program is via OVER-FLOW (at line 870) or MISTAKE (at line 910). TSX transfers a copy of the stack pointer to the X register
120–140	Display ? prompt, and get data from keyboard into buffer at &700
150–240	Initialise the relevant memory locations
250–300	If the first character is a minus sign, set bit 7 of INDIC to 1. Line 300 always results in a branch to 350
320–330	If the first character is not a plus sign, skip to 370

350   If first character was a +/− sign, increment buffer to begin at &701

370–390 If end of number (signalled by carriage return), go to check the sign at line 800

400–460 Otherwise, multiply the current contents of the four-byte location NUMBER by 2 and save on the stack with least significant byte last in (and so first out in line 540)

470–480 Multiply NUMBER by 4 more, giving a total multiplication of 8

490–590 Add the four bytes on the stack (deposited in 400–460) to the current contents of NUMBER. This is equivalent to 2 * NUMBER + 8 * NUMBER, that is, it multiplies NUMBER by ten

600   If overflow occurs into bit 31, jump to error exit at 870

610–660 Load the current buffer character into the accumulator, and subtract &30 to convert to a digit from 0 to 9. If the result is not 0 to 9, go to error exit at 910

670–740 Add this digit to the current contents of NUMBER. (Note that CLC is unnecessary since C must be zero to get past line 660)

750   As line 600, but overflow into bit 31 is signalled after INC by the N flag

770–780 Increment the pointer to the next character in the buffer, and branch always to line 370

790   This section alters the sign of the result if required

800–820 If (INDIC)$_7$ = 1, convert NUMBER to its negative counterpart at line 1090

840–850 C= 0 will indicate 'no error' to the main program. Always branch to line 950

860–890 This is entered if overflow has occurred. Set (INDIC)$_6$ to 1 to indicate 'overflow error' to main program

910–920 If any error has occurred, restore stack pointer to the old value on entry, just after the registers were saved. This is a precaution in case an error was encountered while the stack still contained some data for the conversion (for example, at line 1060).

930   Set C = 1 to indicate 'error'

950–1000 Restore registers (note the reverse order from 50–90) and return

1010–1060 A subroutine to multiply the four-byte NUMBER by 2, and to check for overflow

1080–1190 A subroutine to reverse the sign of NUMBER, leaving its numerical value unchanged. The method used is to subtract from &00000000. This is quicker than using EOR #&FF on each byte plus CLC: ADC #1 at the end

Notice that we cannot use CPX #4 since this affects carry. So we have a second counter in Y which goes from 4 to 0 using DEY, since this does not affect carry.

The general algorithm is very simple: begin with NUMBER equal to &00000000. Then continue to multiply by ten and add the next digit (0 to 9) in the buffer until carriage return is met. For example, 312 is evaluated as $((0 \times 10 + 3) \times 10 + 1) \times 10 + 2$.

If at any point an error occurs, we clear the stack of any unwanted data, signal the error and return. The possible errors are 'invalid number' (for example, 31C2) or overflow (for example, 10,000,000,000).

An error is signalled to the main program which calls this as a subroutine, by setting the carry flag. Here, we use BASIC to test the program in lines 1200–1230. Notice that we are able to differentiate between the type of error, and also differentiate between positive and negative overflow.

The carry flag is the best flag to use for indicating error: it is easy to set and to clear (SEC and CLC). It is also very easy to test: BCS Error, in this example. If a second flag is required, the overflow is best, since this can easily be cleared with CLV. How we set it will be discussed in a moment. If a third flag is required, use the N flag: we will consider in a moment how to set and clear this.

Now in this program we need to use only one flag to indicate error, since we already have the location INDIC at our disposal to convey the other information. But how do we discover the contents of bits 6 and 7 of INDIC? Bit 7 seems straightforward: just use LDA INDIC: BPL... , but what about bit 6, which we need to test first in this case?

There is an instruction BIT which will do everything for us. Just writing BIT INDIC sets the N flag to bit 7 of INDIC and the V flag to bit 6. Moreover, it sets the Z flag to 1 if "ANDing' the accumulator and INDIC (that is, $A \wedge (INDIC)$) is zero; Z is set to zero otherwise. This last use of BIT is not needed here, but it is useful when we wish to test certain bits of a whole series of locations. The reason for this is that BIT leaves the accumulator unchanged, whereas AND changes the accumulator. In a way, BIT is a sort of logical equivalent to CMP. So, if we wanted to see if either bits 2 or 4 of any of four locations were one we could write: LDA #&14: BIT LOC1: BNE ONE: BIT LOC2: BNE TWO, etc. This is particularly useful in interrupt processing.

However, the main use of BIT is to access bits 6 and 7 of a location easily and moreover without affecting the accumulator. A main program calling this subroutine would first test C. If C is 1 it goes to 'Error' where the following will occur: BIT INDIC : BVC INVALCHAR : BPL TOOBIG :.... . If bit 6 of INDIC is zero, INVALCHAR will print a message like 'Not a valid number'; otherwise if bit 7 of INDIC is zero, there is positive overflow, and TOOBIG will print 'Number too large'. IF bit 7 is 1, we pass through to some code which prints 'Number too small'. After this, the main program will return to the subroutine to try again. In this way, errors are easily dealt with.

It is important to signal errors in this way, preferably using flags unless memory locations are available, as here. If we wish to use V and perhaps N this is how we can set and clear them

SET N and V	BIT &FFFC	(&FFFC contains &FF)
SET V, clear N	BIT &FFF7	(&FFF7 contains &6C)
SET N, clear V	BIT &FFEC	(&FFEC contains &A0)
CLEAR N and V	BIT &FFF9	(&FFF9 contains &02)
CLEAR V, N immaterial	CLV	(N will be unchanged by this)

In all of these, the contents of the accumulator will be unaffected. When return is made to the main program, it is important that tests are made immediately if N is being used, since it is extremely sensitive to almost every instruction.

One last point on setting flags. Is it possible to set V leaving N unchanged? It is, but to do it we need to introduce two new instructions: PHP and PLP. PHP copies the processor status register to the stack; PLP copies the top item on the stack to the processor status register. So we write

PHP : PLA : ORA #&40 : PHA : PLP

Transfer the status register to the accumulator. Put a 1 into bit 6, the V flag, leaving all other bits unchanged. Transfer the accumulator back to the status register. All transfers between P and A have to be done via the stack.

The *User Guide* explains how to append listing 9.3 to another program. The listing will need to be on tape, renumbered from 30,000 onwards: lines 10–40, 1190–1230 will not be required. The program will end with RTS and line 30,000 will give a list of all the variables used (that is, it will be line 10 without the location assignments). The main program can now fix memory locations for these variables, and a quick check can be made to ensure that no labels are used twice. To help with this, it is best if common labels like LOOP, NOCARRY, etc. are used only in main programs. In the case of NUMBER, however, it is probably preferable to use this variable name in the main program too, to facilitate the easy passing of parameters. Line 30,000 can then be deleted, and the entire program renumbered.

If subroutines are always saved with at least one copy numbered from 30,000, and if no main program has a greater line number than 30,000, then it is easy to append as many subroutines as required, since after appending, renumbering can be used and the next subroutine appended (32767 is the highest line number allowable).

Listing 9.4: A Subroutine to convert hex to decimal

```
 10 NUMBER=&70:OSWRCH=&FFEE:OSNEWL=&FFE7
 20 DIM START 100                            360      INX
 30 FOR I%=0 TO 2 STEP 2:P%=START            370      LDA NUMBER
 40   [OPTI%                                  380      ORA NUMBER+1
 50 PHA                                       390      ORA NUMBER+2
 60 TXA                                       400      ORA NUMBER+3
 70 PHA                                       410      BNE CONVERT
 80 TYA                                       420      .DISPLAY
 90 PHA                                       430      PLA
100 LDA NUMBER+3                              440      JSR OSWRCH
110 BPL PLUS                                  450      DEX
120 LDA #ASC("-")                            460      BNE DISPLAY
130 JSR OSWRCH                                470      JSR OSNEWL
140 JSR FLIPSIGN                              480      PLA
150 .PLUS                                     490      TAY
160 LDX #0                                    500      PLA
170 .CONVERT                                  510      TAX
180 LDY #32                                   520      PLA
190 LDA #0                                    530      RTS
200 .TENDIV                                   540      .FLIPSIGN
210 ASL NUMBER                                550      LDY #4
220 ROL NUMBER+1                              560      LDX #0
230 ROL NUMBER+2                              570      SEC
240 ROL NUMBER+3                              580      .FLIP
250 ROL A                                     590      LDA #0
260 CMP #10                                   600      SBC NUMBER,X
270 BCC LESS                                  610      STA NUMBER,X
280 SBC #10                                   620      INX
290 INC NUMBER                                630      DEY
300 .LESS                                     640      BNE FLIP
310 DEY                                       650      RTS:]NEXTI%
320 BNE TENDIV                                660 REPEAT
330 CLC                                       670      INPUT"Number",!NUMBEF
340 ADC #&30                                  680      CALLSTART
350 PHA                                       690      UNTIL FALSE
```

Listing 9.4 contains the program and the details are

50–90	Save registers on the stack
100–140	If number is negative, output a minus sign and make the number positive (at line 550)
160	Set digit counter to zero
180–190	Set bit counter to 32 and initialise the accumulator
210–320	Divide current contents of the four-byte NUMBER by 10, using the method described in section 8.9
330–350	The remainder is in the accumulator, and this digit is the next digit to be output, reading from right to left. Convert to ASCII and save on the stack
360–410	Increment digit count. NUMBER now contains the result of dividing by 10 in lines 210–320. If NUMBER is not zero, go back and divide by 10 again to get the next digit
430–470	Output digits from the stack. They will now be in the correct order, since the last one in was the digit furthest to the left
480–530	Replace registers and return
550–650	As 1090–1190 in listing 9.3

The algorithm used here is again simple: keep dividing by 10, saving the remainders on the stack. Output them in reverse order when the dividend becomes zero. For example, applying this to &BC7 gives: remainder 5, dividend &12D; remainder 1, dividend &1E; remainder 0, dividend 3; remainder 3, dividend 0. Now restoring the remainders in reverse order gives 3015.

Exercise 9.2

1. Use PHP and PLP to set or clear N and V without affecting the Z flag.

2. Use PHP and PLP to perform the same function as lines 260–300 of listing 7.7, but dispensing with the X register. Which method is more efficient?

9.7 Further Uses of the Stack

We have seen in the last section two uses of the stack to store temporary information. In the first, it was convenient to put the interim result of 2 * NUMBER on the stack. We could have saved it temporarily in memory but it would have taken up zero page memory.

In the second example, not only did the stack act as a temporary storage area but it also reversed the data for us into the correct order. This is an important use of the stack.

There have been many occasions throughout this book where the instruction STA TEMP has been used, with LDA TEMP following some time later. In such cases PHA and PLA would have saved space. Consider the answer to the first part of question 3 of exercise 5.3 again. Using the stack we could write instead

PHA : TXA : SEC : SBC M : TAX : PLA

This is more economical: it also solves the problem for a program written in ROM.

Listing 9.5

```
 10  COLUMNS=&70:ROWS=&71:SCREENLEFT=&72:SCREENRIGHT=&74:
     TEMP=&76:OSBYTE=&FFF4
 20  FOR I%=0 TO 2 STEP2
 30     P%=&D01
 40     [OPTI%
 50     LDX #4
 60     LDA #&85
 70     JSR OSBYTE
 80     STY MEMLOC+1
 90     LDA #&84
100     JSR OSBYTE
```

```
110      STX SCREENRIGHT
120      STY SCREENRIGHT+1
130      .MEMLOC
140      CPY #0 Dummy operand
150      BNE ZEROMODE
160      LDA #39
170      BNE FOURMODE
180      .ZEROMODE
190      LDA #79
200      .FOURMODE
210      STA COLUMNS
220      LDA #32
230      STA ROWS
240      .BEGIN
250      LDY #7
260      .LOOP1
270      LDA (SCREENRIGHT),Y
280      PHA
290      DEY
300      BPL LOOP1
310      LDX COLUMNS
320      .LOOP2
330      LDA SCREENRIGHT+1
340      STA SCREENLEFT+1
350      LDA SCREENRIGHT
360      STA SCREENLEFT
370      CLC
380      ADC #8
390      STA SCREENRIGHT
400      BCC NOCARRY1
410      INC SCREENRIGHT+1
420      .NOCARRY1
430      LDY #7
440      .LOOP3
450      LDA (SCREENRIGHT),Y
460      STA (SCREENLEFT),Y
470      DEY
480      BPL LOOP3
490      DEX
500      BNE LOOP2
510      LDY #0
520      .LOOP4
530      PLA
540      STA (SCREENRIGHT),Y
550      INY
560      CPY #8
570      BNE LOOP4
580      LDA SCREENRIGHT
590      CLC
600      ADC #8
610      STA SCREENRIGHT
620      BCC NOCARRY2
630      INC SCREENRIGHT+1
640      .NOCARRY2
650      DEC ROWS
660      BNE BEGIN
```

```
670    RTS:JNEXTI%
680    time%=TIME
690    FOR I%=1 TO 100:CALL&DO1
700    NEXTI%:time%=TIME-time%:PRINTtime%/10000 - .001;
       "secs per shift left"
```

Listing 9.5 gives one more example of the use of the stack. This program rotates the high-resolution screen one character to the left. Refer to section 8.6 for the discussion on high-resolution graphics organisation, if you need to. The details are

50–80	As 80–110, listing 8.6 (Y stored at line 140)
90–120	As 120–150, listing 8.6, except that we store starting address in SCREENRIGHT
140–150	As 170–180, listing 8.6
160–170	Put the number of columns less one of mode 4 into the accumulator and branch to 210
190	The number of columns less one for mode 0
210	Store number of columns less one in COLUMNS, a permanent location
220–230	Number of rows in ROWS
250	Initialise byte counter for left-most character square (8 rows, one byte per row)
270–300	Put the first character on the left of the current row on the stack
310	Initialise column counter
330–410	SCREENRIGHT refers to the address of the right-most character of the current pair and SCREENLEFT the left-most. This section of code increments these addresses by 8, so that they point to the next pair
430	Byte counter for current character square
440–480	Move the right-most character of the pair into the left-most character position
490–500	Continue for the 79 or 39 columns (not including the last column)
510	Byte counter for right-most character square
530–570	Get left-most character square from the stack and store in right-most character position
580–630	Increase SCREENRIGHT to the address of the beginning of the next row
650–670	Continue for 32 rows, then return

The idea is to store the first character of the row on the stack (in lines 270 to 300), shift all the rest one place to the left, and then restore the contents of the stack into the last character position (in lines 530–570). Notice how the reversing property of the stack is a slight inconvenience here: it necessitates a forward loop with a CPY at 560. Nevertheless, the stack saves memory here but not time. Why this is so we will consider in the next section.

Exercise 9.3

1. Rewrite 1(i) and 2 of exercise 5.3 so that they would work in ROM.

2. Rewrite the second part of questions 3 and 4 of exercise 5.3, using the stack as much as possible.

9.8 Timing

Appendix 1 contains information on the timing for each instruction. For example, PHA takes 3 cycles, the same as STA TEMP, where TEMP is in zero page. PLA takes 4 cycles, one more than LDA TEMP. It is therefore slightly quicker, on average, to use zero page memory than the stack, but there is a memory cost both in zero page and in the program itself (PHA and PLA are both one-byte instructions). Moreover, there can be a time saving using the stack. In listing 9.3, if we used zero page memory in lines 270–300 instead of the stack, we would need to use indexed addressing (STA TEMP, Y): this takes five cycles, two more than PHA. However, to be fair there is a corresponding saving in lines 530–560: we can move backward through the loop, by replacing PLA by LDA TEMP, Y and can thus eliminate CPY #8. This saves 2 cycles altogether (CPY #8 is 2 cycles, PLA and LDA TEMP, Y are both 4 cycles), which cancels out the extra two in the temporary storage loop.

You will have noticed that the average time taken per shift in mode 4 is about 0.1067 seconds in listing 9.5. The 6502 microprocessor in the BBC computer runs at 2 MHz, that is, 2 million cycles per second. It follows that listing 9.5 uses up about 200,000 machine cycles! Where do they all go?

In order to answer this we will analyse the timing involved in listing 9.5. Table 9.2 gives the details. The column labelled 'Multiplication factor' gives the number of times the instruction is used in the program. In the most used loop, LOOP3, each instruction is used 10,240 times! This underlines the importance of making loops as economical as possible.

In certain cases we have had to estimate the factor: line 630 is an example. With branches, there is a problem since if the branch occurs, the

Table 9.2   Timing for listing 9.5.

Line number	Time for instruction	Multiplication factor	Total
50	2	1	
60	2	1	
70	6	1	
80	4	1	
90	2	1	
100	6	1	
110	3	1	
120	3	1	45
140	2	1	
150	2	1	
160	2	1	
170	3	1	
190	2	0	
210	3	1	
220	2	1	
230	3	1	
250	2	32	64
270	5		
280	3		3328
290	2	32 × 8	
300	3		
310	3	32	96
330	3		
340	3		
350	3		
360	3	40 × 32	28160
370	2		
380	2		
390	3		
400	3		
410	5	40	200
430	2	40 × 32	2560
450	5		
460	6	40 × 32 × 8	163840
470	2		
480	3		
490	2	40 × 32	640
500	3		
510	2	32	64
530	4		
540	6		
550	2	32 × 8	4352
560	2		
570	3		
580	3		
590	2		
600	2	32	416
610	3		
620	3		
630	5	6	30
650	5	32	256
660	3		6
670	6	1	
		Total	204,057

time involved is 3 instead of 2 cycles. We have used the method of assigning the time of the most frequent occurrence — the results should then average out. In this case all branches are given the value of 3: this will involve only a slight overestimate overall (we take no account of page crossing, which gives an additional cycle to a branch, and of indexed addressing, since it will not occur in this program — this is why we have begun at &D01 rather than use DIM START 150). In cases where exactness is important (we shall meet one in a moment) we shall need to be more accurate in our allocation.

From our analysis we see that over 80 per cent of the time is spent on the loop in lines 450–480! Unfortunately, indirect indexed addressing is used twice in this loop and this is costly in time (the reason for this difference in time would take us into hardware considerations outside the scope of this book). But even if we could have got away with zero page indexed addressing, we would save only 3 cycles per loop, which would result in an overall saving of 15 per cent. And of course in mode 0, the time is very nearly doubled.

This sort of analysis does not need to be done with many programs, but it is very revealing in this case. There is a general principle stemming from this: worry about saving time only in loops — initialisations and very small loops take up a negligible amount of time anyway, and are not worth the time-saving effort.

Even with such economy, this rotation program is rather slow for some purposes: for greater speed, the properties of the 6845 chip and screen ULA would have to be used, but these are outside our scope.

To end this section let us try to devise a piece of code that will result in a pause of *precisely* 1 millisecond (that is, 2000 machine cycles). In doing so, we will introduce our last new instruction: NOP. This instruction does nothing: it just takes up 2 cycles of processor time, and is useful for the fine tuning of timing loops, as we shall see.

To begin with we must set the interrupt disable: the interrupt routine takes time and will muddle our timing. We will not clear the disable as part of the code, since that would be done after the operation for which the pause was required has been completed.

Consider the loop

```
LOOP  DEX
      BNE LOOP
```

This takes up $5 * X - 1$ cycles (minus 1 since the last branch will not occur). The maximum value of this is 1279, which falls below our 2000 mark.

Consider instead

```
LOOP  DEC DELAY
      BNE LOOP
```

This take up $8 * (DELAY) - 1$ cycles assuming zero page. We are in range here, so let us now consider the initialisation. We have

```
SEI
PHP
PHA
LDA#Count
STA DELAY
```

and at the end we will need PLA : PLP.

We do not want our delay loop to affect any of the workings of the rest of the program, so we save the accumulator and status register on the stack. All of this adds up to 21 cycles: we therefore require $8 * \text{Count} - 1 = 1979$, and the nearest we can get to this is Count = 247, which leaves us 4 cycles to find. This is where NOP comes in. So our 1 millisecond delay is

```
         SEI
         PHP
         PHA
         LDA #247
         STA DELAY
LOOP DEC DELAY
         BNE LOOP
         NOP
         NOP
         PLA
         PLP
```

Exercise 9.4

Show that if we wish to generalise this to a *t* millisecond delay by using the X register containing *t*, then, assuming we will save the X register on the stack, we will need to load DELAY with the greatest integer not more than $(1991t - 28)/8t$.

Include suitable code to give a precise pause of 10 milliseconds.

9.9 Screen Scrolling: How it Operates

If we consider again the operation of listing 9.5, something rather odd will be noticed. To slow things down a little, insert a line 695 F = INKEY(25) in the program.

Clear the screen in mode 4, begin listing the program and press escape before any scrolling occurs. Now type RUN, and you will notice the screen shuffling along from the top. Now type LIST again, and after a few scrolls press escape. Type RUN again, and you will notice that the screen shuffles along again, but this time it begins somewhere around the middle. Remove line 695 and repeat these experiments: you will see the same effects happening more quickly. In the second case, some of the lines will seem to be indented as the rotation occurs.

To understand what is happening here, we need to perform one more experiment. Keeping listing 9.5, add the following line

1   FOR I% = HIMEM TO &7FFF: ?I% = &AA: F = INKEY(5): NEXT

(use &3FFF in a model A)

Clear the screen and type RUN. The screen will begin filling up from the top. Press escape, and list the program to get some scrolling. Type RUN again and watch the screen fill up starting at the middle! Now clear the screen again, list a little without scrolling, and press return enough times to put the cursor at the bottom of the screen. Now type RUN, and one scroll will occur. The screen will begin to fill up from the bottom. Try this again, but with one scroll before typing RUN and the next to bottom line will start filling; with two scrolls plus RUN, it begins filling two lines from the bottom; and so on.

It is scrolling that causes this to happen. Let us consider what happens in scrolling. Imagine that the whole screen is full and that the cursor is now at

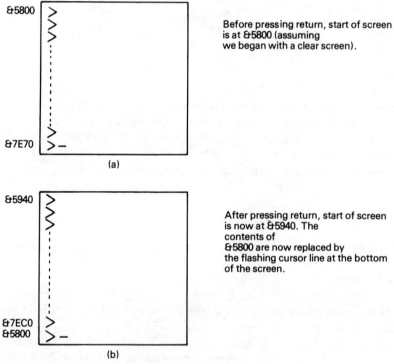

(a)

Before pressing return, start of screen is at &5800 (assuming we began with a clear screen).

(b)

After pressing return, start of screen is now at &5940. The contents of &5800 are now replaced by the flashing cursor line at the bottom of the screen.

Figure 9.8: Scrolling in mode 4 (model B addresses)

the bottom of the screen. At this stage we type in something and press return: what must happen now is that the line at the top of the screen disappears to accommodate the new flashing cursor line. One way to do this is to move up all the other lines so that line two is now at HIMEM (that is, &1800 or &5800), but this is rather slow. A simpler approach is to replace the contents of the top line on the screen by the flashing cursor line (that is, > followed by blanks). All we need to do then is to redefine the start of the screen as the location of the present line one (which is the old line two), that is, &5940 (or &1940) in mode 4. It follows then that &5800 is now the location for the bottom line of the screen. Figure 9.8 shows this.

The screen memory is hence treated as a sort of cylinder, rather like our method in section 6.5, when we implemented the queue. All modes are treated like this, not only mode 4.

The situation with mode 7 is slightly different, since there are 24 unused locations in screen memory. As scrolling takes place, the 24 locations that are unused will change. Figure 9.9 illustrates this. Here, the cylinder principle is even more obvious. Similar considerations apply to modes 3 and 6 also.

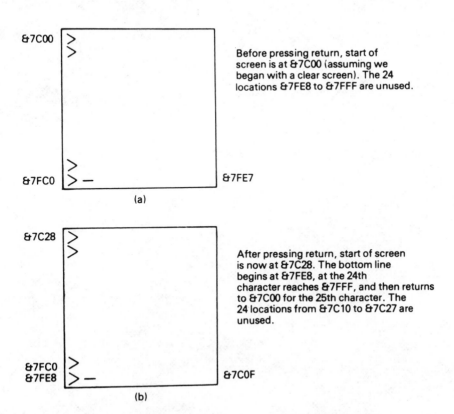

Before pressing return, start of screen is at &7C00 (assuming we began with a clear screen). The 24 locations &7FE8 to &7FFF are unused.

After pressing return, start of screen is now at &7C28. The bottom line begins at &7FE8, at the 24th character reaches &7FFF, and then returns to &7C00 for the 25th character. The 24 locations from &7C10 to &7C27 are unused.

Figure 9.9: Scrolling in mode 7 (model B addresses)

There are a pair of memory locations which are set aside to hold the information of where the start of the screen is at any particular time: the low byte is in &350 and the high byte in &351. Incidentally, the figure given for each mode is the same whether or not a model B is in use. So, a clear screen in mode 7 gives &7C00 for both model A and model B. However, the BBC Computer copes with this in a rather novel way: in a model A machine, all references to location &4000 to &7FFF are treated as references to &0 to &3FFF. In this way, the computer can store one set of parameters in ROM which will work for either machine.

Exercise 9.5

Rewrite listing 8.6 so that it will cope with scrolling.

10 Some Utility Programs

10.1 Introduction

The principal purpose of this chapter is to draw together all the preceding ideas in the past nine chapters into a series of example programs. As a bonus, these programs will be found to be particularly useful to you in your work with BASIC and with assembly language. In this sense they may be called *utility programs*. This is not to imply that programs in the rest of the book are not useful (for example listing 8.6 is certainly of use if you have a printer). But the earlier programs were chosen to make specific pedagogical points: the programs here try to draw together all the points already made. If you purchase the cassette available with this book you will find some other utility programs. It contains an assembly program to find and list the lines containing any section of code in a BASIC program (FIND-CODE) and another to replace any section of code by any other section in a BASIC program (REPLACE).

10.2 Program 1: RETRIEVE

The purpose of this program is to allow you to recover most or all of a program that has been corrupted in some way. It may be that you cannot get all the program from a damaged tape; or it may be that one of your machine code programs went a little wrong! In such cases, when you try to list the program you get the message 'Bad program'. In order to understand what happens here, we need to look a little into the workings of BBC BASIC.

Each line of a BASIC program, when it is stored in memory, begins with 4 bytes. The first is always &0D (ASCII for carriage return); the next is the high byte of the line number (which must not exceed &7F, that is, bit 7 must be zero); the next is the low byte of the line number; and the last is the number of bytes used in this particular line (including these four). This means that line numbers can range from 0 to 32767, and that the number of bytes allowed in a line, apart from the first four, is 251.

Now, apart from these first four, any line consists of two sorts of bytes: those with ASCII values between &20 and &7E, and those with values from &80 to &FF (the control codes from 0 to &1F and the delete code

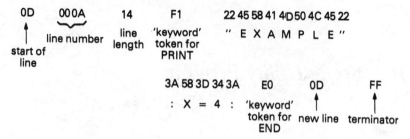

Figure 10.1: How the program 10 PRINT "EXAMPLE": ×=4: END is stored in memory.

&7F will not be found in a BASIC program line). Those from &80 to &FF outside quotes represent keywords, and a list of these is given in your *User Guide*. Figure 10.1 shows how the line

10 PRINT "EXAMPLE": X=4: END

will go into memory (ignore the last byte for a moment). Notice how this method of storage makes the BASIC program entirely relocatable.

Now when you try to save or list a program, or when an error occurs (including ESCAPE) the interpreter first checks that the program is valid. It does this by seeing if the first byte is &0D: if not, it falls at the first hurdle. It now takes the next byte and checks its sign (BMI or BPL): if it is minus (that is, bit 7 is 1) it knows that it has reached the end of the program. This is because &FF is used as a terminator to the program, but any negative byte will do.

If it has not reached the end of the program, it adds the fourth byte (the line length) to the address of &0D and expects to find &0D at this new address—if it does not it outputs 'Bad program'. It repeats this process until either it finds the negative terminator or it outputs 'Bad program'.

Now our program RETRIEVE goes through a program making the same check, but when it comes to a point where the interpreter would output 'Bad program' it is much more friendly: it puts the terminator &FF at that point. In this way you have retrieved some (or all) of your program.

One last point: it is possible to start a program at any page by using the PAGE command. Location &18 contains the current page, and so we can use RETRIEVE on a program anywhere in memory, by first setting PAGE to the correct point.

Listing 10.1

```
10 LASTLINE=&70:THISLINE=&72
20 FOR I%=0 TO 2 STEP2:P%=&D01
30   [OPTI%
40   LDA #0
```

```
  50    STA THISLINE
  60    STA LASTLINE
  70    LDA &18
  80    STA THISLINE+1
  90    STA LASTLINE+1
 100    .LOOP
 110    LDY #0
 120    LDA (THISLINE),Y
 130    CMP #&0D
 140    BNE FAULTFOUND
 150    LDA THISLINE+1
 160    STA LASTLINE+1
 170    LDA THISLINE
 180    STA LASTLINE
 190    LDY #3
 200    CLC
 210    ADC (THISLINE),Y
 220    STA THISLINE
 230    BCC LOOP
 240    INC THISLINE+1
 250    BCS LOOP
 260    .FAULTFOUND
 270    INY
 280    LDA #&FF
 290    STA (LASTLINE),Y
 300    RTS:]NEXTI%
```

The program is in listing 10.1, and the details are

40–90	Initialise the low bytes of the pointers to the beginning of the last line analysed and to the present line under analysis, to zero; and the respective high bytes to the current page
110	Initialise the byte pointer to the current line
120–140	If the first byte of the line is not &0D we have found the fault—go to 270 to put in the terminator
150–180	Otherwise put the address of the present line into the last line pointer
190–250	And add to the present line pointer the length of the present line, storing this new address back into the present line pointer. Always branch back to 110
270–300	Once the fault has been found, put the terminator &FF at the end of the last line and return. This will work even if the entire program can be recovered

The program is relocatable, but is assembled into &D01. Save a machine code copy, and use it when you need to (which will not be very often, I hope).

10.3 Program 2: INTSORT

We saw in listing 7.7 how to sort a set of up to 256 32-bit integers, and in exercise 7.3 how to generalise this to deal with more than 256 such integers. However, a major limitation to that program was that it could not sort an integer array created in a BASIC program, for example, by DIM ARRAY% (500), say. In this section we will see how to remedy this.

One feature of CALL that we have not yet considered is its ability to pass parameters, or more precisely to pass addresses of parameters. For example, if we write CALL ANYTHING, Integer%, FPOINT, where ANYTHING is the start of the program, Integer% is an already declared integer variable and FPOINT an already declared decimal or floating-point variable (see appendix 4), then a parameter block table will be set up starting at address &600. Figure 10.2 shows what it looks like.

The first byte gives the number of parameters passed; and then each group of three following gives the address of the relevant parameter together with its type: 4 is integer (4 bytes are used for an integer, so we expect &1256 to &1259 to contain our four byte Integer%); 5 is floating-point (FPOINT will occupy 5 bytes from &1282 to &1286). It is also possible to pass a single byte (for example, ?BYTE) code 0 (1 would have been more sensible), and a string at a defined address (for example, $TEXT) code 128, but both of these seem rather pointless since by definition we know where they are stored: in such cases, indirect indexed is the best course. Finally, as we shall see in the next section, we can pass string variables (for example, String$).

Now it turns out that arrays are always arranged consecutively by the interpreter, so that we can pass information about the whole of an integer array like one defined in DIM ARRAY% (500) by writing CALL ANYTHING, ARRAY% (0). From then on, we can add four to the address to get the next item in the array.

&600	2	Number of parameters passed
&601	56	} Address of first parameter is
&602	12	} &1256
&603	4	First parameters is an integer variable (4 bytes)
&604	82	} Address of second parameter is
&605	12	} &1282
&606	5	Second parameter is a floating-point variable (5 bytes)

Figure 10.2: The parameter block table in response to CALL ANYTHING, Integer %, FPOINT

In our integer sorting program we need to pass one more item of information: the number of integers to be sorted. So we assume that our program is called from BASIC with the statement CALL &D01, NUMBER%, ARRAY% (0) (the names NUMBER and ARRAY are arbitrary, but the % sign is essential).

Listing 10.2

```
 10 TEMP=&70:FIRST=&71:SECOND=&73:NUMBER=&75:LOOPCOUNT
    =&77:OSWRCH=&FFEE
 20 FOR I%=0 TO 2 STEP 2:P%=&D01
 30    [OPTI%
 40    LDA &600
 50    CMP #2
 60    BNE MISTAKE
 70    LDA &603
 80    CMP #4
 90    BNE MISTAKE
100    LDA &606
110    CMP #4
120    BEQ OK
130    .MISTAKE
140    LDA #ASC("?")
150    JSR OSWRCH
160    RTS
170    .OK
180    LDY #0
190    LDA &601
200    STA FIRST
210    LDA &602
220    STA FIRST+1
230    LDA (FIRST),Y
240    SEC
250    SBC #1
260    STA NUMBER
270    INY
280    LDA (FIRST),Y
290    SBC #0
300    STA NUMBER+1
310    .START
320    LDA &604
330    STA SECOND
340    LDA &605
350    STA SECOND+1
360    LDA #0
370    STA LOOPCOUNT
380    STA LOOPCOUNT+1
390    .BEGIN
400    LDY #0
410    LDA SECOND+1
420    STA FIRST+1
430    LDA SECOND
440    STA FIRST
450    CLC
```

```
460     ADC #4
470     STA SECOND
480     BCC NOCARRY
490     INC SECOND+1
500     .NOCARRY
510     LDX #4
520     SEC
530     .LOOP1
540     LDA (SECOND),Y
550     SBC (FIRST),Y
560     INY
570     DEX
580     BNE LOOP1
590     BVC NOOVFLOW
600     EOR #&80
610     .NOOVFLOW
620     EOR #0
630     BPL OVER
640     DEY
650     .LOOP2
660     LDA (FIRST),Y
670     STA TEMP
680     LDA (SECOND),Y
690     STA (FIRST),Y
700     LDA TEMP
710     STA (SECOND),Y
720     DEY
730     BPL LOOP2
740     .OVER
750     INC LOOPCOUNT
760     BNE NTZERO
770     INC LOOPCOUNT+1
780     .NTZERO
790     LDA LOOPCOUNT
800     CMP NUMBER
810     BNE BEGIN
820     LDA LOOPCOUNT+1
830     CMP NUMBER+1
840     BNE BEGIN
850     DEC NUMBER
860     BEQ LOWZERO
870     LDA NUMBER
880     CMP #&FF
890     BNE START
900     DEC NUMBER+1
910     BPL START
920     .LOWZERO
930     LDA NUMBER+1
940     BNE START
950     RTS:]NEXTI%
960 CLS:INPUT"How many numbers",N%:DIM A%(N%)
970 FOR I%=0 TO N%-1:A%(I%)=RND:NEXTI%
980 PRINT"Numbers assigned.   Sorting now":time%=TIME:
    CALL&D01,N%,A%(0):time%=TIME-time%:PRINTtime%/100
    "secs":PRINT"Done.   Checking now."
```

```
990 FOR I%=0 TO N%-2:IF A%(I%)>A%(I%+1) THEN PRINT
    "ERROR AT "STR$(I%):END
1000   NEXTI% :PRINT"Checking O.K.":END
```

The program is listing 10.2 and the details are

40–60	If there are not two parameters, something is wrong
70–120	And if they are not both integers, something is wrong
140–160	In these cases, output a query sign and return
180–300	Store the address of NUMBER% in a temporary location (FIRST will be used for other things later). Subtract one from the contents of that address and store in NUMBER. Store the byte from the next address in NUMBER + 1 (adjusting it if any borrow had occurred on the previous subtraction)
320–350	Store the address of the first integer (ARRAY%(0)) temporarily in SECOND
360–380	Initialise the integer counter
400–730	Identical to 120–450 of listing 7.7. Notice how in 670 and 700 we do not use PHA and PLA since they cost one cycle in a very often used loop
750–760	If the lower byte of the integer count is not zero, go straight to 790 where we can compare it to the lower byte of NUMBER
770	If it is zero, increment the higher byte of the count first
790–810	If the lower bytes do not agree, we cannot be finished with the present cycle through the integers. Go back to 400
820–840	Even if the lower bytes agree, equality cannot occur unless the higher bytes agree too. Go back to 400
850–910	At the end of the present cycle, decrement the lower byte of NUMBER by 1. If it is not zero, examine whether it has gone through zero: if so, decrement the high byte of NUMBER by 1. Return to 320 in all cases, unless the high byte of NUMBER has passed through zero (which will never happen—see 930–950)
930–950	This checks if the high byte of NUMBER has got to zero as well as the low byte of NUMBER, since entry to 930 is from 860 only. In this case, (NUMBER) equals 0 and we have finished; otherwise return to 320

Notice how much more code is necessary for decrementing NUMBER when the number of integers can exceed 255: 6 lines of code for fewer than 256 integers, 18 lines for more than 256 integers. The principal problem is that we need to allow the case where the low byte of NUMBER equals zero in every cycle, except the one where the high byte is also zero (and for fewer than 256 integers this will be the only such case where the lower byte is zero). Hence, we need to check if the high byte of NUMBER is zero every time that the low byte reaches zero.

This is not the fastest machine code sort possible, but it is simple and still pretty quick. To sort 2000 integers in BASIC using the bubble sort would take all day: see how long it takes in machine code. In practice, though, you are not likely to want to sort more than about 500 integers, and this takes only a sixteenth of the time. (The reason for the sixteen-fold increase from 500 to 2000 is that the number of comparisons with 500 is $\frac{1}{2} \times 500 \times 501 = 125,250$, whereas with 2000 it is $\frac{1}{2} \times 2000 \times 2001 = 2,001,000$, almost 16 times as great.)

10.4 Program 3: STRINGSORT

Let us now do the same thing for listing 7.8 as we did for listing 7.7. There is a slight complication when we pass a string variable via CALL. The address we get is not of the string, but of another block of information called a String Information Block. This consists of four bytes: the first two give the starting address of the string and the last one the length of the string. This is essential because a string variable does not end in &0D unlike $TEXT.

The third byte is of no use to us here, but it is quite interesting: it denotes the maximum length of string possible without reallocation of space. When a string variable is first defined in BBC BASIC it is given a bit more space than it actually needs: this amount of space is stored in the third variable. The reason for doing this is to cut down on what are called garbage collection problems. When we define A$ to be "ABC" and then later define it to be A$ + A$ + A$ + A$ + A$, this new string will have to be stored somewhere else in memory: the old "ABC" remains where it was. What will happen here is that the String Information Block will have its contents changed to point to the new string (but the block itself will not need to be moved). If we do this a lot, we will run out of memory, but a lot of memory will be old discarded strings—in other words, garbage. So all this garbage will need to be collected up and thrown away; and this is a slow process, even in machine code. By careful programming, however, we can assign enough space to our original string to circumvent this. So long as our new allocation does not exceed byte three, we will not have to use up any more memory to store our new string: we just overwrite the old one. So, if we know that a string is unlikely to be much more than about 25 characters, define it initially as A$ = STRING$(25, "*").

Back now to our immediate task. So far as we are concerned then, a string array will be a continuous set of bytes in memory, each element of the array corresponding to four of those bytes (the String Information

Block). The strings themselves can be anywhere else in memory: the first two bytes in the String Information Block point to the starting point of the string. It follows that the first half of listing 7.8 has already been done for us by the interpreter: the list of pointers already exists, we do not have to create it. However, we must remember that when we swap pointers there are four bytes to swap: the address plus the two string length bytes. We shall assume that there are no null strings in the set of strings that we shall be sorting. A null string is denoted by zeros in the String Information Block.

Listing 10.3

```
 10 LOOPCOUNTH=&70:FIRST=&71:SECOND=&73:TEMP=&75:ADDRESS
    =&76:NUMBER=&78:STORE1 =&7A:STORE2=&7C:LGTH1=&7E:LGTH2=
    &7F:OSWRCH=&FFEE
 20 FOR I%=0 TO 2 STEP 2:P%=&D01
 30    [OPTI%
 40    LDA &600
 50    CMP #2
 60    BNE MISTAKE
 70    LDA &603
 80    CMP #4
 90    BNE MISTAKE
100    LDA &606
110    CMP #&81
120    BEQ OK
130    .MISTAKE
140    LDA #ASC("?")
150    JSR OSWRCH
160    RTS
170    .OK
180    LDA &601
190    STA FIRST
200    LDA &602
210    STA FIRST+1
220    LDY #0
230    LDA (FIRST),Y
240    SEC
250    SBC #1
260    STA NUMBER
270    INY
280    LDA (FIRST),Y
290    SBC #0
300    STA NUMBER+1
310    .LOOP3
320    LDA &604
330    STA STORE2
340    LDA &605
350    STA STORE2+1
360    LDX #0
370    STX LOOPCOUNTH
380    .LOOP4
390    LDY #0
400    LDA STORE2+1
```

```
410    STA  STORE1+1
420    LDA  STORE2
430    STA  STORE1
440    CLC
450    ADC  #4
460    STA  STORE2
470    BCC  NOCARRY3
480    INC  STORE2+1
490    .NOCARRY3
500    LDA  (STORE1),Y
510    STA  FIRST
520    LDA  (STORE2),Y
530    STA  SECOND
540    INY
550    LDA  (STORE1),Y
560    STA  FIRST+1
570    LDA  (STORE2),Y
580    STA  SECOND+1
590    LDY  #3
600    LDA  (STORE1),Y
610    STA  LGTH1
620    LDA  (STORE2),Y
630    STA  LGTH2
640    LDY  #0
650    .LOOP5
660    LDA  (FIRST),Y
670    CMP  (SECOND),Y
680    BCC  NEWRECORD
690    BNE  SWAP
700    INY
710    CPY  LGTH1
720    BEQ  NEWRECORD
730    CPY  LGTH2
740    BEQ  SWAP
750    BNE  LOOP5
760    .PIVOT1
770    BPL  LOOP3
780    .PIVOT2
790    BNE  LOOP3
800    .SWAP
810     LDY  #3
820    .LOOP6
830    LDA  (STORE1),Y
840    STA  TEMP
850    LDA  (STORE2),Y
860    STA  (STORE1),Y
870    LDA  TEMP
880    STA  (STORE2),Y
890    DEY
900    BPL  LOOP6
910    .NEWRECORD
920    INX
930    BNE  NTZERO
940    INC  LOOPCOUNTH
950    .NTZERO
960    CPX  NUMBER
```

```
 970      BNE LOOP4
 980      LDA LOOPCOUNTH
 990      CMP NUMBER+1
1000      BNE LOOP4
1010      DEC NUMBER
1020      BEQ LOWZERO
1030      LDA NUMBER
1040      CMP #&FF
1050      BNE LOOP3
1060      DEC NUMBER+1
1070      BPL PIVOT1
1080      .LOWZERO
1090      LDA NUMBER+1
1100      BNE PIVOT2
1110      RTS
1120      .TEXT:]NEXTI%
1130 CLS:INPUT'"How many records",N%
1140 DIM A$(N%-1)
1150 PRINT'"Setting up strings now"
1160   S=0:FOR I%=0 TO N%-1:R=RND(10):A$="":FOR J%= 0 TO
       R-1:A$=A$+CHR$(RND(26)+ 64):NEXTJ%:S=S+R:A$(I%)=
       A$:NEXTI%
1170 PRINT"Sorting now.":time%=TIME:CALL&DO1,N%,A$(0):
     time%=TIME-time%:PRINTtime%/100"secs":PRINT
     "Checking."
1180 FOR I%=0 TO N%-2:IF A$(I%)>A$(I%+1) THEN PRINT
     "ERROR AT "STR$(I%):END
1190    NEXT:PRINT"O.K.":END
```

The program is in listing 10.3 and the details are

40–160	Check that the parameters are of the right type. The code for a string variable is &81. If there are any mistakes output a query and return
180–300	As listing 10.2
320–350	As 400–430 of listing 7.8 except that we do not need STORE: the information is in &604 and &605
360–370	Low byte of string count is in X which is not otherwise required in the program
390–580	As 460–650 of listing 7.8 except that we need to add 4 not 2 to get the next pointer
590–630	Store the lengths of the respective strings being compared in LGTH1 and LGTH2
640–700	As 660–720 of listing 7.8
710–720	If we have reached the end of the first string and there is still equality, no swap is needed
730–740	By contrast, if the end of the second string is reached a swap is required
750	If we get to here, the branch will always occur
760–790	See 920–1100

810–900   As 750–840 of listing 7.8 except that we swap four bytes not
            two
920–1100   As 750–940 of listing 10.2, except that the low byte of the
            count is in X, not in LOOPCOUNT, and LOOPCOUNT+1
            is replaced by LOOPCOUNTH. Using X is quicker, and
            allows a saving at 960 (compared to 790 and 800 of listing
            10.2)

            Lines 1070 and 1100 are necessary in order to create a
            relocatable program. The jump is just too far for a straight
            branch, and so we use pivots at 760–790. Listing 10.2 was
            slightly easier to make relocatable than this one, but the cost
            is still small, and is certainly worth it for a program of this
            sort (no pun intended!).

Try it for 1000 strings. Again, it is not the fastest sort possible, but still
very reasonable compared to BASIC (BASIC takes long enough to set up
the test strings!). (Again there are ½ × 1000 × 1001 = 500,500 comparisons.)

10.5 Program 4: REMSPACE

When you type a BASIC program into your computer it is useful to leave a
liberal number of spaces to aid legibility. For example, IF X > 3 THEN
PRINT   "MORE"   is   much   easier   to   read   than
IFX>THENPRINT"MORE". Moreover, in a case like IF X > Y THEN
100, the space between Y and THEN is essential otherwise BASIC will
look for a variable YTHEN.
    Again, to aid understanding it is useful to put in the occasional REM
statement either in a full line, such as

10   REM This is a full line

or a part line like

50 X = 0 : Y = 0 : REM This is a part line

The problem with both these strategies is that they take up memory
space; and in a microcomputer like the BBC Micro, space can be crucial in
high-resolution modes.
    The purpose of our next program is to solve this problem. All spaces and
all REM statements will be extracted from any program (of course, spaces
occurring between quotes will be left). You can therefore keep two copies
of a program: one for running and one for documentation purposes. (If you

have REPLACE, available on the cassette, you can reduce the program still further by replacing all variables by single letter variables.)

Once a statement like IF X > Y THEN 100 is translated into BASIC, using tokens for IF and THEN, it is perfectly alright to remove all the spaces, so no precautions are needed here. This assumes that you do not use lines like .LABEL DEY, for if you do, when the space is removed the computer will treat it as .LABELDEY and the DEY instruction will be lost into the label. If you must use this, write .LABEL: DEY. Again, DEFPROCYN Y% = −1 will lead to difficulties, since the procedure will take on the new name YNY% and you will get a 'no FN/PROC' error. There is no need to use this formulation—use DEFPROCYN: Y% = −1; it is much easier to read anyway.

When full line REMs are removed any GOTO, etc. will point to the wrong place if it hitherto pointed to the REM. My own preference is never to point to a REM statement in this way; but if your own preference is different, you will have to change all the line numbers yourself (or write a utility to do it for you!).

The program is shown in listing 10.4. It is not relocatable because to do without the subroutine MVEMEM would be a substantial hardship. However, if you want it to be relocatable, you can put the subroutine permanently at location &75 onwards (it takes up 8 bytes) and define MVEMEM to be &75 in line 10. Delete lines 820 to 870, and insert the following 16 lines, after writing 21 [OPT I%

```
22          LDA    #&B1
23          STA    &75
24          LDA    #&72
25          STA    &76
26          LDA    #&91
27          STA    &77
28          LDA    #&70
29          STA    &78
30          LDA    #&C8
31          STA    &79
32          LDA    #&C9
33          STA    &7A
34          LDA    #&0D
35          STA    &7B
36          LDA    #&60
37          STA    &7C
```

Now, every time that the program is run, it will write the subroutine MVEMEM into &75 to &7C, no matter where you put the program. My own preference is not to go to these extremes to create relocatable code, but I offer this solution to those of you who feel more strongly about it.

In the program, two main variables are used: NEWLINE is the address of the first byte of the current line of the new program (that is, the program with spaces and REMs removed); OLDLINE is the address of the current byte of the 'old' program less the pointer to the current byte of the 'new' program (which is stored in Y), that is, NEWLINE + Y = current byte of 'new' program; OLDLINE + Y = current byte of 'old' program.

The method used is to transfer the program byte by byte, not transferring spaces or REM statements. In a sense, the program is transferred back into its own memory space, but it will take up less of that space at the end. OLDLINE is incremented by one every time that a space is met or $(FLAGREM)_7$ is set. $(FLAGREM)_7$ is set to one if a REM has been met. This will cause all further bytes of the 'old' line to be passed over: OLDLINE is incremented but not Y, the 'new' line byte pointer.

Listing 10.4

```
  10 NEWLINE=&70:OLDLINE=&72:FLAGREM=&74
  20 FOR I%=0 TO 2 STEP2:P%=&D01
  30    [OPTI%
  40    LDA #0
  50    STA NEWLINE
  60    STA OLDLINE
  70    LDA &18
  80    STA NEWLINE+1
  90    STA OLDLINE+1
 100    .LOOP1
 110    LDA #0
 120    STA FLAGREM
 130    LDY #1
 140    JSR MVEMEM
 150    CMP #&FF
 160    BEQ FINISH
 170    JSR MVEMEM
 180    JSR MVEMEM
 190    .LOOP2
 200    LDA (OLDLINE),Y
 210    BIT FLAGREM
 220    BPL NTSET
 230    CMP #&0D
 240    BNE SPACE
 250    JSR MVEMEM
 260    BEQ ENDLINE
 270    .NTSET
 280    CMP #&20
 290    BEQ SPACE
 300    CMP #&F4
 310    BNE NTREM
 320    DEY
 330    LDA #&80
 340    STA FLAGREM
```

```
350     BNE SPACE
360     .NTREM
370     JSR MVEMEM
380     BEQ ENDLINE
390     CMP #&22
400     BEQ QUOTES
410     BNE LOOP2
420     .SPACE
430     INC OLDLINE
440     BNE LOOP2
450     INC OLDLINE+1
460     BNE LOOP2
470     .ENDLINE
480     DEY
490     TYA
500     PHA
510     CPY #3
520     BEQ NOCARRY
530     LDY #3
540     STA (NEWLINE),Y
550     CLC
560     ADC NEWLINE
570     STA NEWLINE
580     BCC NOCARRY
590     INC NEWLINE+1
600     .NOCARRY
610     PLA
620     CLC
630     ADC OLDLINE
640     STA OLDLINE
650     BCC LOOP1
660     INC OLDLINE+1
670     BNE LOOP1
680     .QUOTES
690     JSR MVEMEM
700     BEQ ENDLINE
710     CMP #&22
720     BNE QUOTES
730     BEQ LOOP2
740     .FINISH
750     LDA NEWLINE
760     CLC
770     ADC #2
780     STA &12
790     LDA NEWLINE+1
800     ADC #0
810     STA &13
820     RTS
830     .MVEMEM
840     LDA (OLDLINE),Y
850     STA (NEWLINE),Y
860     INY
870     CMP #&OD
880     RTS:]NEXT
```

The details are

40–90	Put address of beginning of program to be 'compacted', into the pointers
110–120	Set the 'REM-found' flag to zero initially, at the beginning of each line of the program to be compacted
130–140	Move the high byte of the address from the 'old' to the 'new' line
150–160	If this high byte is &FF, the end of the program is reached
170–180	Otherwise, move the low byte of the address and the line length byte from the 'old' to 'new' lines
200	Put the current byte of the 'old' line of the program into the accumulator
210–220	If FLAGREM not set (that is, bit 7 = 0) branch to 280
230–240	Otherwise check if end of line, and if not, branch to 430
250–260	If end of line is reached, move &0D into the 'new' line and always branch to 480
280–290	Check if space, and if so branch to 430
300–310	Check if REM token, and if not skip over to 370
320	Otherwise reduce 'new' line byte pointer by one, so that the colon before the REM is written over by &0D in lines 250–260. If this is a full line REM, this decrement is irrelevant, but will be performed anyway
330–360	Set bit 7 of FLAGREM and always branch to 430
370–380	Move a byte from 'old' to 'new' line, and branch to 480 if end of line is reached
390–410	If quote met, branch to 690; otherwise go back to 200
430–460	Increment the pointer to the 'old' line by one and return to 200
470	Routine when end of line reached
480–500	Reduce the 'new' line byte pointer by one (it was incremented unnecessarily in 860) and transfer to the stack
510–520	If this pointer is 3, a full line REM was met, so skip over update of NEWLINE by going straight to 610
530–540	Store this pointer as new line-length byte in the 'new' line
550–590	Update NEWLINE to beginning of next 'new' line
610–670	Update OLDLINE to beginning of next 'old' line
680	Routine entered when quote encountered
690–730	As long as another quote is not met, keep moving bytes from the 'old' to 'new' line, checking for end of line at each stage. Return to 200 if another quote met
750–820	Reset TOP location (&12 and &13) to point to top of the 'new' program, and return to call
840–870	Move a byte from the 'old' to the 'new' line, increment the 'new' line byte pointer by 1, and set Z to 1 if end of line reached

10.6 Program 5: MEMORYHUNT

Our next program searches any section of memory for any set of bytes and displays the addresses (if any) of their location in that section of memory.

It is particularly useful if you want to analyse the workings of the BBC Micro's firmware. Used in conjunction with a disassembler, it offers a powerful tool for understanding how the interpreter and operating system work. It differs in its structure a little from the rest of the programs in this chapter in that it is a mixture of BASIC and assembly language. We use BASIC to perform all the inputs, error checking and initialisation; and we use assembly language to search very speedily through memory.

Listing 10.5

```
 10 GOSUB 240:*KEY9"GOTO 100!M"
 20 VDU12:PRINT''"Do you want to search for a
    string,"'"some machine code or some
    assembly"'"code (S/M/A)?"
 30 A$=GET$:IFA$="A"THENPRINT''"Input the assembly
    code in line 130"'"of this program. When you
    have"'"finished press key f9":END
 40 IFA$="S"THEN80ELSEIFA$<>"M"THEN30
 50 INPUT"How many bytes",BYTES%:PRINT"Input them one
    by one in order."'"Hex is assumed so do not prefix
    with &."'
 60 FORI%=1TOBYTES%:PRINT"BYTE";STR$(I%);:INPUTA$:
    ?(&6F+I%)=EVAL("&"+A$):NEXT
 70 GOTO90
 80 INPUT"What is the string",A$:FORI%=1TOLEN(A$):
    ?(&6F+I%)=ASC(MID$(A$,I%,1)):NEXT
 90 BYTENUMBER=I%-1:GOTO150
100 GOSUB240
110  ON ERROR PRINT"Assembly error: correct line"'"130
     and press f9":END
120 FORI%=0TO2STEP2:P%=&70:[OPTI%
130    JMP (&206):REM MNEMONICS SEARCHED PUT HERE
140    ]NEXT:BYTENUMBER=P%-&70
150 ON ERRORPRINT'"Hex is assumed so do not prefix
    with &."
160 PRINT'"The default starting and finishing"'
    "addresses of memory to be searched"'"are &8000
    to &FFFF."'"Is this alright (Y/N)?"
170 A$=GET$:IFA$="Y"THENA$="8000":B$="FFFF" ELSEIFA$=
    "N"THENPRINT''"What are the starting and finishing":
    INPUT"addresses of memory to be searched",A$,B$
    ELSEG OTO170
180   START%=EVAL("&"+A$):FINISH%=EVAL("&"+B$):?&8E=
      START%MOD256:?&8F=START%DIV 256:ON ERROR OFF
190 PRINT'"Print out display (Y/N)?";:A$=GET$:IF A$=
    "Y" THEND%=0 ELSE IF A$="N " THEN D%=1 ELSE 190
200   SUM%=FINISH%-START%+1:IFSUM%=&10000THENSUM%=&FFFF
210   ?&8C=SUM%MOD256:?&8D=SUM%DIV256:?&89=BYTENUMBER:
      VDU12,D%+2:CALL START:IFD %=0 THENVDU1,13,3
220 PRINT'"E  To end        R  To rerun program"
```

```
230 A$=GET$:IFA$="R"THEN20ELSEIFA$<>"E"THEN230ELSEEND
240 VDU12:DIM START 250:BYTECOUNT=&89:MATCHBASE=&8A:
    MEMTOTAL=&8C:SEARCHBASE=&8E:OSNEWL=&FFE7:OSWRCH=
    &FFEE
250 FORI%=0TO2STEP2:P%=START
260   [OPTI%
270   JSR OSNEWL
280   LDY #0
290   LDA MEMTOTAL+1
300   BEQ NOHIGH
310  .LOOP1
320   JSR COMPARE
330   INY
340   BNE LOOP1
350   INC SEARCHBASE+1
360   DEC MEMTOTAL+1
370   BNE LOOP1
380  .NOHIGH
390   LDA MEMTOTAL
400   BEQ DONE
410  .LOOP2
420   JSR COMPARE
430   INY
440   DEC MEMTOTAL
450   BNE LOOP2
460  .DONE
470   RTS
480  .COMPARE
490   LDA (SEARCHBASE),Y
500   CMP &70
510   BEQ MATCH
520   RTS
530  .MATCH
540   LDX #0
550   TYA
560   PHA
570   LDY #0
580   CLC
590   ADC SEARCHBASE
600   STA MATCHBASE
610   LDA SEARCHBASE+1
620   ADC #0
630   STA MATCHBASE+1
640  .LOOP3
650   INX
660   CPX BYTECOUNT
670   BEQ FOUND
680   INY
690   LDA (MATCHBASE),Y
700   CMP &70,X
710   BEQ LOOP3
720   PLA
730   TAY
740   RTS
750  .FOUND
```

```
 760      LDA  MATCHBASE+1
 770      JSR  HEXASC
 780      LDA  MATCHBASE
 790      JSR  HEXASC
 800      LDA  #&20
 810      JSR  OSWRCH
 820      PLA
 830      TAY
 840      RTS
 850     .HEXASC
 860      PHA
 870      LSR  A
 880      LSR  A
 890      LSR  A
 900      LSR  A
 910      JSR  CONVT
 920      PLA
 930      AND  #&0F
 940      JSR  CONVT
 950      RTS
 960     .CONVT
 970      SED
 980      CLC
 990      ADC  #&90
1000      ADC  #&40
1010      CLD
1020      JSR  OSWRCH
1030      RTS:JNEXT
1040  RETURN
```

The program is in listing 10.5. The BASIC part is from 10 to 230. The idea is that we can input the bytes simply as a series of bytes (lines 50–60) or as a string (line 80) or as assembler mnemonics (lines 30 and 100–140). In this latter case, we must leave the program to input the mnemonic code in line 130, and then re-enter at 100 using the programmable f_9 key. The machine code routine will have to be reassembled (GOSUB 240) in this case to deal with destruction of dynamic memory caused by the rewriting of 130. In the case of bytes and strings, no reassembly is necessary and we may continue to rerun the program (from line 220) without doing a GOSUB 240. The rest of the BASIC program sets up all the values required by the machine code routine, deals with the various input requirements and then calls the machine code.

Lines 270–1030 contain the assembly program. The program is written in such a way that if we are searching for the string ABA then it will be found twice in ABABA. This is the best strategy for a memory-searching problem of this type. The code to be searched for is put in &70 onwards and BYTENUMBER contains the number of bytes. There are three variables used for the searching process. MEMTOTAL contains the total number of bytes to be searched. SEARCHBASE contains the base address of the memory to be searched. It is used in conjunction with the index register Y and, employing indirect indexed addressing, the high byte is incremented every 256 bytes. MATCHBASE contains the address of the current section of memory being compared to the code searched, where the first byte of this section is the same as the first byte of the code to be searched.

The details are

270	Print a new line to guard against overscanning on ordinary TVs (which tends to obscure the top line)
280	Set pointer to current byte at zero
290–300	If fewer than 256 bytes are to be searched, jump to 390
320	See if first byte of code searched matches current byte (at 490)
330–340	Loop for 256 bytes
350–370	Increment base pointer to memory searched, decrement byte total and return to loop if high byte of total still not zero
390–400	If low byte zero, finish
420	Again compare first byte of code to current byte (at 490)
430–470	Increment pointer, decrement low byte of total and continue until zero, when return
490–520	Compare current byte to first byte of code looked for. If it matches, go to 540; otherwise, return to the searching of memory
540	Set pointer to code looked for at zero
550–560	Save Y on the stack
570	Treat Y as a pointer relative to current match position and set to zero
580–630	Store address of current match position in MATCHBASE
650	Increment pointer to code looked for
660–670	If all bytes have been matched, jump to address print-out (at 760)
680–710	Otherwise load next byte of memory, compare with next byte of code looked for, and if equal loop back to 650
720–740	If not equal, match unsuccessful. Restore value of Y before entry to MATCH routine, and return to searching of memory
750	Routine to print out the address of the first byte where match achieved
760–810	Display high and low bytes of beginning of match in memory, followed by a space
820–840	Restore the old value of Y prior to entry to MATCH, and return to searching of memory. This ensures that if we are looking for, say, ABA then it is found twice in ABABA. If Y were set to the position immediately following the end of the match, ABA would only be located once, since the search

	would resume at the beginning of the second BA, instead of at the beginning of the first BA, as here
850	Routine to display byte on the screen
860–910	Save byte on the stack, move top nybble to bottom nybble position, and go to conversion routine (at 970)
920–950	Retrieve byte from the stack, set top nybble to zero, go to conversion routine and return
960	Converts a single hex digit to ASCII and prints it on the screen
970–990	Using BCD, add 90. If digit is between 0 and 9, no carry is generated. If between A and F, a carry is generated into the top nybble and thence to the carry flag (for example, OB → 1 01)
1000	Add 40 with carry BCD. For 90 to 99 this gives 30 to 39. For 1 00 to 1 05, this gives 41 to 46
1010–1030	Clear BCD flag, output the ASCII digit and return

10.7 Program 6: MC-MONITOR

When working in assembly language or machine code it is very important to be able to monitor the progress of a program, especially if it does not work in quite the way you wanted it to. What is required is a program that will at least

(i) display all the registers—SP, X, Y, A and each bit of the flag (status) register;

(ii) display the contents of the stack;

(iii) display any memory location, but especially the zero page locations from &70 to &8F;

(iv) allow you to alter the X, Y, A or P registers or any memory location; and

(v) allow you to go to any subroutine and return to the display in (i)–(iii) above.

In addition, if it is to be an effective debugging tool, it must allow you to jump into it from the program that you are trying to debug, and to return to the same point in the program when you are ready.

This is the purpose of our last program, shown in listing 10.6. It is a very much bigger program than any other in this book, occupying about 800 bytes, and it is assembled into the top of memory using the HIMEM method (see section 2.5). If you do not already have the program on tape, type it in and save it on tape. We shall look first at what the program does; and then at how it works.

Listing 10.6

```
 10 HIMEM=HIMEM-&330
 20 OSWRCH=&FFEE:OSRDCH=&FFEO:OSNEWL=&FFE7:OSASCI=&FFE3:
    OSBYTE=&FFF4
 30 S%=HIMEM:FORI%=0 TO 2 STEP 2
 40     P%=S%
 50     [OPTI%
 60     .START
 70     PHP
 80     PHA
 90     TYA
100     PHA
110     TXA
120     PHA
130     CLD
140     CLI
150     LDA#12
160     JSR OSWRCH
170     LDX #0
180     JSR OUTPUT
190     TSX
200     TXA
210     CLC
220     ADC #6
230     PHA
240     TAX
250     INX
260     BEQ NOSTACK
270     .STACK
280     LDA &100,X
290     JSR HEXASC
300     LDA#&20
310     JSR OSWRCH
320     JSR OSWRCH
330     JSR OSWRCH
340     INX
350     BNE STACK
360     .NOSTACK
370     JSR OSNEWL
380     LDX #(TEXT2-TEXT)
390     JSR OUTPUT
400     LDA #&20
410     JSR OSWRCH
420     JSR OSWRCH
430     TSX
440     LDY #4
450     .REGST
460     INX
470     LDA &100,X
480     JSR HEXASC
490     LDA #&20
500     JSR OSWRCH
510     DEY
```

```
520       BNE REGST
530       INX
540       LDA &100,X
550       LDX #8
560       .STATUS
570       ASL A
580       PHA
590       LDA #&30
600       BCC ZERO
610       LDA #&31
620       .ZERO
630       JSR OSWRCH
640       PLA
650       DEX
660       BNE STATUS
670       JSR OSNEWL
680       LDX #(TEXT3-TEXT)
690       JSR OUTPUT
700       LDA #0
710       STA MEMLOC2+1
720       STA MEMLOC4+2
730       LDA #&70
740       STA MEMLOC3+1
750       STA MEMLOC4+1
760       JSR MEMOUT
770       .MENU
780       LDX #(TEXT4-TEXT)
790       JSR OUTPUT
800       LDX #(TEXT5-TEXT)
810       JSR OUTPUT
820       .CHAR
830       JSR INCHAR
840       CMP #2
850       BEQ CONTROL
860       CMP #3
870       BEQ CONTROL
880       CMP #14
890       BEQ CONTROL
900       CMP #15
910       BNE NTCONTROL
920       .CONTROL
930       JSR OSWRCH
940       .NTCONTROL
950       CMP #ASC("E")
960       BNE ENOT
970       LDX #&FD
980       TXS
990       RTS
1000      .ENOT
1010      CMP #ASC("C")
1020      BNE CNOT
1030      PLA
1040      PLA
1050      TAX
1060      PLA
1070      TAY
```

```
1080     PLA
1090     PLP
1100     RTS
1110     .CNOT
1120     CMP  #ASC("M")
1130     BEQ  MTYPE
1140     CMP  #ASC("G")
1150     BEQ  GTYPE
1160     CMP  #ASC("R")
1170     BEQ  RTYPE
1180     CMP  #ASC("A")
1190     BNE  CHAR
1200     JSR  MORA
1210     STX  MEMLOC8+1
1220     JSR  BYTE
1230     STX  MEMLOC8+2
1240     JSR  INBYTE
1250     .MEMLOC8
1260     STX  &FFFF  Dummy
1270     JMP  NOSTACK
1280     .MTYPE
1290     JSR  MORA
1300     STX  MEMLOC4+1
1310     STX  MEMLOC3+1
1320     JSR  BYTE
1330     STX  MEMLOC2+1
1340     STX  MEMLOC4+2
1350     JSR  MEMOUT
1360     JMP  MENU
1370     .GTYPE
1380     JSR  MORA
1390     STX  MEMLOC9+1
1400     JSR  BYTE
1410     STX  MEMLOC9+2
1420     PLA
1430     PLA
1440     TAX
1450     PLA
1460     TAY
1470     PLA
1480     PLP
1490     .MEMLOC9
1500     JSR  &FFFF  Dummy
1510     JMP  START
1520     .RTYPE
1530     LDX  #(TEXT8-TEXT)
1540     JSR  OUTPUT
1550     .GTREG
1560     JSR  INCHAR
1570     CMP  #&0D
1580     BEQ  JUMP
1590      TSX
1600     INX
1610     INX
1620     CMP  #ASC("X")
1630     BEQ  REGGOT
```

```
1640      INX
1650      CMP #ASC("Y")
1660      BEQ REGGOT
1670       INX
1680      CMP #ASC("A")
1690      BEQ REGGOT
1700      INX
1710      CMP #ASC("P")
1720      BNE GTREG
1730      .REGGOT
1740      JSR OSWRCH
1750      TXA
1760      PHA
1770      JSR INBYTE
1780      TXA
1790      TAY
1800      PLA
1810      TAX
1820      TYA
1830      STA &100,X
1840      .JUMP
1850      JMP NOSTACK
1860      .MORA
1870      PLA
1880       STA RETADRL3+1
1890      PLA
1900      STA RETADRH3+1
1910      .NTENOUGH2
1920      LDX #(TEXT6-TEXT)
1930      JSR OUTPUT
1940      JSR HEXINPUT
1950      CPY #5
1960      BEQ OK2
1970      CPY #1
1980      BNE PULL2
1990      PLA
2000      JMP NOSTACK
2010      .PULL2
2020      PLA
2030      DEY
2040      BNE PULL2
2050      JSR MISTAKE
2060      JMP NTENOUGH2
2070      .OK2
2080      PLA
2090      JSR OSNEWL
2100      JSR BYTE
2110      .RETADRH3
2120      LDA #0 Dummy
2130      PHA
2140      .RETADRL3
2150      LDA #0 Dummy
2160      PHA
2170      RTS
2180      .HEXINPUT
2190      PLA
```

```
2200      STA RETADRL2+1
2210      PLA
2220      STA RETADRH2+1
2230      .AGAIN
2240      LDY #0
2250      .DIGIT
2260      JSR INCHAR
2270      CMP #&7F
2280      BEQ OVERCHECK
2290      CMP #&0D
2300      BEQ OVERCHECK
2310      CMP #&30
2320      BCC DIGIT
2330      CMP #&47
2340      BCS DIGIT
2350      CMP #&3A
2360      BCC OVERCHECK
2370      CMP #&41
2380      BCC DIGIT
2390      .OVERCHECK
2400      JSR OSASCI
2410      CMP #&7F
2420      BNE NTDEL
2430      DEY
2440      BMI AGAIN
2450      PLA
2460      JMP DIGIT
2470      .NTDEL
2480      PHA
2490      INY
2500      CMP #&0D
2510      BNE DIGIT
2520      .RETADRH2
2530      LDA #0 Dummy
2540      PHA
2550      .RETADRL2
2560      LDA #0 Dummy
2570      PHA
2580      RTS
2590      .OUTPUT
2600      JSR OSNEWL
2610      .MEMLOC1
2620      LDA TEXT,X
2630      JSR OSASCI
2640      INX
2650      CMP #&0D
2660      BNE MEMLOC1
2670      RTS
2680      .MEMOUT
2690      LDY #4
2700      .MEMLOC2
2710      LDA #0 Dummy
2720      JSR HEXASC
2730      .MEMLOC3
2740      LDA #0 Dummy
2750      JSR HEXASC
```

```
2760      LDA  #&3A
2770      JSR  OSWRCH
2780      LDA  #&20
2790      JSR  OSWRCH
2800      LDX  #0
2810      .MEMLOC4
2820      LDA  &FFFF,X Dummy
2830      JSR  HEXASC
2840      LDA  #&20
2850      JSR  OSWRCH
2860      INX
2870      CPX  #8
2880      BCC  MEMLOC4
2890      JSR  OSNEWL
2900      .INCMEM
2910      INC  MEMLOC3+1
2920      INC  MEMLOC4+1
2930      BNE  NTZERO
2940      INC  MEMLOC2+1
2950      INC  MEMLOC4+2
2960      .NTZERO
2970      DEX
2980      BNE  INCMEM
2990      DEY
3000      BNE  MEMLOC2
3010      JSR  OSNEWL
3020      RTS
3030      .BYTE
3040      PLA
3050      STA  RETADRL1+1
3060      PLA
3070      STA  RETADRH1+1
3080      PLA
3090      TAX
3100      PLA
3110      JSR  HEXCON
3120      ASLA
3130      ASLA
3140      ASLA
3150      ASLA
3160      STA  MEMLOC5+1
3170      TXA
3180      JSR  HEXCON
3190      .MEMLOC5
3200      ORA  #0 Dummy
3210      TAX
3220      .RETADRH1
3230      LDA  #0 Dummy
3240      PHA
3250      .RETADRL1
3260      LDA  #0 Dummy
3270      PHA
3280      RTS
3290      .HEXCON
3300      CMP  #&40
3310      BCC  LESS
```

```
3320    SBC #7
3330    .LESS
3340    SEC
3350    SBC #&30
3360    RTS
3370    .HEXASC
3380    PHA
3390    LSRA
3400    LSRA
3410    LSRA
3420    LSRA
3430    JSR CONVT
3440    PLA
3450    AND #&0F
3460    JSR CONVT
3470    RTS
3480    .CONVT
3490    SED
3500    CLC
3510    ADC #&90
3520    ADC #&40
3530    CLD
3540    JSR OSWRCH
3550    RTS
3560    .MISTAKE
3570    LDA #11
3580    JSR OSWRCH
3590     LDA #ASC("?")
3600    JSR OSWRCH
3610    LDA #7
3620    JSR OSWRCH
3630    JSR OSNEWL
3640    RTS
3650    .INBYTE
3660    LDX #(TEXT7-TEXT)
3670    JSR OUTPUT
3680    JSR HEXINPUT
3690    CPY #3
3700    BEQ OK1
3710    .PULL1
3720    PLA
3730    DEY
3740    BNE PULL1
3750    JSR MISTAKE
3760    JMP INBYTE
3770    .OK1
3780    PLA
3790    JSR BYTE
3800    RTS
3810    .INCHAR
3820    JSR OSRDCH
3830    CMP #&1B
3840    BNE NTESC
3850    LDA #&7E
3860    JSR OSBYTE
3870    JMP INCHAR
```

```
3880    .NTESC
3890     RTS
3900    .TEXT:]
3910    LGTH=0:TEXT1=FNTEXT("STACK")
3920    TEXT2=FNTEXT("  SP  X   Y   A   NV-BDIZC")
3930    TEXT3=FNTEXT("ZERO PAGE")
3940    TEXT4=FNTEXT("C CONTINUE E END M MEMORY")
3950    TEXT5=FNTEXT("A ALTER R REGISTERS G GO")
3960    TEXT6=FNTEXT("ADDRESS (4 DIGITS)?")
3970     TEXT7=FNTEXT("ALTER TO (2 DIGITS)?")
3980    TEXT8=FNTEXT("WHICH (X,Y,A,P)?")
3990    NEXTI%
4000  VDU12:PRINT"************BBC MONITOR************"''
4010  PRINT"Access from assembler with JSR S%"''"Access
      from BASIC with CALL S%"
4020  *KEY10"OLD¦MHIMEM=HIMEM-&330¦M"
4030  END
4040  DEF FNTEXT(A$)
4050  L=LGTH:LGTH=LGTH+LEN(A$)+1
4060  $(TEXT+L)=A$
4070  =TEXT+L
```

Run the program and enter the monitor with CALL 5% (CALL HIMEM would do just as well if you ever want to use 5%). The first heading is a display of the stack just prior to the instruction that called the monitor. Here, the stack is empty (apart from the bug-byte return address which was deposited when CALL entered the monitor.

Next we see the registers, with each flag of the status register visible. We have not displayed the program counter for reasons that I shall explain in a moment.

The contents of &70 to &8F are the final display, followed by the menu. C is used in conjunction with the JSR S% entry, which we will consider in a moment. E returns to BASIC at the point of a CALL (but not a USR) instruction. M displays any section of memory; and A allows you to alter any section of memory. R allows you to alter X, Y, A or P. G allows you to go to any subroutine that you like. Pressing any other letter will do nothing. However, you can press CTRL-N (page mode on), CTRL-O (page mode off), CTRL-B (printer on) and CTRL-C (printer off) and it will be accepted.

Let us now look at M, A, R and G in more detail. Press M, and you are asked for the starting address of the 32 bytes to be displayed. This address must be given as 4 hex digits (so that even 0 must be given as 0000). If you type in any number of digits apart from 4, an indication of error will be displayed: try it. If you attempt to input a non-digit it will not be accepted (this is true of A, R and G also): try this too. Finally, if you realise that you pressed M by mistake you can return to the display (from the registers onwards) by pressing carriage return immediately. This will work with A, R and G too. Try some addresses now, and display their contents.

Pressing A will allow you to alter the contents of any memory location. Again 4 digits exactly are required for the address, and 2 for the contents.

Try 0070, and alter it to 8A; then 0071 and alter to A8; and then 0072 altering it to 60. Notice how, if it is user zero page that you are altering (which is the most usual), then the altered contents are shown immediately.

Pressing R will allow you to alter X, Y, A or P. Let us alter A to 50, X to E3 and P to 81. Notice that these register contents are activated only when you use C or G. Let us try G: go to 0070, which now contains TXA: TAY: RTS and see what happens. Is this what you expected? One final experiment in this phase: alter 01FE to CF, 01FF to 78 and type E. Why does this happen? Press the break key to get out of this, and notice the effect of line 4020.

Let us now examine how we can use the monitor to aid debugging. Load listing 10.5 into the computer now (make sure that you have a copy of listing 10.6 on tape or disc) and insert this line: 335 JSR S%. Type RUN, and search for the bytes 60 EA. You can follow the program through LOOP1 by pressing C after you have inspected the display in the monitor: if you want to, you can change any locations that you like. In this way, you can easily see if the logic of the problem is what you expect it to be.

On first entry, the stack is 16 8F; this holds the return address to the CALL at line 210 (which is &8F17). Zero page holds the correct data, with MEMTOTAL and SEARCHBASE both &8000 and BYTECOUNT with 2. At this stage, MATCHBASE is immaterial, since the accumulator indicates C9 as the current item of memory. Press C again: now Y is 2, and A is 01. Press C again twice giving Y:3, A:F0; and Y:4, A:1F. Now press C again and look at MATCHBASE: it is &8004, so 60 must have been located here. A is 4 since it contains the old value of Y (from line 730). Type M and then &8000 to check that the operation is correct.

Type E to exit the monitor and rerun MEMORYHUNT, searching this time for E9 00. You enter the monitor once again at 8000 with Y equals 1.

This time use A to alter &8E to 35 and &8F to DC and use R to set Y to 01. Press C, and see what happens. There has been a match, but print-out was too rapid to see; but X is equal to BYTECOUNT and this is the clue. Use M to verify that DC36 and DC37 contain E9 00.

Let us monitor the print-out operation now: delete 335, and put JSR S% at 1005. Search again for E9 00. We enter the monitor when MATCH-BASE is &8689. Let us examine the stack: EA 17 is the return address to line 920; 86 is the high byte of the match (put on at 860); D5 17 is the return address to line 780; 89 is the value of Y at the beginning of the match; and 93 17 is the return address to line 330. We note that A contains 38, the ASCII code for 8. C again puts 36 in the accumulator (ASCII for 6). Press C twice more, and check the registers, especially A and P. Continue in this way to monitor the print-out of the address &8689.

You should now have a good idea how the monitor can help you to debug programs. By putting JSR S% into sensible points you can quickly determine a fault. You will find this monitoring process much easier if you have a copy of the program being monitored (a printer is very useful in assembly code work, but copying out by hand is not very laborious except for programs of the monitor's length). Indicate by pencil on your copy where your JSR S% has been put, so you can follow through the logic. Since putting in a JSR S% upsets the address location of the program, there is little advantage following the contents of the PC through, and so little advantage in displaying the PC. You can, of course, use more than one JSR S% at the same time, but in many cases you will find it easier to take each small section of the program separately with just one JSR S%. However, there are times when you want to single-step through some small section of code, and this is easily done by putting a JSR S% after each line that you want to monitor. Do not be tempted to single-step through large sections of code, however. It is a very slow process, and is not usually very revealing. By using your intimate knowledge of the program being debugged, you will be able to pinpoint the area where monitoring will be most efficacious.

When you write assembly programs of even moderate complexity you will often find that they do not work first time! The break key is a boon at these moments (which is why line 4020 programs it to safeguard the relevant locations). The monitor too will be very useful to you, but it should not be used as a first resort. There are some simple checks that you should always make first. In order of regularity they are

(a) Missing off the # in immediate statements; for example, LDA 10 instead of LDA #10.
(b) Missing off the & for hex; for example, STA 70 instead of STA &70.
(c) Forgetting to clear or set carry in ADC or SBC instructions.
(d) Forgetting to save a result after addition or subtraction; for example, LDA &70: CLC: ADC #1: BCC NOCARRY: LDA &71... etc. Here, we have forgotten to put STA &70 after the ADC #1.
(e) Forgetting that INC and DEC do not put anything into the accumulator.
(f) Forgetting that CMP, CPX and CPY affect the carry flag.
(g) Using BMI and BPL where BCC and BCS should be used.
(h) Missing off the NEXT in a two-pass assembly (so only getting one pass).
(i) Not allocating enough room in DIM START statements.

If none of these is the cause, then it is the time to use the monitor. Pay particular attention to the indexes in arrays and in indirect indexed addressing: monitor code containing these first. Be patient, systematic and sensible and debugging will not take you long: approach it randomly, hoping for good luck, and it could take you ages.

Let us finish now by looking at the details of the program itself. Notice in particular the use of the function at 4040 to 4070: its purpose is to allow us to use multi-outputs (here there are eight) without having to calculate their lengths. We could change the contents of any of lines 3910 to 3980 and no other changes will be required to the program. It is easier in this case to use this function than to use EQUS.

The program is written so as to be as self-contained as possible. In particular, apart from the stack and registers, *no memory locations outside the space of the program itself are used. Hence, the monitor cannot corrupt any memory locations*, a very important consideration. Only two system routines are needed (OSWRCH and OSRDCH), and since these are provided on all computers, the program can, with very little modification, be used as a monitor on any 6502 computer.

The program details are

70–120	Put registers on the stack in the order P,A,Y,X
130–140	Clear decimal and interrupt flags (if set they will be reset when P is retrieved from the stack)
150–160	Clear screen
170–180	Put heading "STACK"
190–230	Save adjusted stack pointer on the stack (adjusted by 6 to skip over the four pushes in 70–120 plus the two-byte return address)
240–250	Point to last item on the stack before entry to MONITOR, and put in X register. (Remember that SP points to next free location—hence the need for INX)
260	Jump to 370 if stack empty
280–350	Otherwise print out contents of stack in hex. Leave three spaces between each item
370–390	Output a new line and print out register headings
400–520	Print out contents of SP, X, Y and A under headings
530–660	Output 8 bits of P in the order most significant to least significant. Prior to line 600, the accumulator always contains ASCII zero. If C = 1, this is replaced in 610 by ASCII one
670–690	Output a new line and print "ZERO PAGE"
700–760	Pass parameters to subroutine MEMOUT (at 2680). These will cause 32 bytes to be output from location &0070 onwards
780–810	Print out menu
830	Get a character from the keyboard (at 3820)
840–940	Allow page and printer control codes to get through
950–990	If E pressed, set stack pointer to point to return to BASIC (that is, first two bytes on the stack) and return
1010–1100	If C pressed, restore registers in order X, Y, A, P and return to calling program. (1030 throws away the adjusted stack pointer put on stack at 190–230)
1120–1170	Branch to relevant section if M, G or R
1180–1190	If not A, return to 830

1200–1270 Coding if A pressed

1200   Go to 'get address' routine at 1870 (used by M or A)

1210   Put low byte of address (stored in X after return from M or A) in low byte position of line 1260

1220–1230 Put high byte of address (in X from BYTE at line 3040) in high byte position of 1260

1240   Get a byte from the keyboard (at 3660)

1260–1270 Put keyboard byte (stored in X) in address defined by 1210–1230, and return to zero page display, etc.

1290–1360 Coding if M pressed

1290–1310 Go to 'get address' routine at 1870; store low byte in 2820 and in 2740

1320–1340 Store high byte in 2820 and in 2710

1350–1360 Display 32 bytes from the address specified in 1290–1340, and return to the menu

1380–1510 Coding if G pressed

1380–1390 Go to 'get address' routine in 1870; store low byte in 1500

1400–1410 Store high byte in 1500

1420–1480 Restore registers (as 1010–1100)

1500–1510 Jump to subroutine specified in 1380–1410 and on return go to the start of the program

1530–1840 Coding if R pressed

1530–1540 Print out "WHICH (X,Y,A,P)?"

1560–1580 Get a character from keyboard (at 3820). If carriage return, jump to display via 1850

1590   Put stack pointer plus 2 into X (plus 2 to skip over adjusted stack pointer)

1620–1720 Registers in stack are in the order X, Y, A, P. Increment X to point to relevant point on the stack or else return to 1560

1740   Output the letter X, Y, A or P typed in

1750–1770 Save X register on stack (used in INBYTE), and go to get a byte from the keyboard

1780–1820 Achieves the result X → A, top of stack → X

1830–1840 Put new value of register (now in A) in relevant position in the stack (pointed to by X set in 1620–1720) and return to display

1860–3890 Subroutines

1860   The 'get address' routine used by M or A

1870–1900 Save return address in lines 2120 and 2150. This allows stack to be used to pass parameters on return

1920–1930 Print "ADDRESS" (4 DIGITS)?"

1940   Go to routine which puts digit plus CR on to stack (at 2190)

1950–1960 If five characters, input is OK

1970–2000 If just CR, pull off stack and return to display

2020–2060 If there are not five characters, pull them all off the stack, signal the mistake (at 3570) and ask for address again (at 1920)

2080–2170 If five characters, throw CR away from the stack, output a new line, translate low byte of address from ASCII to hex (at 3040), put return address on the stack (stored from 1880–1900) and return

2180   Routine to input a series of hex digits in ASCII from the keyboard

2190–2220 As 1870–1900, but store in 2530 and 2560

2240   Set digit count to zero

2260–2300 Get a character from the keyboard. If delete or CR, skip over check for a hex digit

2310–2340 If less than &30 or more than &46, cannot be a digit

2350–2360 If less than &3A will be 0 - 9

2370–2380 If more than &40 will be A–F

2400   If character is suitable (that is, it passes tests in 2260–2390) print it out (giving a new line if CR)

2410–2460 If delete, throw away last member input to the stack (2440 checks that input not empty). Decrement the character count (in Y) and return to 2260 for next character

2480–2580 If not delete, increment character count. If CR, return from subroutine after restoring return address. Otherwise return to 2260 for another digit

2600–2670 Routine to output string whose starting address is indexed by X. The CR is output also

2680   Routine to display 32 bytes. Starting address of bytes is passed to line 2820 prior to entry. The low byte is also passed to 2740 and the high byte to 2710 prior to entry

2710–2790 Display address of current 8 bytes followed by a colon and a space

2800–2890 Display current 8 bytes, terminated by a new line

2910–2980 Increment low bytes in lines 2740 and 2820 by 8, incrementing by one high byte of 2820 and 2710 if necessary

2990–3020 Repeat for four sets of 8 bytes, output a new line and return

3030   Routine to convert a byte in ASCII to a hex byte

3040–3070 As lines 1870–1900 except store in 3230 and 3260

3080–3100 Put top of stack in X (this is the top hex digit of the byte), and next item of stack in A (the bottom hex digit of the byte)

3110–3160 Convert bottom ASCII digit to hex digit (at 3300), shift bottom nybble to top nybble and store temporarily in 3200

3170–3210 Convert top ASCII digit to hex digit, combine with bottom digit already at 3200 and transfer to X

3220–3280 Return

3290   Routine to convert single ASCII digit to hex

3300–3320 If more than &40 (that is, A–F) subtract 7; for example, A (= &41) → &3A (= &30 + &0A)

3340–3360 Subtract &30 to give hex digit in accumulator and return

3370–3550 Displays byte on the screen (see 850–1030 of listing 10.5)

3560   Give visual and aural indication of an error

3570–3630 Move cursor up, display a question mark, output a short bleep and a new line, and return

3650   Routine to accept a single byte from the keyboard and convert it to hex

3660–3670 Print "ALTER TO (2 DIGITS)"

3680   Get a series of hex digits in ASCII from the keyboard (at 2190)

3690–3760 If not 3 characters, pull characters offte to hex (at 3040) and return

3810   Accept a character from the keyboard

3820–3890 Get a character. If ESCAPE, acknowledge with &7E through OSBYTE and ignore. Otherwise return

Exercise 10.1

(So that you can prove to yourself how much you have learnt, no solutions will be provided for this exercise. That your programs work will be proof enough!)

1. Modify RETRIEVE so that instead of putting FF immediately, it first checks if the next line would have had a valid line number (that is, greater than the last one). If so, it then searches the next 250 bytes for 0D. If it comes across any of the bytes 00 to 1F it replaces them by zero. And if it finds 0D, it modifies the line length byte, accepts the line, and continues to examine the next one.

2. Modify INTSORT and STRINGSORT so that a flag is set to zero at the start of each scan through the data, and set to one if any swap is made during that scan. Thus, if at the end of any scan the flag is still zero, the sort can be terminated. Do you still need to check that NUMBER equals zero with this modification? Under what conditions is the sort speeded up significantly by this change?

3. Modify REMSPACE so that

(i) it deals with multi-line assembler statements, for example

.LOOP LDA #3: .LOOP1 LDX #0

(ii) it removes assembler comments, for example

LDA HIGH / Load high byte: LDX LOW

(Remember that unlike REM, / does not cause all later text to be ignored by the assembler, and that in some cases / can be replaced by a space.)

(iii) it deals with line number references to REM statements.

4. Incorporate the byte-searching routine of MEMORYHUNT into the MONITOR, with suitable commands added to the menu.

Appendix 1:   6502 Instruction Set

It is convenient to divide up the 56 instructions into four groups, depending upon how many of the bits in their op codes are fixed.

Group 1: Five Bits Fixed

Instructions in this group have fixed (f) and variable (v) bits as follows

fffvvvff

There are two subgroups to consider.

Group 1A: 8 Addressing Modes

These modes are

vvv	Mode
000	Indexed indirect (see appendix 3)
001	Zero page
010	Immediate (not STA)
011	Absolute
100	Indirect indexed
101	Zero page, indexed X
110	Absolute, indexed Y
111	Absolute, indexed X

The instructions in this group are

ADC, AND, CMP, EOR, LDA, ORA, SBC, STA

Group 1B: 5 Addressing Modes

The modes are

vvv	Mode
000	Immediate (not ASL, LSR, ROL, ROR)
001	Zero page
010	Accumulator (not LDX, LDY)
011	Absolute
101	Zero page, indexed X (indexed Y in LDX)
111	Absolute, indexed X (indexed Y in LDX)

The instructions in this group are

ASL, LDX, LDY, LSR, ROL, ROR

Group 2: Six Bits Fixed

There are two subgroups.

Group 2A

These have fixed (f) and variable (v) bits as follows

fffvvfff

The addressing modes are

vvv	Mode
00	Zero page
01	Absolute
10	Zero page, indexed X (indexed Y in STX)
11	Absolute, indexed X (not STX, STY)

The instructions in this group are

DEC, INC, STX, STY

Group 2B

These have fixed (f) and variable (v) bits as follows

ffffvvff

The addressing modes are

vv	*Mode*
00	Immediate
01	Zero page
11	Absolute

The instructions in this group are

CPX, CPY

Group 3: Seven Bits Fixed

There are two subgroups.

Group 3A

This has a fixed (f) and variable (v) bit pattern of

ffffvfff

The modes are

v	*Mode*
0	Zero page
1	Absolute

The only instruction in this group is BIT.

Group 3B

This has a fixed (f) and variable (v) bit pattern of

ffvfffff

The modes are

v	Mode
0	Absolute
1	Indirect

The only instruction in this group is JMP.

Group 4: All Bits Fixed

These are the implied and relative addressing mode instructions

BCC, BCS, BEQ, BMI, BNE, BPL, BRK, BVC, BVS, CLC, CLD, CLI, CLV, DEX, DEY, INX, INY, NOP, PHA, PHP, PLA, PLP, RTI, RTS, SEC, SED, SEI, TAX, TAY, TSX, TXA, TXS, TYA. Also the absolute mode for JSR.

As an example of this, consider LDA. This is in group 1A, and the fixed bits are 101vvv01. Taking each set of values for vvv in turn we arrive at the op codes A1, A5, A9, AD, B1, B5, B9 and BD.

In the detailed summary that follows, the fixed bytes will be given for each mnemonic, and then each addressing mode will have attached its own variable bits. This information is useful if one wishes to construct an assembler or disassembler, for example.

Abbreviations in Table A1.1

*	Plus 1 cycle if page boundary crossed
†	Plus 1 cycle if branch occurs; plus 2 cycles if branch crosses into another page
n	Number of bytes comprising the op code and operand
t	Number of machine cycles needed to complete instruction
v	A variable bit in the op code
M	An arbitrary memory location (that is, an address)
(M)	The contents of M
M_6	The contents of bit 6 of M
$\overline{M}$	The one's complement of (M)
r	A signed byte (that is, &00 to &7F is +0 to +127; &80 to &FF is −128 to −1)
LOOP	An arbitrary label (that is, an address)
N	The negative flag
Z	The zero flag
C	The carry flag
V	The overflow flag
I	The interrupt disable flag
D	The decimal mode flag
B	The break flag
A	The accumulator
X,Y	The index registers
P	The processor status register
S	The stack pointer
PC	Program counter (containing the address of the *first byte of the instruction*)
→	Copy to memory location or register
↑	Copy to stack (that is, push)
↓	Transfer from stack (that is, pull)
∨	OR
∧	AND
∀	Exclusive-OR
⊕	Signed addition (that is, second byte is treated as a signed byte)
√	Flag is affected by instruction
—	Flag is not affected by instruction

Table A.1.1 Alphabetical summary of instruction set

ADC

Description of ADC M

Add the contents of M to the accumulator, together with any carry bit. Store the result in the Accumulator and any carry in the carry flag.

Symbolic operation of ADC M

$$A + (M) + C \rightarrow A$$
$$\text{Carry} \rightarrow C$$

Flags affected

N	Z	C	V
✓	✓	✓	✓

Fixed bit pattern 011VVV01

		Immediate	Zero Page	Absolute	Zero pageX	Absolute X	Absolute Y	(Indirect) Y	Accumulator	(Indirect X)
OP CODE	n	69 2	65 2	6D 3	75 2	7D 3	79 3	71 2		61 2
t	VVV	2 010	3 001	4 011	4 101	4* 111	4* 110	5* 100		6 000

AND

Description of AND M

Perform the logical AND operation bit by bit on the corresponding bits of (M) and the accumulator, leaving the results in the accumulator

Symbolic operation of AND M

$$A \wedge (M) \rightarrow A$$

∧	0	1
0	0	0
1	0	1

Flags affected

N	Z	C	V
✓	✓	—	—

Fixed bit pattern 001VVV01

		Immediate	Zero Page	Absolute	Zero pageX	Absolute X	Absolute Y	(Indirect) Y	Accumulator	(Indirect X)
OP CODE	n	29 2	25 2	2D 3	35 2	3D 3	39 3	31 2		21 2
t	VVV	2 010	3 001	4 011	4 101	4* 111	4* 110	5* 100		6 000

ASL

Description of ASL M

Move the contents of M left one bit : bit 7 goes into carry. Zero goes into bit 0.
The result is in M.

Symbolic operation of ASL M

$M_7\ M_6\ M_5\ M_4\ M_3\ M_2\ M_1\ M_0 \leftarrow 0$, with bit 7 going into C.

Flags affected

N	Z	C	V
✓	✓	✓	—

Fixed bit pattern 000VVV10

		Immediate	Zero Page	Absolute	Zero pageX	Absolute X	Absolute Y	(Indirect) Y	Accumulator	(Indirect X)
OP CODE	n		06 2	0E 3	16 2	1E 3			0A 1	
t	VVV		5 001	6 011	6 101	7 111			2 010	

BCC

Description of BCC LOOP	Symbolic operation of BCC r	Addressing mode	Opcode	n	t
If C=0, branch to the instruction labelled LOOP	If C = 0: PC + 2 ⊕ r → PC If C = 1: no operation	Relative	90	2	$2^{\dagger}$

Flags affected

N	Z	C	V
—	—	—	—

BCS

Description of BCS LOOP	Symbolic operation of BCS r	Addressing mode	Opcode	n	t
If C = 1, branch to the instruction labelled LOOP	If C=1: PC + 2 ⊕ r → PC If C=0 no operation	Relative	B0	2	$2^{\dagger}$

Flags affected

N	Z	C	V
—	—	—	—

BEQ

Description of BEQ LOOP	Symbolic operation of BEQ r	Addressing mode	Opcode	n	t
If Z = 1, branch to the instruction labelled LOOP	If Z = 1: PC + 2 ⊕ r → PC If Z = 0 no operation	Relative	F0	2	$2^{\dagger}$

Flags affected

N	Z	C	V
—	—	—	—

BIT

Description of BIT M

The logical AND of M and A is performed, the result not being stored. Z is set to 1 if the result is zero, otherwise Z is zero. Finally bits 6 and 7 of M are copied to V and N. A is unchanged.

Symbolic operation of BIT M

$$\overline{A \wedge (M)} \rightarrow Z$$
$$M_6 \rightarrow V$$
$$M_7 \rightarrow N$$

Flags affected

N	Z	C	V
M_7	✓	—	M_6

Fixed bit pattern

0010V100

		Immediate		Zero Page		Absolute		Zero page X		Absolute X		Absolute Y		(Indirect) Y		Accumulator		(Indirect X)	
OP CODE	n			24	2	2C	3												
t	v			3	0	4	1												

BMI

Description of BMI Loop	Symbolic operation of BMI r	Addressing mode	Opcode	n	t	Flags affected
If N=1, branch to the instruction labelled Loop	If N=1: Pc+2⊕r → Pc If N=0: no operation	Relative	30	2	$2^†$	N: — Z: — C: — V: —

BNE

Description of BNE Loop	Symbolic operation of BNE r	Addressing mode	Opcode	n	t	Flags affected
If Z=0, branch to the instruction labelled Loop	If Z=0: Pc+2⊕r → Pc If Z=1: no operation	Relative	D0	2	$2^†$	N: — Z: — C: — V: —

BPL

Description of BPL Loop	Symbolic operation of BPL r	Addressing mode	Opcode	n	t	Flags affected
If N=0, branch to the instruction labelled Loop	If N=0: Pc+2⊕r → Pc If N=1: no operation	Relative	10	2	$2^†$	N: — Z: — C: — V: —

BRK

Description of BRK	Symbolic operation of BRK	Addressing mode	Opcode	n	t	Flags affected
A software interrupt.	↑ Pc+2 S−2→S ↑ P S−1→S (FFFF ; FFFE) → Pc	Implied	00	1	7	N: — Z: — C: — V: —

B is set to 1 before P is pushed onto the stack.

I is set to 1 after P is pushed onto the stack.

BVC

Description of	Symbolic operation of	Addressing mode	Opcode	n	t	Flags affected			
BVC LOOP	BVC r					N	Z	C	V
If V = 0, branch to the instruction labelled LOOP	If V = 0: PC + 2 @r → PC If V = 1: no operation	Relative	50	2	2^t	—	—	—	—

BVS

Description of	Symbolic operation of	Addressing mode	Opcode	n	t	Flags affected			
BVS LOOP	BVS r					N	Z	C	V
If V = 1, branch to the instruction labelled LOOP	If V = 1: PC + 2 @r → PC If V = 0: no operation	Relative	70	2	2^t	—	—	—	—

CLC

Description of	Symbolic operation of	Addressing mode	Opcode	n	t	Flags affected			
CLC	CLC					N	Z	C	V
The carry flag is set to zero (cleared)	0 → C	Implied	18	1	2	—	—	0	—

CLD

Description of	Symbolic operation of	Addressing mode	Opcode	n	t	Flags affected			
CLD	CLD					N	Z	C	V
The decimal flag is set to 0 (cleared). All arithmetic will now be standard binary	0 → D	Implied	D8	1	2	—	—	—	—

D is set to zero

CLI

Description of CLI	Symbolic operation of CLI	Addressing mode	Opcode	n	t	Flags affected
The interrupt mask bit is set to Zero, So enabling interrupts.	$0 \rightarrow I$	Implied	58	1	2	N Z C V — — — —

I is set to 0

CLV

Description of CLV	Symbolic operation of CLV	Addressing mode	Opcode	n	t	Flags affected
The overflow flag is set to Zero (cleared)	$0 \rightarrow V$	Implied	B8	1	2	N Z C V — — — 0

CMP

Description of CMP M

(M) is subtracted from A, but the result is not stored and A is unchanged. Z is 1 on equality, C is 1 if (M) does not exceed A, N is 1 if bit 7 of the result is 1.

Symbolic operation of CMP M

$A - (M) \rightarrow$ result (not stored)
if $A < (M)$, $Z=0$, $C=0$
if $A = (M)$, $Z=1$, $C=1$
if $A > (M)$. $Z=0$, $C=1$
$N =$ result$_7$

Flags affected

N	Z	C	V
✓	✓	✓	—

Fixed bit pattern

110VVV01

		Immediate		Zero Page		Absolute		Zero page X		Absolute X		Absolute Y		(Indirect) Y		Accumulator	(Indirect X)	
OP CODE	n	C9	2	C5	2	CD	3	D5	2	DD	3	D9	3	D1	2		C1	2
t	VVV	2	010	3	001	4	011	4	101	4*	111	4*	110	5*	100			6	000

CPX

Description of CPX M

(M) is subtracted from X, but the result is not stored and X is unchanged. Z is 1 on equality, C is 1 if (M) does not exceed X, N is 1 if bit 7 of the result is 1.

Symbolic operation of CPX M

$X - (M) \rightarrow$ result (not stored)
if $X < (M)$, $Z=0$, $C=0$
if $X = (M)$, $Z=1$, $C=1$
if $X > (M)$, $Z=0$, $C=1$
$N =$ result$_7$

Flags affected

N	Z	C	V
✓	✓	✓	—

Fixed bit pattern

110VV00

		Immediate		Zero Page		Absolute		Zero page X	Absolute X	Absolute Y	(Indirect) Y	Accumulator	(Indirect X)
OP CODE	n	E0	2	E4	2	EC	3						
t	VV	2	00	3	01	4	11						

CPY

	Description of CPY M	Symbolic operation of CPY M	Flags affected	Fixed bit pattern

Description of CPY M

(M) is subtracted from Y but the result is not stored and Y is unchanged. Z is 1 on equality, c is 1 if (M) does not exceed X. N is 1 if bit 7 of the result is 1.

Symbolic operation of CPY M

$Y-(M) \to$ result (not stored)
if $Y<(M)$, $Z=0$, $C=0$
if $Y=(M)$, $Z=1$, $C=1$ } $N = $ result$_7$
if $Y>(M)$, $Z=0$, $C=1$

Flags affected

N	Z	C	V
✓	✓	✓	—

Fixed bit pattern

1100VV00

		Immediate	Zero Page	Absolute	Zero page X	Absolute X	Absolute Y	(Indirect) Y	Accumulator	(Indirect X)
OP CODE	n	C0 2	C4 2	CC 3						
t	vv	2 00	3 01	4 11						

DEC

Description of DEC M

The contents of M is decreased by 1. (If (M) is zero it becomes &FF.) The result is stored in M.

Symbolic operation of DEC M

$(M)-1 \to M$

Flags affected

N	Z	C	V
✓	✓	—	—

Fixed bit pattern

110VV110

		Immediate	Zero Page	Absolute	Zero page X	Absolute X	Absolute Y	(Indirect) Y	Accumulator	(Indirect X)
OP CODE	n		C6 2	CE 3	D6 2	DE 3				
t	vv		5 00	6 01	6 10	7 11				

DEX

Description of DEX

The contents of X is reduced by 1. (If X is zero it becomes &FF.)

Symbolic operation of DEX	Addressing mode	Opcode	n	t	Flags affected			
$X-1 \to X$	Implied	CA	1	2	N ✓	Z ✓	C —	V —

DEY

Description of DEY

The contents of Y is reduced by 1. (If Y is zero it becomes &FF.)

Symbolic operation of DEY	Addressing mode	Opcode	n	t	Flags affected			
$Y-1 \to Y$	Implied	88	1	2	N ✓	Z ✓	C —	V —

EOR

Description of EOR M

Perform the exclusive - OR operation bit by bit on the corresponding bits of (M) and the accumulator, leaving the result in the accumulator.

Symbolic operation of EOR M

$$A \wedge (M) \rightarrow A$$

A		
A	0	1
0	0	1
1	1	0

Flags affected

N	Z	C	V
✓	✓	—	—

Fixed bit pattern

010VVV01

		Immediate	Zero Page	Absolute	Zero pageX	Absolute X	Absolute Y	(Indirect) Y	Accumulator	(Indirect X)
OP CODE	n	45 2	45 2	4D 3	55 2	5D 3	59 3	51 3		41 2
t	vvv	2 010	3 001	4 011	4 101*	4* 111	4* 110	5* 100		6 000

INC

Description of INC M

The contents of M is increased by 1. (If (M) is &FF it becomes zero.) The result is stored in M.

Symbolic operation of INC M

$$(M) + 1 \rightarrow M$$

Flags affected

N	Z	C	V
✓	✓	—	—

Fixed bit pattern

111VV110

		Immediate	Zero Page	Absolute	Zero pageX	Absolute X	Absolute Y	(Indirect) Y	Accumulator	(Indirect X)
OP CODE	n		E6 2	EE 3	F6 2	FE 3				
t	vv		5 00	6 01	6 10	7 11				

INX

Description of INX

The contents of X is increased by 1. (If X is &FF it becomes zero).

Symbolic operation of INX

$$X + 1 \rightarrow X$$

Addressing mode	Opcode	n	t	Flags affected
Implied	E8	1	2	N Z C V ✓ ✓ — —

INY

Description of INY

The contents of Y is increased by 1. (If Y is &FF it becomes zero).

Symbolic operation of INY

$$Y + 1 \rightarrow Y$$

Addressing mode	Opcode	n	t	Flags affected
Implied	C8	1	2	N Z C V ✓ ✓ — —

JMP

Description of JMP Loop	Symbolic operation of JMP Loop	Flags affected	Fixed bit pattern

The address represented by the label Loop is loaded into the program counter causing a jump to occur to the instruction at that address.

Loop → PC

N	Z	C	V
—	—	—	—

01v01100

		Immediate	Zero Page	Absolute	Zero page X	Absolute X	Absolute Y	(Indirect) Y	Accumulator	(Indirect X)	Indirect
OP CODE	n			4C 3							6C 3
t	v			3 0							5 1

JSR

Description of JSR Loop	Symbolic operation of JSR Loop	Addressing mode	Opcode	n	t	Flags affected

The program counter plus 2 (the address minus one of the instruction following the JSR) is saved on the stack. The address represented by Loop is loaded into the program counter.

PC + 2 ↑
Loop → PC

Absolute   2o   3 6

N	Z	C	V
—	—	—	—

LDA

Description of LDA M	Symbolic operation of LDA M	Flags affected	Fixed bit pattern

The contents of M is copied into the accumulator.

(M) → A

N	Z	C	V
✓	✓	—	—

101vvv01

		Immediate	Zero Page	Absolute	Zero page X	Absolute X	Absolute Y	(Indirect) Y	Accumulator	(Indirect X)
OP CODE	n	A9 2	A5 2	AD 3	B5 2	BD 3	B9 3	B1 2		A1 2
t	vvv	2 010	010 3	001 4	011 4	101 4*	111 4*	110 5*	100	6 000

LDX

Description of LDX M	Symbolic operation of LDX M	Flags affected	Fixed bit pattern
The contents of M is copied into X.	$(M) \rightarrow X$	N Z C V / ✓ ✓ — —	101vvv10

		Immediate	Zero Page	Absolute	Zero pageY	Absolute X	Absolute Y	(Indirect) Y	Accumulator	(Indirect X)
OP CODE	^	A2 2	A6 2	AE 3	B6 2		BE 3			
t	vvv	2 000	3 001	4 011	4 101		4* 111			

LDY

Description of LDY M	Symbolic operation of LDY M	Flags affected	Fixed bit pattern
The contents of M is copied into Y.	$(M) \rightarrow Y$	N Z C V / ✓ ✓ — —	101vvv00

		Immediate	Zero Page	Absolute	Zero pageX	Absolute X	Absolute Y	(Indirect) Y	Accumulator	(Indirect X)
OP CODE	^	A0 2	A4 2	AC 3	B4 2	BC 3				
t	vvv	2 000	3 001	4 011	4 101	4* 111				

LSR

Description of LSR M	Symbolic operation of LSR M	Flags affected	Fixed bit pattern
Move the contents of M right one bit: bit 0 goes into carry. Zero goes into bit 7. The result is in M.	$M_7\,M_6\,M_5\,M_4\,M_3\,M_2\,M_1\,M_0$ → C	N Z C V / 0 ✓ ✓ —	010vvv10

		Immediate	Zero Page	Absolute	Zero pageX	Absolute X	Absolute Y	(Indirect) Y	Accumulator	(Indirect X)
OP CODE	^		46 2	4E 3	56 2	5E 3			4A 1	
t	vvv		5 001	6 011	6 101	7 111			2 010	

NOP

Description of NOP	Symbolic operation of NOP	Addressing mode	Opcode	n t	Flags affected
Does Nothing for 2 cycles.	—	Implied	EA	1 2	N Z C V / — — — —

ORA.

Description of ORA M	Symbolic operation of ORA M	Flags affected	Fixed bit pattern

Perform the inclusive-OR operation bit by bit on the corresponding bits of (M) and the accumulator, leaving the result in the accumulator.

$$A \lor (M) \rightarrow A$$

V	0	1
0	0	1
1	1	1

N	Z	C	V
✓	✓	–	–

000VVV01

		Immediate	Zero Page	Absolute	Zero page X	Absolute X	Absolute Y	(Indirect) Y	Accumulator	(Indirect X)
OP CODE	n	09 2	05 2	0D 3	15 2	1D 3	19 3	11 2		01 2
t	vvv	2 010	3 001	4 011	4 101	4* 111	4* 110	5* 100		6 000

PHA

Description of PHA	Symbolic operation of PHA	Addressing mode	Opcode	n	t	Flags affected

The contents of the accumulator is copied to the stack, and the stack pointer is decreased by one.

↑A
$$S - 1 \rightarrow S$$

Implied   48   1   3

N	Z	C	V
–	–	–	–

PHP

Description of PHP	Symbolic operation of PHP	Addressing mode	Opcode	n	t	Flags affected

The contents of the status register is copied to the stack, and the stack pointer is decreased by 1.

↑P
$$S - 1 \rightarrow S$$

Implied   08   1   3

N	Z	C	V
–	–	–	–

PLA

Description of PLA	Symbolic operation of PLA	Addressing mode	Opcode	n	t	Flags affected

The contents of the accumulator is filled by the last byte pushed on the stack, and the stack pointer is increased by one.

↓A
$$S + 1 \rightarrow S$$

Implied   68   1   4

N	Z	C	V
✓	✓	–	–

PLP

Description of	Symbolic operation of	Addressing mode	Opcode	n	t	Flags affected
PLP	PLP					N Z C V

The status register is filled with the last byte pushed onto the stack, and the stack pointer is increased by one.

$\downarrow P$

$S+1 \rightarrow S$

Implied   28   1 4

N	Z	C	V
✓	✓	✓	✓

B.D and I are also affected.

ROL

Description of ROL M

Move the contents of M left one bit: bit 7 goes into carry after the present contents of carry has gone into bit 0. The result is in M.

Symbolic operation of ROL M

$M_7 M_6 M_5 M_4 M_3 M_2 M_1 M_0$

C

Flags affected

N	Z	C	V
✓	✓	✓	—

Fixed bit pattern

001VVV10

		Immediate	Zero Page	Absolute	Zero page X	Absolute X	Absolute Y	(Indirect) Y	Accumulator	(Indirect X)
OP CODE	n		26 2	2E 3	36 2	3E 3				2A 1	
t	VVV		5 001	6 011	6 101	7 111				2 010	

ROR

Description of ROR M

Move the contents of M right one bit: bit 0 goes into carry after the present contents of carry has gone into bit 7. The result is in M.

Symbolic operation of ROR M

$M_7 M_6 M_5 M_4 M_3 M_2 M_1 M_0$

C

Flags affected

N	Z	C	V
✓	✓	✓	—

Fixed bit pattern

011VVV10

		Immediate	Zero Page	Absolute	Zero page X	Absolute X	Absolute Y	(Indirect) Y	Accumulator	(Indirect X)
OP CODE	n		66 2	6E 3	76 2	7E 3				6A 1	
t	VVV		5 001	6 011	6 101	7 111				2 010	

RTI

Description of	Symbolic operation of	Addressing mode	Opcode	n	t	Flags affected
RTI	RTI					N Z C V

Return to main program after an interrupt has been serviced. The status register and program counter are restored from the stack, and the stack pointer is adjusted.

$\downarrow P$

$S+1 \rightarrow S$

$\uparrow PC$

$S+2 \rightarrow S$

Implied.   40   1 6

N	Z	C	V
✓	✓	✓	✓

B.D and I are also affected.

RTS

Description of	Symbolic operation of	Addressing mode	Opcode	n	t	Flags affected

RTS

RTS

Return to calling program from a subroutine. The return is to the instruction following the call (ie. following JSR). The program counter is restored from the stack and incremented by 1. The stack pointer is adjusted.

↓ PC
S + 2 → S
PC + 1 → PC

Implied   60   1   6

N	Z	C	V
—	—	—	—

SBC

Description of SBC M	Symbolic operation of SBC M	Flags affected	Fixed bit pattern

Subtract the contents of M together with any borrow from the accumulator. The result is left in the accumulator and any borrow in the carry flag.

$A - (M) - \bar{C} \rightarrow A$

$\overline{Borrow} \rightarrow C$

N	Z	C	V
✓	✓	✓	✓

111vvv01

		Immediate	Zero Page	Absolute	Zero page X	Absolute X	Absolute Y	(Indirect) Y	Accumulator	(Indirect X)
OP CODE	n	E9 2	E5 2	ED 3	F5 2	FD 3	F9 3	F1 2		E1 2
t	vvv	2 010	3 001	4 011	4 101	4* 111	4* 110	5* 100		6 000

SEC

Description of	Symbolic operation of	Addressing mode	Opcode	n	t	Flags affected

SEC

SEC

The carry flag is set to one

$1 \rightarrow C$

Implied   38   1   2

N	Z	C	V
—	—	1	—

SED

Description of	Symbolic operation of	Addressing mode	Opcode	n	t	Flags affected

SED

SED

The decimal flag is set to one. All arithmetic is now in BCD (ie. ADC and SBC operate according to BCD)

$1 \rightarrow D$

Implied   F8   1   2

N	Z	C	V
—	—	—	—

D is set to 1.

SEI

Description of	Symbolic operation of	Addressing mode	Opcode	n	t	Flags affected

SEI

SEI

The interrupt mask bit is set to 1, so disabling interrupts.

$1 \rightarrow I$

Implied   78   1   2

N	Z	C	V
—	—	—	—

I is set to 1.

STA

Description of STA M	Symbolic operation of STA M	Flags affected	Fixed bit pattern
The contents of the accumulator is put into the location M.	A → M	N Z C V – – – –	100vvv01

	Immediate	Zero Page	Absolute	Zero page X	Absolute X	Absolute Y	(Indirect) Y	Accumulator	(Indirect X)
OP CODE n		85 2	8D 3	95 2	9D 3	99 3	51 2		81 2
t vvv		3 001	4 011	4 101	5 111	5 110	6 100		6 000

STX

Description of STX M	Symbolic operation of STX M	Flags affected	Fixed bit pattern
The contents of X is put into the location M.	X → M	N Z C V – – – –	100vv110

	Immediate	Zero Page	Absolute	Zero page Y	Absolute X	Absolute Y	(Indirect) Y	Accumulator	(Indirect X)
OP CODE n		86 2	8E 3	96 2					
t vv		3 00	4 01	4 10					

STY

Description of STY M	Symbolic operation of STY M	Flags affected	Fixed bit pattern
The contents of Y is put into the location M.	Y → M	N Z C V – – – –	100vv100

	Immediate	Zero Page	Absolute	Zero page X	Absolute X	Absolute Y	(Indirect) Y	Accumulator	(Indirect X)
OP CODE n		84 2	8C 3	94 2					
t vv		3 00	4 01	4 10					

TAX

Description of TAX	Symbolic operation of TAX	Addressing mode	Opcode	n	t	Flags affected
The contents of the accumulator is copied into the X register.	A → X	Implied	AA	1	2	N Z C V ✓ ✓ – –

TAY

Description of	Symbolic operation of	Addressing mode	Opcode	n	t	Flags affected

TAY

Description of	Symbolic operation of	Addressing mode	Opcode	n	t	N	Z	C	V
The contents of the accumulator is copied into the Y register.	A → Y	Implied	A8	1	2	✓	✓	—	—

TSX

Description of	Symbolic operation of	Addressing mode	Opcode	n	t	N	Z	C	V
TSX	TSX								
The contents of the stack pointer is copied into the X register	S → X	Implied	BA	1	2	✓	✓	—	—

TXA

Description of	Symbolic operation of	Addressing mode	Opcode	n	t	N	Z	C	V
TXA	TXA								
The contents of the X register is copied to the accumulator	X → A	Implied	8A	1	2	✓	✓	—	—

TXS

Description of	Symbolic operation of	Addressing mode	Opcode	n	t	N	Z	C	V
TXS	TXS								
The contents of the X register is copied to the stack pointer	X → S	Implied	9A	1	2	—	—	—	—

TYA

Description of	Symbolic operation of	Addressing mode	Opcode	n	t	N	Z	C	V
TYA	TYA								
The contents of the Y register is copied to the accumulator.	Y → A	Implied	98	1	2	✓	✓	—	—

Table A1.2 Instruction set in numerical order of opcodes

In this table the following abbreviations are used:

ZP	Zero page addressing mode
Abs	Absolute addressing mode
Imm	Immediate addressing mode
ZP,X ⎫ ZP,Y ⎬	Zero page indexed addressing mode
Abs,X ⎫ Abs,Y ⎬	Absolute indexed addressing mode
(Ind),Y	Indirect indexed addressing mode
(Ind,X)	Indexed indirect addressing mode
(Ind)	Indirect addressing mode
A	Accumulator addressing mode
LSN	Least significant nybble (for example, A in &EA)
MSN	Most significant nybble (for example, E in &EA)
—	Reserved for future expansion

MSN ↓	0	1	2	3	4	5	6	7	8	9	A	B	C	D	E
0	BRK	ORA (Ind,X)	—	—	—	ORA ZP	ASL ZP	—	PHP	ORA Imm	ASL A	—	—	ORA Abs	ASL Abs
1	BPL	ORA (Ind),Y	—	—	—	ORA ZP,X	ASL ZP,X	—	CLC	ORA Abs,Y	—	—	—	ORA Abs,X	ASL Abs,X
2	JSR	AND (Ind,X)	—	—	BIT ZP	AND ZP	ROL ZP	—	PLP	AND Imm	ROL A	—	BIT Abs	AND Abs	ROL Abs
3	BMI	AND (Ind),Y	—	—	—	AND ZP,X	ROL ZP,X	—	SEC	AND Abs,Y	—	—	—	AND Abs,X	ROL Abs,X
4	RTI	EOR (Ind,X)	—	—	—	EOR ZP	LSR ZP	—	PHA	EOR Imm	LSR A	—	JMP Abs	EOR Abs	LSR Abs
5	BVC	EOR (Ind),Y	—	—	—	EOR ZP,X	LSR ZP,X	—	CLI	EOR Abs,Y	—	—	—	EOR Abs,X	LSR Abs,X
6	RTS	ADC (Ind,X)	—	—	—	ADC ZP	ROR ZP	—	PLA	ADC Imm	ROR A	—	JMP (Ind)	ADC Abs	ROR Abs
7	BVS	ADC (Ind),Y	—	—	—	ADC ZP,X	ROR ZP,X	—	SEI	ADC Abs,Y	—	—	—	ADC Abs,X	ROR Abs,X
8	—	STA (Ind,X)	—	—	STY ZP	STA ZP	STX ZP	—	DEY	—	TXA	—	STY Abs	STA Abs	STX Abs
9	BCC	STA (Ind),Y	—	—	STY ZP,X	STA ZP,X	STX ZP,Y	—	TYA	STA Abs,Y	TXS	—	—	STA Abs,X	—
A	LDY Imm	LDA (Ind,X)	LDX Imm	—	LDY ZP	LDA ZP	LDX ZP	—	TAY	LDA Imm	TAX	—	LDY Abs	LDA Abs	LDX Abs
B	BCS	LDA (Ind),Y	—	—	LDY ZP,X	LDA ZP,X	LDX ZP,Y	—	CLV	LDA Abs,Y	TSX	—	LDY Abs,X	LDA Abs,X	LDX Abs,Y
C	CPY Imm	CMP (Ind,X)	—	—	CPY ZP	CMP ZP	DEC ZP	—	INY	CMP Imm	DEX	—	CPY Abs	CMP Abs	DEC Abs
D	BNE	CMP (Ind),Y	—	—	—	CMP ZP,X	DEC ZP,X	—	CLD	CMP Abs,Y	—	—	—	CMP Abs,X	DEC Abs,X
E	CPX Imm	SBC (Ind,X)	—	—	CPX ZP	SBC ZP	INC ZP	—	INX	SBC Imm	NOP	—	CPX Abs	SBC Abs	INC Abs
F	BEQ	SBC (Ind),Y	—	—	—	SBC ZP,X	INC ZP,X	—	SED	SBC Abs,Y	—	—	—	SBC Abs,X	INC Abs,X

Appendix 2: Full Block Diagram of 6502 Architecture

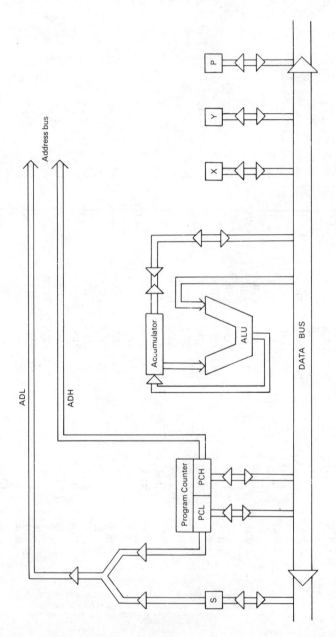

Internal address pathways for the program counter are omitted.

Appendix 3: Indexed Indirect Addressing

There is one more 6502 addressing mode which we have not covered in the book: *indexed indirect addressing*. This omission is quite deliberate, for you are not likely to want to use this mode of addressing in your work on the BBC Micro. The designers of the 6502 included indexed indirect for a very specific purpose: *multiple peripheral programming*.

In this appendix we shall first describe briefly the operation of the indexed indirect mode, and then describe the sort of application for which it is suitable.

Consider a list of pointers stored consecutively in memory. Then the contents of the location to which any pointer is referencing can be loaded into the accumulator by writing LDA (PNTER,X), where PNTER is the base address of the pointers and X is a suitable even number. Similarly STA (PNTER,X) stores a copy of the accumulator in the location pointed to by (PNTER,X). Only the X register can be used for this purpose, just as only the Y register can be used for indirect indexed addressing. Again, like indirect indexed addressing, indexed indirect requires the location PNTER *to be in zero page*.

The diagram below illustrates the pair of instructions LDA (PNTER1,X): STA (PNTER2,X), where X equals 6.

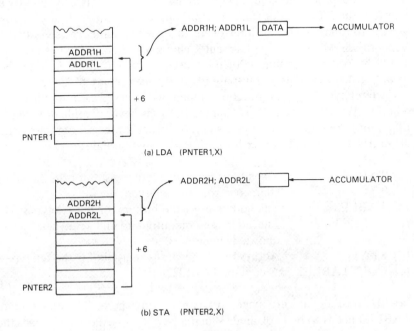

(a) LDA (PNTER1,X)

(b) STA (PNTER2,X)

6, the contents of X, is added to the base address PNTER1 to give the location containing the low byte of the address, the content of which is ADDR1L. The next location will always contain the high byte of the address, in (a) ADDR1H. Hence the contents of the address ADDR1H; ADDR1L are put into the accumulator. Similarly, in (b) the accumulator is put into ADDR2H; ADDR2L.

Now, the indexed indirect addressing mode cannot be usefully used to access strings in memory by referring to a list of pointers to those strings, such as we constructed in section 7.6. The reason for this is that each character of the string could then be accessed only by using ordinary indexed addressing, and we cannot combine both modes in the same instruction. That is, we cannot write LDA (BASE,X),Y (it is unfortunate that we cannot do this—it would be a most powerful combination). Because most lists of pointers in the sort of assembly programs that we are likely to write will be used to access a base address from which we will index, indexed indirect is not of much use to us. The methods used in section 7.6 are still the best ones to use in these cases.

However, it is worth understanding the sort of applications where indexed indirect is useful—the sort of application, indeed, for which the addressing mode was designed. Consider a whole series of peripheral devices, say teletypes, each of which will be serviced by one 6502 microprocessor. Each teletype is connected up to its own specific VIA port. Each teletype is sending a message to the microprocessor, which will be terminated by a carriage return. As each character of the message is ready to be processed, the VIA to which the teletype is connected will interrupt the 6502. At this stage, the microprocessor will enter an interrupt service routine which will interrogate in turn the status registers of the VIAs to see which teletype has sent a character. Since teletypes are very slow, the order of polling is of no consequence: any multiple interrupt would be dealt with quite transparently to the user of any of the teletypes.

Each teletype has a small section of memory reserved for it which acts as a buffer. We shall assume here that the buffer is never overfilled. Five sets of pointers are required for this system, the order for the set of tables being arbitrary, although the order for each table must be the same.

(a) TABLE1   The addresses of the input register for the incoming character from the teletype
(b) TABLE2   The addresses of the buffers for the teletypes
(c) TABLE3   The addresses of output to the teletypes for acknowledgement
(d) STATUS   Addresses of the status registers for the teletypes
(e) COPYTABLE2   A copy of TABLE2

(a)–(d) must be in zero page, (e) can be anywhere. The function of TABLE3 needs to be explained. When a key is pressed on a teletype, the action of the print-hammer is caused not directly by this key but by the computer reflecting the key. In this way, an instant verification is performed to confirm that the correct data has been received.

Here, now, is the simplified code for performing this polling sequence (we simplify by ignoring parity checking, among other things)

```
 1                 LDX    #2 * (NUMBER − 1)
 2 LOOP1           LDA    (STATUS,X)
 3                 BMI    STOREDATA
 4                 DEX
 5                 DEX
 6                 BPL    LOOP1
 7                 BMI    OUT
 8 STOREDATA  LDA    (TABLE1,X)
 9                 STA    (TABLE3,X)
10                 CMP    #&0D
11                 BEQ    ENDSTRING
12                 STA    (TABLE2,X)
13                 INC    TABLE2,X
14                 BNE    OUT
15                 INC    TABLE2+1,X
16                 BNE    OUT
17 ENDSTRING  LDA    COPYTABLE2,X
18                 STA    TABLE2,X
19                 LDA    COPYTABLE2+1,X
20                 STA    TABLE2+1,X
21                 JSR    ANALYSE
22 OUT                   ·
                        ·
                        ·
                        ·
                        ·
```

In line 1, NUMBER is the number of teletypes connected. The beauty of this program is that it will work for up to 32 teletypes, with no change whatsoever being required in the program ($32 \times 2 \times 4 = 256$, the limit of zero page).

In lines 2 to 7 we examine the status register of each VIA in turn, beginning with the one at the top of the STATUS list. If bit 7 is 1, this indicates that the teletype to which this VIA is attached has sent a character, and we go to line 8 to process it. Otherwise, we decrease X by 2, and look at the next status register down the list. If we happen to go through the entire list without finding the source of the interrupt (a 'phantom' interrupt) we go to some suitable exit code at line 22 onwards

Assuming that we find the appropriate teletype, we then load the contents of the input and store it in the buffer (lines 8 and 9). Notice how indexed indirect allows us to recover the appropriate set of pointers by using just one index value (this is why the tables must be arranged in the same order, of course). If we have reached the end of the message (lines 9 and 10) we go to perform some analysis in lines 17–21. Lines 17–20 reset the pointers in TABLE2, which have been altered in lines 13–15, and line 21 jumps to a subroutine which performs some analysis on the basis of the message (and which will output a line feed, when the analysis is complete). During this analysis, interrupts will be enabled so that further input can be received. One function of the ANALYSIS routine will be to deal with the case where 2 or more teletypes have messages to be analysed simultaneously, using some time-sharing principle which need not concern us here.

If the end of the message is not yet reached, the current character will be stored in the buffer (line 12) and then the address of the buffer will be incremented by one to point to the next free space. This is slower and more cumbrous than the indirect indexed method used in section 7.6, but it is suitable in this case since teletypes are relatively slow anyway, and relatively few increments are required (at least compared to the sorting requirements of section 7.6).

The size of this program is very small considering the complex task it performs, and this is due entirely to the use of the indexed indirect mode. The overall speed of processing is very favourable too, and this is why the designers of the 6502 included this addressing mode. Unfortunately, we are unlikely to be able to profit from it on the BBC Micro. Probably the only time that we are likely to use it, is in the case where we want a simple indirect mode and the Y register is not available. In this case, using indexed indirect with X equal to zero will suffice, since LDA (BASE),Y and LDA (BASE,X) give identical results when X and Y are both zero.

Appendix 4: Floating-point Representation

In this book we have considered only the integer (or fixed point) representation of numbers. The discussion of the *floating-point* representation has been outside our scope. However, for the sake of completeness, we will here discuss this representation, although we will not be considering how arithmetic may be performed upon such numbers.

The number four in base two is 100; if we divide by two we obtain 10, or more suggestively 10.0; divide by two again and we get 1.0, which is one, of course. Now it would seem reasonable to write the result of dividing by two again as 0.1, by two yet again at 0.01, and by two still again as 0.001; and so on. Hence 0.1 is ½, 0.01 is ¼, 0.001 is ⅛; and so on. This is *bicimal* representation, the direct counterpart to the base ten decimal; and we refer to the point as the *bicimal point.*

Any decimal can be written in bicimal; and any bicimal in decimal. For example, 0.75 is 0.11 in bicimal; and 0.0101 in bicimal is 0.3125. Now, fractions that can be written as terminating decimals may give recurring bicimals. For example, ⅕ is $0.00\dot{1}\dot{1}$ in bicimal. However, any fraction that terminates in bicimal will terminate in decimal, because all such fractions will have denominators of a power of two, all of which terminate in decimal (just keep halving 0.5 until you get there). It follows that there may be a loss of precision in translating from decimal to bicimal if we cannot use the recurrence notation (the dots over the relevant repeating digits). Moreover, bicimal takes up many more places than decimal, so we may have to round to get our decimal into a fixed number of bicimal places. Hence, we see that a possible error can be introduced in translating from decimal to bicimal (and vice versa if the number of significant figures allocated to decimal output is fixed). This must be borne in mind when dealing with floating-point numbers (in assembler *or* in BASIC), for in certain circumstances these rounding errors can compound considerably, resulting in significant errors.

When storing bicimal numbers in a computer it is convenient to write them first in a *normalised form.* So, we write 11011.01011 as 0.1101101011 $\times 2^5$, and 0.00010101011 as 0.10101011 $\times 2^{-3}$, for example. The convention is to move the bicimal point until the most significant digit is the one just after the point: that is, move it right or left until all digits to the left of the point are zero and the first digit to the right of the point is one. The power of two attached to this adjusted number reflects the number of moves that the bicimal point has had to make. Applying this power to the adjusted number will set the bicimal point back to its correct place (5 places rightwards in the first case, that is, $0.\overset{\frown}{1101101011} \rightarrow 11011.01011$ as required, and 3 places leftwards in the second). Thus the point is allowed to *float* across so that a normalised form is achieved, and so we call the representation the *floating-point representation*. Whole numbers can also be represented in this way, of course. For example, 110001011 is 0.110001011×2^9.

The BBC Micro and most other microcomputers use 5 bytes to represent such numbers. The least significant byte represents the power, or as it is usually called, the *exponent*. The next four bytes represent the number, or as it is usually called, the *mantissa*. The exponent is in two's complement form with one difference: the sign bit is reversed. Hence an exponent of &90 represents &10 or 16, while &70 represents −&10 or −16. The reason for this is connected with the representation for zero. Clearly zero gives a zero mantissa (which cannot be normalised since there is no one). It is logical to have the minimum exponent associated with this, which is the maximum negative exponent. This is reasonable since a maximum negative exponent is associated with the smallest number that can be represented for any given mantissa. Without the change in the sign bit this would give &80 00 00 00 00; with the change it gives &00 00 00 00 00, which is much more sensible.

Apart from zero, *all* mantissas will have their most significant bits as one. We can therefore *assume* that the most significant bit is one, and use the actual bit in this position to reflect the sign of the number: 0 is positive, 1 is negative.

Figure A4.1 shows the format for a floating-point number: notice that the byte on the extreme left (carrying the exponent) is the *lowest* in memory of the five. Moreover, in the next four, the most significant byte is *lowest* in memory, and the least significant, *highest* in memory. This is in distinction to integer (fixed point) numbers, where the most significant

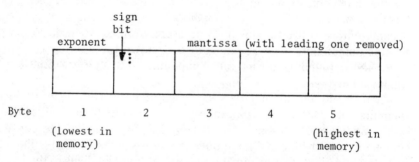

Figure A4.1: Floating point storage in the BBC Micro

byte is the highest in memory. The convention with integers is chosen to fit in with the 6502 convention; with floating-point, there are standard routines for arithmetic and there is no gain in using the specific convention of the 6502 microprocessor.

The largest numerical values are, on the positive side FF 7F FF FF FF and on the negative FF FF FF FF FF (that is, $\pm 1.70141183 \times 10^{38}$ to 9sf, the limit of precision in the BBC Micro). The smallest numerical values (apart from zero) are 00 00 00 00 01 and 00 80 00 00 01 (that is, $\pm 1.46936794 \times 10^{-39}$ to 9sf).

In order to acquaint yourself with this representation, load the monitor (listing 10.6) and use CALLS%,X, with X set at various values. For example

$$X = 2500: \text{CALLS\%,X}$$

Now type M 0600 and the address pointed to should be &25E4. M 25E4 gives 8C 1C 40 00 00, which is $\&0.9C4 \times 2^{12}$ (that is, 0.1001 1100 0100 $\times$ 2^{12}). Now moving the hexadecimal point across each hex digit is equivalent to multiplying by 2^4, so we obtain &9C4, which is indeed 2500.

Again, X = -2500: CALLS%,X, gives 8C 9C 40 00 00, that is, $-\&0.9C4 \times 2^{12}$ or $-\&9C4$, as required. Remember, the sign bit of the second byte is the sign of the whole number.

Finally, X = 0.3175: CALLS%,X gives 7F 20 00 00 00, which is &0.A0 $\times 2^{-1}$, that is, 0.0101, as required.

Try more yourself—you will soon become very familiar with this form of storage.

Appendix 5: Flowchart Symbols and Conventions Used in This Book

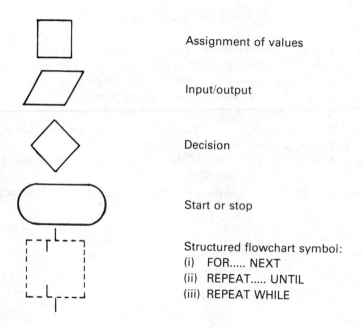

Assignment of values

Input/output

Decision

Start or stop

Structured flowchart symbol:
(i)   FOR..... NEXT
(ii) REPEAT..... UNTIL
(iii) REPEAT WHILE

Appendix 6: Further Uses of OPT

You may wish to use your BBC Micro as a development machine to produce machine code programs which you want to put on EPROMs. To do this you will need an EPROM programmer add-on. But this will not be enough: it is likely that you will want your programs on EPROM to occupy space above &8000, the usual ROM and EPROM locations. However, you have no RAM in this area on the BBC Micro, so how can you do it?

The answer is to use OPT4 to OPT7. If you do this you can make use of *two* assembly location variables: P% is still the program counter, but now O% is also available, and this indicates where the code will *physically* go in your BBC Micro. Hence you can set P% above &8000 with O% at a usual RAM location.

As an example, consider listing 4.2 again. Change

    20 to 20 P%=&9000:O%=START

and

    30 to 30 [OPT7 (the equivalent of OPT3)

and RUN the program.

Notice that it assembles using addresses from &9000 onwards

           9000 LDA NUM
           9002 .BACK etc.

However, now type in

    FOR I%=0 TO 8: PRINT~START?I%:NEXT

and note that you get the machine code. Hence, while the assembler uses *addresses* beginning from P%, it assembles *into* the address contained in O%. This is exactly what we require for EPROM programming.

Appendix 7: The User Port

The user port on a model B is part of a 6552 Versatile Interface Adapter (VIA). This is a fairly complex input/output chip, which provides two ports, handshaking, interrupts, two timers and a serial register. It is quite possible to write a book on the applications of this chip, and there is not space here to do this, However, information on the VIA in accessible and digestible form is not easy to come by and, in this appendix, a brief but full account is given of its workings. This should allow you to do most of what you want with the user port.

A7.1 Overview of the 6522 VIA

(This section may be read quickly on first reading, and returned to later.)
   The VIA which is used to create the centronics printer port and the user port is memory mapped into the locations &FE60 to &FE6F. Table A7.1 shows the purpose of each location. Since *port A* is used exclusively for the printer, we shall not consider it or its associated control lines in any detail (though if you require up to 10mA of buffered 'sink' current, port A could be used without modification to the circuits).

Table A7.1   User port and printer VIA

Address	Function
FE60	Port B
FE61	Port A, with handshaking (printer)
FE62	Data direction register for port B
FE63	Data direction register for port A (printer)
FE64	Timer1 counter, low byte
FE65	Timer1 counter, high byte
FE66	Timer1 latch, low byte
FE67	Timer1 latch, high byte
FE68	Timer2 counter, low byte
FE69	Timer2 counter, high byte
FE6A	Serial shift register
FE6B	Auxiliary control register
FE6C	Peripheral control register
FE6D	Interrupt flag register
FE6E	Interrupt enable register
FE6F	Port A, no handshaking (printer)

Port B at &FE60 has each of its bits connected to a corresponding pin on the user port. There are also two *control lines*, CB1 and CB2, which are connected to the other two pins on the user port: your User Guide contains the relevant circuit diagram. Each bit of the port can either be used for output or for input: the *data direction register* at &FE62 controls this.

The 6522 contains two timers, *timer1* being more complex than *timer2*, and both are available for use. The VIA supports interrupts on both these timers, and also on each of the control lines (CB1 and CB2 for the user port). There is also a *serial register* which can output and accept bits one at a time and shift them accordingly, and this can also generate interrupts. In the BBC computer *all* IRQ interrupts vector first through an address contained in &0204 and &0205 (that is, JMP (&0204) is performed). Interrupts from the user port will not be dealt with by this service routine: instead, the routine is exited with a JMP (&206). Hence, one can write one's own servicing routine for the user port by putting the address of this routine in &206 and &207 (that is, at IRQ2, compare section 9.3). So the user can write his own interrupt service routines in connection with port B, the serial register and the timers. The *interrupt enable register* (&FE6E) controls which interrupts are allowed: the *interrupt flag register* (&FE6D) displays which items are calling for an interrupt (regardless of whether they are enabled), and bit 7 of this register is one if an interrupt is asked for and enabled. Tables A7.2 and A7.3 show these registers.

Table A7.2   Interrupt enable register

7	6	5	4	3	2	1	0
Set or clear control bit	T1	T2	CB1	CB2	SR	CA1	CA2

1 = interrupt enabled; 0 = interrupt disabled (bits 0 to 6)
1 = writing a one sets that bit to 1 ⎫
0 = writing a one sets that bit to 0 ⎭ (bit 7)

Table A7.3   Interrupt flag register

7	6	5	4	3	2	1	0
IRQ	T1	T2	CB1	CB2	SR	CA1	CA2

Bit 7 is 1 if any of bits 0–6 are set to 1 in both this register and the interrupt enable register.

Bits 0–6 are set and cleared by the following operations:

Bit	Set by	Cleared by*
0	Active transition on CA2	Reading or writing &FE61
1	Active transition on CA1	Reading or writing &FE61
2	Completion of 8 shifts (not in free-running mode)	Reading or writing &FE6A
3	Active transition of CB2	Reading or writing &FE60
4	Active transition of CB1	Reading or writing &FE60
5	Time-out of Timer2	Reading &FE68 or writing &FE69
6	Time-out of Timer1	Reading &FE64 or writing &FE65

*Note that interrupt flags can also be cleared by writing 1 into the bit position.

There are two control registers: the *peripheral control register* is concerned with the operation of the four control lines (CA1, CA2, CB1, CB2); the top nybble controls CB1 and CB2, the bottom CA1 and CA2 (which are reserved for the printer port). The *auxiliary control register* determines how the input ports, serial register and the timers behave. Tables A7.4 and A7.5 give the details.

Table A7.4   Peripheral control register (bits 4–7 only; bits 0–3 are identical in function but are for port A)

Bit 4:　　0　Active transition on CB1 is high to low ⎫ Bit 4 of interrupt flag
　　　　　1　Active transition on CB1 is low to high ⎬ register is set on
　　　　　　　　　　　　　　　　　　　　　　　　⎭ active transition

Bits 5–7:　000　CB2 handshake input mode ⎫ Active transition on CB2 is high to low ⎫
　　　　　001　CB2 independent input mode ⎬ ⎪
　　　　　010　CB2 handshake input mode ⎫ Active transition on CB2 is low to high ⎬ Bit 3 of interrupt flag register is set on active transition
　　　　　011　CB2 independent input mode ⎬ ⎪
　　　　　100　CB2 handshake output mode ⎫ Active transition on CB2 is high to low ⎪
　　　　　101　CB2 pulse output mode ⎬ ⎭
　　　　　110　Constant low output on CB2
　　　　　111　Constant high output on CB2

Table A7.5   Auxiliary control register

Bit 0:	0	Disable input latch on port A
	1	Enable input latch on port A
Bit 1:	0	Disable input latch on port B
	1	Enable input latch on port B
Bits 2–4:	000	Disable shift register
	001	Shift in at timer2 rate
	010	Shift in at machine clock rate
	011	Shift in at external clock rate on CB1
	100	Free-running output at timer2 rate
	101	Shift out at timer2 rate
	110	Shift out at machine clock rate
	111	Shift out at external clock rate on CB1
Bit 5:	0	Decrement timer2 in single-interval mode using machine clock
	1	Decrement timer2 on external pulses via bit 6 of port B
Bit 6:	0	Single-interval mode on timer1
	1	Free-running mode on timer1
Bit 7:	0	Disable output via bit 7 of port B — timer1 only
	1	Enable output via bit 7 of port B — timer1 only

Bits 2–4 grouping: 001–100 — All output on CB2; 101–111 — All input on CB2

A7.2   Configuring the 6522 for input/output

Each bit of each port of a VIA can be programmed to act as an input source or an output source. The data direction registers at &FE62 and &FE63 are used to specify this. A *one* in the relevant position in the data direction register specifies *output* for the corresponding bit in the port. A *zero* in the data direction register specifies *input* for the corresponding bit in the port. Using zero for input is a safeguard, for momentary power failures, faults, resets etc. usually zeroise memory locations, and random output is far more dangerous than random input.

Location &FE63 contains &FF, since all the bits on port A are to be outputs to the printer and this location should not usually be touched by the programmer. Location &FE62 controls the user port and is at the disposal of the programmer. Here are some examples:

```
(a) All bits inputs:   LDA   #0
                       STA   &FE62
(b) Bottom nybble outputs, top nybble inputs:   LDA   #&0F
                                                STA   &FE62
(c) Odd bits outputs, even bits inputs:   LDA   #&AA
                                          STA   &FE62
(d) Bit 7 output, rest inputs:   LDA   #&80
                                 STA   &FE62
```

You can read the contents of port B even if one or more of its bits are designated as outputs; that is, LDA &FE60 will always give a valid reflection of the contents of &FE60. This is not true of port A, however, where the bits can be validly read only if they are designated inputs — fortunately, port B and not port A is the user port (port B is also a more powerful driver, and with suitable circuits, can drive solenoids etc.).

A7.3 Handshaking

Suppose we wish to send data to a teletype. The teletype has a parallel buffer which can store 8 bits, we shall assume. So we configure the user ports to be all output (that is, LDA #&FF: STA &FE62). We deposit the byte we wish to send into port B (STA &FE60, assuming that the byte is in the accumulator), wait until the teletype has processed the byte, and then send the next one. But how do we know when the teletype is ready? And how does it know when we are ready to send the next byte? The answer lies in the concept of *handshaking*.

Port B has two control lines, CB1 and CB2. CB1 is *always* an *input*, and so will be used to transmit the signal from the teletype: CB2 can be an input or an output, and in this case we will use it as an ouput (how we specify this will become clear in a moment).

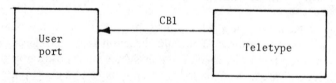

(a)   The teletype is ready to receive data.

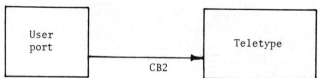

(b)   The microprocessor deposits a byte in Port B, and signals to the teletype (the handshake).

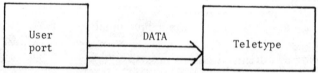

(c)   The data is transmitted and processed (for example, a character is printed)

Figure A7.1: An output handshake

Refer to figure A7.1. The idea is that, when the teletype is ready to receive a byte, it sends a signal on CB1 to the user port (A7.1a). The microprocessor now deposits the byte in port B and sends a signal on CB2 to the teletype indicating that output is now valid (A7.1b). The teletype reads and processes the byte (A7.1c), sends a signal on CB1 asking for the next byte (A7.1a), and so the process continues.

This method of establishing connections between the user port and the teletype (or any other peripheral) is called handshaking: the teletype extends its 'hand' (signal on CB1), and the user port extends its 'hand' in recognition (signal on CB2). Now the information can pass between them. Sometimes CB1 and CB2 are referred to as *strobes* in this context; a strobe is simply an input and/or output line that indicates the availability of data to be transferred or the occurrence of a successful transfer. A strobe is usually a short pulse, one or two cycles long.

Figure A7.2 shows the same idea when port B is used for input (perhaps again from a teletype). When data is ready to be sent, the teletype sends a signal on CB1 indicating that data is ready (A7.2a). The user port responds by reading in the data (A7.2b), and sending a signal on CB2 indicating that the data has been successfully read (A7.2c) — this is the handshake. Again the process continues, with the teletype signalling the next byte is ready for transmission (A7.2a).

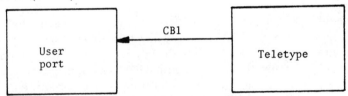

(a)   The teletype signals that it is ready to send data

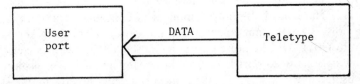

(b)   The data is transmitted and perhaps processed

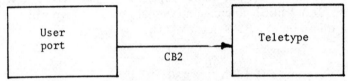

(c)   The microprocessor signals that data has been successfully received (the handshake)

Figure A7.2: An input handshake

Notice that for output the handshake takes place *before* the data is sent, but that for input the handshake takes place *after* the data has been read. This is because the handshake is always finalised by the microprocessor.

Now the user port needs to provide the following facilities for these handshaking activities (we focus here only on port B — port A has almost identical features, but it is reserved for the printer in the BBC Computer):

(a) To designate CB2 as an input or output line.

(b) To fix the *levels* of input of CB1 and CB2 if relevant (that is, whether a signal is to be interpreted as high to low voltage — a falling edge, *negative transition* — or vice versa — a rising edge, *positive transition*).

These and other functions are the purpose of the top nybble of the peripheral control register (&FE6C): Table A7.4 shows the 8 possible configurations of bits 5–7, which control CB2, and the two configurations of bit 4 which control CB1.

You will notice in this table reference to the interrupt flag register. Bit 3 of this register will be set to 1 if there is an active transition (as defined by the peripheral control register) on CB2 and bit 4 if there is an active transition on CB1. Table A7.3 shows the entire register, and we will consider other flags later.

The difference in table A7.4 between the handshaking and independent input modes of CB2 lies in this: in the handshaking mode, reading or writing to port B will clear bit 3 of the interrupt flag register automatically (to make way for the next handshaking operation), whereas in the independent mode one can read or write to port B without the interrupt flag being cleared (this is useful if CB2 is being used for a purpose unconnected with what occurs on port B).

However, in our applications here we are interested in the output modes of CB2. The handshake output mode sets CB2 low when data is written into port B by the microprocessor, and sets it high again on an active transition of CB1. The pulse output mode sets CB2 low for one clock cycle following a write to port B (a brief strobe). The last two constant modes are useful if we wish to provide output signals directly under software control, independently of what occurs at port B.

Now let us consider our output application again. We begin with LDA #&FF: STA &FE62, to create an output port at B. We will assume that active transition of CB1 is negative. Thus we write

```
LDA   #&80
ORA   &FE6C
STA   &FE6C
```

to configure CB1 and CB2 as required (ORA then STA, so as to preserve the information for port A). The handshaking sequence is now

```
1          BEGIN   LDA     #&10
2          WAIT    BIT     &FE6D
3                  BEQ     WAIT
4                  LDA     OUTPUT
5                  STA     &FE60
```

Repeating this, with suitable changes in line 4, is all that is needed to output as much data as required. Lines 1–3 wait until CB1 goes active, signalled by bit 4 of the interrupt flag register being set. At this stage, CB2 is automatically high (a feature of handshake output mode). Line 5 sets CB2 low and also clears the CB1 interrupt flag, all automatically. We can now return to line 1 to wait for the next CB1 signal. The signal on CB2, negative transition, has automatically occurred at line 5, and no doubt the teletype will respond in due course.

Consider now the input function. We set port B to input, and configure CB1 and CB2 as before. Lines 1–3 of the handshake are as before. We then write

```
4          LDA     &FE60
5          STA     &FE60
6          STA     OUTPUT
```

We have to write the data back to port B in line 5 in order to activate the CB2 line: in handshake output mode CB2 is only activated on a write (port A does not have this limitation, however, CA2 being activated by a read or write).

One final point in this section. To guard against changes in input before the input port is read — this is especially important if the microprocessor is doing much more than just the wait sequence in lines 1–3 — it is important to hold the input stable. To achieve this, the VIA is provided with *latches* which can protect input from corruption by changes on the input lines. To set the latch on port B we write a one into bit one of the auxiliary control register (at &FE6B) before entering the handshake (this need be done only once). Hence we write LDA #&02: STA &FE6B. Other functions of the auxiliary control register will be considered shortly.

A7.4   Interrupts on CB1 and CB2

If we consider the input application above, it is clear that it is rather wasteful of processor time to wait until the teletype sends its next byte.

Few teletypes work faster than about 30 characters per second, so the microprocessor could be doing other things most of the time. One strategy is to inspect the CB1 flag every 1/50 second — we will see how this is done in the next section. Another is to obtain an interrupt on CB1.

This is easily done: the interrupt enable register at &FE6E is the relevant register — see Table A7.2. We need to set bit 4 to 1 to enable interrupts on CB1. Once this bit is set to 1, an interrupt will be generated as soon as bit 4 of the interrupt flag register is set. In this case bit 7 of the flag register will also be set — this is used by the interrupt servicing routine when it is polling the potential causes of interrupt (see section 9.3). In the case of the BBC machine, if this bit is set, a test is made to see if bit 1 of the enable and flag registers are also set. If they are, the printer has caused the interrupt — if not, the user port service routine will be entered by a JMP (&0206).

Since bit 4 of the interrupt flag register may already be one, it is essential to clear it before enabling the interrupt. This can be done either by writing 1 to bit 4 of the flag register (that is, LDA #&10: STA &FE6D), or by reading port B (that is, LDA &FE60). Clearly the latter is slightly quicker, but not if taken together with the enable for we can neatly write LDA #&90: STA &FE6D: STA &FE6E, as we will see below (writing one into bit 7 of the flag register does nothing).

If your interrupt routine is going at location &0D01 onwards, you will write ?&0206 = 1: ?&0207 = &0D. Now all interrupts on CB1 (and on CB2, T1, T2 and SR) will go to a routine at &0D01. The routine will consist of lines 4–6, with 6 suitably amended and expanded if necessary.

Every time an interrupt is routed to &206 and &207 the first thing that *must* be done in one's servicing routine is to save X, Y and the original contents of the accumulator (stored at &FC). Thus, your routine must *always* begin with

```
        TXA
        PHA
        TYA
        PHA
        LDA    &FC
        PHA
```

and end with

```
        PLA
        STA    &FC
        PLA
        TAY
        PLA
        TAX
        JMP    &DE89        (the original contents IRQ2)
```

We take the precaution of saving &FC in case a subroutine is called within the interrupt routine which alters &FC. Note, though, that we do not need to save P: this is done automatically by the 6502 microprocessor itself on interrupt.

The interrupt enable register can be altered only by writing ones into the relevant bit positions: *writing zeros has no effect at all*. To enable CB1 interrupts we must write a one into bit 4 with bit 7 *equal to one*: to disable CB1 interrupts we write a one into bit 4 with bit 7 *equal to zero*. Thus, to enable CB1: LDA #&90: STA &FE6E; and to disable: LDA #&10: STA &FE6E. These operations will only affect the CB1 enable — all other bits will be unaffected.

A7.5 Using the programmed timers

(Note that small inaccuracies in the 6522 timer operation are ignored in this section).

There are two timers in the 6522, and both are at the programmer's disposal. Timer2 is the easier, and we shall consider this first.

Timer 2 has two uses: it can generate a single time interval or it can count pulses input to bit 6 of port B. Bit 5 of the auxiliary control register determines which (see Table A7.5). The timer's counter consists of two bytes: the low byte at &FE68 and the high at &FE69. Always load the low byte first: loading the high byte clears the interrupt flag and starts the timing operation.

Suppose we wish to create an interval of 10,000 (&2710) clock cycles and then generate an interrupt. Here is the coding

```
0       LDA    #&DF  ⎫
1       AND    &FE6B  ⎬   Set bit 5 to zero
2       STA    &FE6B  ⎭
3       LDA    #&A0  ⎫   Clear T2 interrupt flag
4       STA    &FE6D  ⎭
5       STA    &FE6E      Enable T2 interrupts
6       LDA    #&10  ⎫   Load low byte with &10
7       STA    &FE68  ⎭
8       LDA    #&27  ⎫   High byte with &27 and start
9       STA    &FE69  ⎭   the countdown
```

If desired, this configuration can be done from BASIC using the query (?) operator.

In the service routine at &D01, just before JMP &DE89 is encountered, the statement LDA &FE68 must appear: this clears the T2 interrupt flag.

Note that a clock cycle here is one-half the 2 MHz machine cycle; for example, 10,000 cycles is 1/100th of a second. This is because the clocking is done by the phase 2 clock which times memory operations, and this runs at 1 MHz.

The pulse counting mode is used to access an external clock or to synchronise with a set of external events.Changing lines 0 and 1 above to LDA #&20: ORA &FE6B will count 10,000 pulses incoming on bit 6 of port B.

Timer1 has more interesting applications. Instead of generating just one time interval it can generate a whole series of intervals. Bit 6 of the auxiliary control register determines this (Table A7.5). When the high byte is loaded countdown will begin: if bit 6 of the auxiliary control register is 1, at the end of countdown the counter will be reloaded with the original contents of the counters which are stored in latches (at &FE66 and &FE67), and countdown will begin again.

Consider the teletype input again. We can generate an interrupt every 1/50th of a second by loading timer1 with 20,000 (&4E20) in continuous mode

0	LDA	#&40	
1	ORA	&FE6B	Set bit 6 to one
2	STA	&FE6B	
3	LDA	#&C0	Clear T1 interrupt flag
4	STA	&FE6D	
5	STA	&FE6E	Enable T1 interrupts
6	LDA	#&20	Load counter and latch with low byte
7	STA	&FE64	
8	LDA	#&4E	Load counter and latch with high
9	STA	&FE65	byte and start count

Again in the service routine at &D01 include LDA &FE64 to clear the T1 interrupt flag. And again, BASIC can be used for the configuration if desired.

It is possible to alter the contents of the latches while the countdown is proceeding without affecting it in its present run. On the next run, however, new contents will be loaded. This is particularly useful with the other feature of timer1, the generation of pulses out of bit 7 of port B (clearly this bit must be configured as output). In the continuous mode (bit 6 = 1), the level on bit 7 of port B will begin low, then at time-out will go high, then at time-out again low, etc. Hence it is possible to create complicated waveforms, if the contents of the latches are also changed.

If we want to generate considerably longer delays, we can build this into our interrupt service routine. Let lines 0–9 be as before, but suppose we require an operation to occur every 1 second. To do this, we will require to reserve one location for the service routine, say &8F. The idea is that we load it with 50 and decrement it every interrupt. When it reaches zero we perform the required operation. However, as we saw in section 9.3, events are much easier to use for this purpose, and are to be preferred.

A7.6 The Shift Register

The 6522 has a shift register (at &FE6A) which will input or output bits one at a time under timed control. The timing can either be provided by an external clock, the internal machine clock or else timer2. Bits 2, 3 and 4 of the auxiliary control register determine which (Table A7.5).

If the teletype in our previous examples lacked a parallel buffer, it would be possible to input and output bits synchronously using timer2 and the shift register. To achieve handshaking, it will be necessary to choose the mode that disables the timer each time, and to provide a suitable set of interrupts. The software turns out to be quite tricky, and it is better to use a UART (such as the 6551 ACIA which does not need an external clock): this will sort out all the parity and framing errors, and provide the stop and start bits. This can generate its own interrupts, but the circuitry might be easier if connections are made to the user port, utilising the VIA's interrupts instead (or by using the expansion bus). Of course, for a 300 baud teletype the computer's own RS423 port can be used, and handshaking here is very simple to implement.

There are really only two main uses for the serial registers as far as we are concerned. One is to provide a source of memory clock pulses, or to receive them from another computer, so as to achieve synchronisation between the computers. Use 010 or 110 at bits 2–4 of the auxiliary control register to achieve this. The other is to output a variety of square waves independently of microprocessor control. This allows frequencies from about 2 Hz (loading the shift register with &0F and timer2 with &FFFF) to 500 KHz (loading the shift register with &55 and timer2 with 1). 0100 at bits 2–5 of the auxiliary control register is the configuration in this case.

Appendix 8: Differences between BASIC 1 and BASIC 2

The new BASIC (BASIC 2) has two major additional features as far as assembly programming is concerned. (Type REPORT to find out which version of BASIC you have. ©1982 implies BASIC 2.) The first is the use of the EQU functions, discussed in chapter 6 and later chapters. The other is the extended use of OPT, described in appendix 6.

This book assumes that BASIC 2 is installed, but includes alternative methods for BASIC 1 where appropriate. In chapter 6 all the addresses given are for BASIC 2. The table below gives the BASIC 1 equivalents:

BASIC 2	BASIC 1
BC05	BC20
BC0D	BC28
BC0F	BC2A

Answers to Exercises

Exercise 1.1

2. (i) The contents need to change.
(ii) The address must be permanently available, even when power is off.

3. There is a limit to the number of pins economically available in a package. Once 40 pins became established, it became very difficult to produce other size packages. Another problem is that, until recently, a 16-bit bus would be too slow—however, 16-bit processors are now a reality.

4. Data can go *into* memory and *out of* memory. A memory location is chosen, however, by sending an address *towards* it. No *address* information needs to come *from* it.

5. Because each instruction needs to be translated every time that it is executed in an interpreted language. With compilation the translation occurs just once, prior to execution.

Exercise 2.1

1. (a) Immediate

&0C00	&0C01
A9	0E

(b) Absolute

&0C00	&0C01	&0C02
AD	40	7F

(c) Zero page

&0C00	&0C01
A5	20

(d) Absolute

&0C00	&0C01	&0C02
8D	72	7A

(e) Zero page

&0C00	&0C01
85	00

(f) Immediate

&0C00	&0C01
A9	12

(g) Zero page

&0C00	&0C01
85	02

(h) Zero page

&0C00	&0C01
A5	0E

(i) Absolute

&0C00	&0C01	&0C02
8D	00	04

2. The contents of NUM1 are already in the accumulator.

$$P\% = \&0C00$$
$$NUM1 = \&70$$
$$NUM2 = \&71$$
LDA   #17
STA   NUM1
STA   NUM2

&0C00	&0C01	&0C02	&0C03	&0C04 ∶	&0C05
A9	11	85	70	85	71

3.

$$P\% = \&0C00$$
$$NUM1 = \&70$$
$$NUM2 = \&71$$
$$NUM3 = \&73$$
LDA   NUM3
STA   NUM1
LDA   NUM2
STA   NUM3
LDA   NUM1
STA   NUM2

Exercise 3.1

```
 10 NUM1=&70:NUM2=&71:NUM3=&72:SUML=&73:SUMH=&74
 20 DIM P% 50
 30 [OPT3
 40 .START
 50 LDA NUM1
 60 CLC
 70 ADC NUM2
 80 STA SUML
 90 LDA #0
100 STA SUMH
110 ADC SUMH
120 STA SUMH
130 LDA SUML
140 CLC
150 ADC NUM3
160 STA SUML
170 LDA #0
180 ADC SUMH
```

```
190 STA SUMH
200 RTS:]
210 REPEAT
220    INPUT"First number to be added",?NUM1
230    INPUT"Second number to be added",?NUM2
240    INPUT"Third number to be added",?NUM3
250    CALLSTART
260    PRINT?NUM1+?NUM2+?NUM3,256*?SUMH+?SUML
270    UNTIL FALSE
```

Exercise 3.2

1.

```
 10 NUM1L=&70:NUM1H=&71:NUM2L=&72:NUM2H=&73:SUM0
    =&74:SUM1=&75:SUM2=&76
 20 DIM P% 50
 30 [OPT3
 40 .START
 50 LDA NUM1L
 60 CLC
 70 ADC NUM2L
 80 STA SUM0
 90 LDA NUM1H
100 ADC NUM2H
110 STA SUM1
120 LDA 30
130 STA SUM2
140 ADC SUM2
150 STA SUM2
160 RTS:]
170 REPEAT
180    INPUT"First number to be added",!NUM1L
190    INPUT"Second number to be added",!NUM2L
200    CALLSTART
210    PRINT256*?NUM1H+?NUM1L+256*?NUM2H+?NUM2L,
       65536*?SUM2+256*?SUM1+?SUM0
220    UNTIL FALSE
```

2.

```
 10 DIM NUM1(3),NUM2(3),RESULT(3)
 20 FOR I%=0 TO 3:NUM1(I%)=&70+I%
 30    NUM2(I%)=&74+I%:RESULT(I%)=&78+I%:NEXTI%
 40 DIM P% 50
 50 [OPT3
 60 .START
 70 LDA NUM1(0)
 80 CLC
 90 ADC NUM2(0)
100 STA RESULT(0)
110 LDA NUM1(1)
120 ADC NUM2(1)
130 STA RESULT(1)
```

```
140 LDA NUM1(2)
150 ADC NUM2(2)
160 STA RESULT(2)
170 LDA NUM1(3)
180 ADC NUM2(3)
190 STA RESULT(3)
200 RTS:]
210 REPEAT
220    INPUT"First number to be added",!NUM1(0)
230    INPUT"Second number to be added",!NUM2(0)
240    CALLSTART
250    PRINT!NUM1(0)+!NUM2(0),!RESULT(0)
260    UNTIL FALSE
```

Symbolic representation is

(NUM1(3); NUM1(2); NUM1(1); NUM1(0)) + (NUM2(3); NUM2(2); NUM2(1); NUM2(0)) → RESULT(3); RESULT(2); RESULT(1); RESULT(0)

Exercise 3.3

1.
```
            LDA    NUM1L
            SEC
            SBC    NUM2L
            STA    DIFFL
            LDA    NUM1H
            SBC    NUM2H
            STA    DIFFH
```

A mathematical demonstration of why this works may be helpful to you. In general, for *any* numbers A and B, $A - B = A + B_c - B_c - B$, where B_c is the two's complement of B, $= (A + B_c) - (B_c + B) = A + B_c$, if we ignore the 'carry'.

Now, if A and B are double bytes, so that A = (AH;AL) and B = (BH;BL) then $B_c = (\bar{B}\bar{H};BL_c)$, where $\bar{B}\bar{H}$ is the one's complement of BH. Hence, $A - B = (AH + \bar{B}\bar{H} + C; AL + BL_c)$, where C is the carry. Now, $AL + BL_c$ is achieved by the first three lines of the program. If this is positive C will be one, if negative C will be zero. Either way, the second part of the program perform $AH + \overline{BH} + C$ as required.

2.

```
10 DIM NUM1(3),NUM2(3),RESULT(3)
20 FOR I%=0 TO 3:NUM1(I%)=&70+I%
30    NUM2(I%)=&74+I%:RESULT(I%)=&78+I%:NEXTI%
40 DIM P% 50
50 [OPT3
```

```
 60 .START
 70 LDA NUM1(0)
 80 SEC
 90 SBC NUM2(0)
100 STA RESULT(0)
110 LDA NUM1(1)
120 SBC NUM2(1)
130 STA RESULT(1)
140 LDA NUM1(2)
150 SBC NUM2(2)
160 STA RESULT(2)
170 LDA NUM1(3)
180 SBC NUM2(3)
190 STA RESULT(3)
200 RTS:]
210 REPEAT
220   INPUT"First number",!NUM1(0)
230   INPUT"Number to be subtracted",!NUM2(0)
240   CALLSTART
250   PRINT!NUM1(0)-!NUM2(0),!RESULT(0)
260   UNTIL FALSE
```

Exercise 3.4

1. (a) $\&18 - \&EE = \&18 + \&12 = \&2A \quad (= 42)$
(b) $\&AA - \&23 = \&AA + \&DD = 1\ \&87\ (= -121)$

Overflow can occur only if the signs of the numbers subtracted are different.

2. -2^{31} to $2^{31} - 1$

3. No adjustments necessary.

IF SUM(3) > 127 THEN RESULT = (((SUM(3) − 255) ∗ 256 + (SUM(2) − 255)) ∗ 256 + (SUM(1) − 255)) ∗ 256 + SUM(0) − 256 ELSE RESULT = ((SUM(3) ∗ 256 + SUM(2)) ∗ 256 + SUM(1)) ∗ 256 + SUM(0)

Exercise 3.5

(a) ORA   #&88
    AND   #&EE

(b) EOR   #&80
    ORA   #&40
    AND   #&E0

Exercise 4.1

```
1.                    LDA   NUM1
                      CLC
                      ADC   NUM2
                      BEQ   ZERO
                      BPL   POSITIVE
         ZERO           .
                        .
                        .
                        .

         POSITIVE       .
                        .
                        .
                        .
                        .


2.                    LDA   NUM1
                      SEC
                      SBC   NUM2
                      BEQ   ZERO
                      LDA   NUM2
                      STA   NUM3
                      LDA   NUM1
                      STA   NUM2
                      LDA   NUM3
                      STA   NUM1
         ZERO           .
                        .
                        .
                        .
                        .


3.                    LDA   NUM1
                      CLC
                      ADC   NUM2
                      BCC   NOCARRY
                      LDA   #0
                      STA   SUM
                      BEQ   OVER        (always branches)
         NOCARRY      STA   SUM
         OVER           .
                        .
                        .
```

Congratulate yourself if you got this. Congratulate yourself even more if you got the following more economical version

```
              LDA   NUM1
              CLC
              ADC   NUM2
              STA   SUM
              BCC   NOCARRY
              LDA   #0
              STA   SUM
NOCARRY             .
                    .
                    .
                    .
                    .
```

Exercise 4.2

1.
```
              LDA   NUM
              CMP   #15
              BEQ   LESSEQ
              BCC   LESSEQ
              LDA   #0
              STA   NUM
LESSEQ              .
                    .
                    .
                    .
                    .
```

2.
```
              LDA   NUM
              BPL   POSITIVE
              CMP   #&F6
              BEQ   EQUAL
              BCS   POSITIVE      (or BPL POSITIVE)
EQUAL         STA   INDIC
              JMP   OVER
POSITIVE      LDA   #0
              STA   NUM
              LDA   #1
              STA   INDIC
OVER                .
                    .
                    .
                    .
```

```
3.                      LDA    NUM1
                        CMP    NUM2
                        BNE    NTEQUAL1
                        LDA    NUM3
                        STA    NUM2
                        JMP    OVER
         NTEQUAL1       LDA    NUM4
                        CMP    #16
                        BEQ    NTEQUAL2
                        BCC    NTEQUAL2
                        STA    NUM2
                        JMP    OVER
         NTEQUAL2       LDA    #0
                        STA    NUM2
                        STA    NUM4
         OVER           .
                        .
                        .
                        .
```

Exercise 4.3

```
1.                      LDA    NUM1L
                        CMP    NUM2L
                        LDA    NUM1H
                        SBC    NUM2H
                        BCC    LESS
                               .
                               .
                               .
                               .
         LESS                  .
```

```
2.                      LDA    NUM1L
                        CMP    NUM2L
                        BNE    NTEQUAL
                        CLC
         NTEQUAL        LDA    NUM1H
                        SBC    NUM2H
                        BCC    LESSEQ
                               .
                               .
                               .
                               .
         LESSEQ                .
```

3.
```
        LDA   NUM1(0)
        CMP   NUM2(0)
        LDA   NUM1(1)
        SBC   NUM2(1)
        LDA   NUM1(2)
        SBC   NUM2(2)
        LDA   NUM1(3)
        SBC   NUM2(3)
        BCS   GTEQUAL
              .
              .
              .
              .
GTEQUAL       .
```

4.
```
        LDA   NUM(0)     The accumulator will at the end
        ORA   NUM(1)     contain ones in the positions
        ORA   NUM(2)     where ones occur in any of the
        ORA   NUM(3)     four bytes tested. Hence, only if
        BEQ   ZERO       all four bytes are zero will the
              .          accumulator be zero.
              .
              .
              .
ZERO          .
```

Exercise 4.4

(a)
```
        LDA   NUM1L
        SEC
        SBC   NUM2
        STA   NUM1L
        LDA   NUM1H
        SBC   #0
        STA   NUM1H
```

(b)
```
        LDA   NUM1L
        SEC
        SBC   NUM2       Three bytes are saved.
        STA   NUM1L
        BCS   NOBORROW
        DEC   NUM1H
```

```
        NOBORROW            .
                            .
                            .
                            .
                            .
```

Exercise 4.5

1.
```
                LDA    NUM1
                SEC
                SBC    NUM2
                BCC    LESSEQ
                CMP    NUM3
                BEQ    LESSEQ
                BCS    GREATER
        LESSEQ              .
                            .
                            .
                            .
                            .
        GREATER            .
```

2.
```
                LDA    #0
                STA    DIFF2
                LDA    NUM1L
                SEC
                SBC    NUM2L
                STA    DIFF0
                LDA    NUM1H
                SBC    NUM2H
                STA    DIFF1
                BCS    NTNEG
                DEC    DIFF2
                            .
        NTNEG              .
                            .
```

3.
```
                LDA    #0
                STA    SUMH
                LDA    NUM1
                CLC
                ADC    NUM2
                STA    SUML
```

```
                    BVC    NOOVFLOW
                    EOR    #&80
        NOOVFLOW    BPL    NTNEG
                    DEC    SUMH
        NTNEG              .
                           .
                           .
                           .
                           .
```

4.
```
                    LDA    #0
                    STA    DIFF2
                    LDA    NUM1L
                    SEC
                    SBC    NUM2L
                    STA    DIFF0
                    LDA    NUM1H
                    SBC    NUM2H
                    STA    DIFF1
                    BVC    NOOVFLOW
                    EOR    #&80
        NOOVFLOW    BPL    NTNEG
                    DEC    DIFF2
                           .
        NTNEG              .
                           .
```

5.
```
                    LDA    NUM1L
                    SEC
                    SBC    NUM2L
                    STA    NUM1L
                    LDA    NUM1M
                    SBC    NUM2H
                    STA    NUM1M
                    BCS    NOBORROW
                    DEC    NUM1H
                    BPL    OVERFLOW
        NOBORROW           .
                           .
                           .
                           .
                           .
        OVERFLOW           .
```

Overflow occurs here if NUM1H goes from &80 to &79, and the N flag will register this. The V flag is not affected by DEC or by INC, since the N flag tells us exactly what we want to know. The OVERFLOW routine here would probably be designed to return some error message.

6.

```
                LDA    #0
                STA    SUMH
                LDA    NUM1L
                CLC
                ADC    NUM2L
                STA    SUML
                LDA    NUM1H
                ADC    NUM2H
                STA    SUMM
                BVC    NOOVFLOW
                EOR    #&80
NOOVFLOW        BPL    NTNEG
                DEC    SUMH
NTNEG            .
                 .
                 .
                 .
                 .
```

7.

```
                LDA    NUM1
                SEC
                SBC    NUM2
                BVC    NOOVFLOW
                EOR    #&80
NOOVFLOW        BPL    GTEQUAL
                 .
                 .
                 .
                 .
GTEQUAL          .
                 .
                 .
```

8.

```
                LDA    NUM1
                SEC
                SBC    NUM2
                BVC    NOOVFLOW
                BPL    LESSEQ          (Since overflow occurred, this
                                       branches if the result is negative,
                                       that is, NUM1–NUM2<0
                BMI    OVER            —and this branches if result
                                       positive
NOOVFLOW        BMI    LESSEQ
OVER            CMP    NUM3            Usual comparison between unsigned
                                       numbers.
                BEQ    LESSEQ
```

```
                    BCS    GREATER
        LESSEQ             .
                          .
                          .
                          .
                          .
        GREATER           .

9.                 LDA    NUM1
                   SEC
                   SBC    NUM2
                   BVC    NOOVFLOW
                   BMI    MORE          Positive overflow must exceed
                                        NUM3.
                   BPL    LESSEQ        Negative overflow must be less
                                        than NUM3.
   NOOVFLOW1 SEC
                   SBC    NUM3
                   BEQ    LESSEQ
                   BVC    NOOVFLOW2
                   EOR    #&80
   NOOVFLOW2 BPL   MORE
   LESSEQ                  .
                          .
                          .
                          .
                          .
        MORE              .
                          .
                          .

10.
                   LDA    NUM1L
                   CMP    NUM2L
                   LDA    NUM1H
                   SBC    NUM2H
                   BVC    NOOVFLOW
                   EOR    #&80
   NOOVFLOW  BPL   GTEQUAL
                          .
                          .
                          .
                          .
        GTEQUAL           .
```

Exercise 5.1

1. Yes they will. For example, FOR X = −2 TO 50 in (e) will result in just one cycle of the loop since it will be understood as FOR X = 254 TO 50.

We solve such problems by using BPL and BMI instead of BCS and BCC after comparisons (so that, if NUM is signed, it is the second program in (d) which is correct). It is not quite this simple in (f), however, since we can get overflow: FOR X = 126 TO 10 STEP 20 is an example; FOR X = 50 TO 100 STEP 40 is another.

Hence we need a test for overflow also, and the solution to question 3 deals with this.

2. (a)
```
              LDX   NUM2
    LOOP        .
                .
                .
                .
                .
              DEX
              CPX   #&FF
              BEQ   OUT
              CPX   NUM1
              BCS   LOOP
    OUT         .
                .
                .
                .
                .
```

(b)
```
              LDX   NUM2
    LOOP        .
                .
                .
                .
                .
              TXA
              SEC
              SBC   NUM3
              BCC   OUT
              TAX
              CMP   NUM1
              BCS   LOOP
    OUT         .
                .
                .
                .
```

3.

```
              LDX   NUM1
LOOP            .
                .
                .
                .
                .

              TXA
              CLC
              ADC   NUM3
              TAX
              BVS   OUT      If overflow, loop must be finished.
              CMP   NUM2
              BMI   LOOP
              BEQ   LOOP
OUT             .
                .
                .
                .
                .
```

It is quicker still to work 'backwards' (although—(NUM3) may turn out to be positive):

```
              LDX   NUM2
LOOP            .
                .
                .
                .
                .

              TAX
              SEC
              SBC   NUM3
              TAX
              BVS   OUT
              CMP   NUM1
              BPL   LOOP
OUT             .
                .
                .
                .
                .
```

Exercise 5.2

1. After LDX #0 put LDA   NUMH
                       BEQ   LOOP2

2. (i) In this case, all that is required is that we create a loop with (NUMH; NUML) + 1 cycles. The most efficient way to do this is

```
                LDX   NUML
        LOOP1         .
                      .
                      .
                      .
                      .

                DEX
                CPX   #&FF
                BNE   LOOP1
                LDY   NUMH
                BEQ   OUT
                INX
        LOOP2         .
                      .
                      .
                      .
                      .

                DEX
                BNE   LOOP2
                DEY
                BNE   LOOP2
        OUT           .
                      .
                      .
                      .
                      .
```

(ii) N cannot be computed in any simple way from (i), since N does not decrease in strict descending order (in LOOP2 &00 precedes &FF). Also the high byte of N is given by Y − 1 in LOOP2.

    We require a loop in strict order where N is (Y;X) in LOOP2 and (NUMH;X) in LOOP1

```
              LDX   NUML
LOOP1               .
                    .
                    .
                    .
                    .

              DEX
              CPX   #&FF
              BNE   LOOP1
              LDY   NUMH
              BEQ   OUT
              DEY
LOOP2               .
                    .
                    .
                    .
                    .

              DEX
              CPX   #&FF
              BNE   LOOP2
              DEY
              CPY   #&FF
              BNE   LOOP2
OUT                 .
                    .
                    .
                    .
                    .
```

Only (i) is an improvement over the forward loop.

Exercise 5.3

1. (a)
```
      TXA              (b)         STX   MEMLOC+1
      SEC                          SEC
      SBC   M        MEMLOC        SBC   #0
      STA   M
```

   (c)
```
      TXA              (d)         STX   MEMLOC+1
      SEC                          SEC
      SBC   M        MEMLOC        SBC   #0
      TAX                          TAX
```

```
(e)                TXA
                   STY    MEMLOC+1
                   CLC
        MEMLOC     ADC    #0


(f)                TXA
                   STY    MEMLOC+1
                   SEC
        MEMLOC     SBC    #0


(g)                STA    MEMLOC+1
        MEMLOC     CPX    #0


(h)                STY    MEMLOC+1
        MEMLOC     CPX    #0


(i)                STX    MEMLOC+1
                   TAX
        MEMLOC     LDA    #0
```

```
2.                 STA    MEMLOC+1
                   TXA
                   CLC
                   ADC    M
                   STA    M
        MEMLOC     LDA    #0
```

```
3.                 STA    MEMLOC+1              STX    MEMLOC
                   TXA                          STA    MEMLOC
                   SEC                          SEC
                   SBC    M         MEMLOC1     SBC    #0
                   TAX                          TAX
        MEMLOC     LDA    #0        MEMLOC2     LDA    #0
```

```
4.                    STY    MEMLOC1 + 1
                      STA    MEMLOC2 + 1
                      TXA
                      CLC
      MEMLOC1         ADC    #0
                      TAX
      MEMLOC2         LDA    #0
```

Note that the use of the stack makes questions 2, 3 and 4 easier to solve. This is considered further in chapter 9.

Exercise 5.4

1.

```
10  TERML=&70:TERMH=&71:NUM=&72:SUM1=&73:SUM2=&74:
    SUM3=&75:?&76=0
20  DIM START 100
30  FOR I%=0 TO 2 STEP 2:P%=START
40      [OPTI%
50      LDA #0
60      TAX
70      STA SUM2
80      STA SUM3
90      STA TERMH
100     LDA #1
110     STA SUM1
120     STA TERML
130     .LOOP
140     INX
150     CPX NUM
160     BEQ FINISH
170     STX MEMLOC+1
180     CLC
190     LDA TERML
200     .MEMLOC
210     ADC #0 Dummy operand
220     STA TERML
230     BCC NOCARRY
240     CLC
250     INC TERMH
260     .NOCARRY
270     LDA TERML
280     ADC SUM1
290     STA SUM1
300     LDA TERMH
310     ADC SUM2
320     STA SUM2
330     BCC LOOP
340     INC SUM3
```

```
350      BCS LOOP
360      .FINISH
370      RTS:JNEXTI%
380 CLS:REPEAT
390      INPUT"How many terms",?NUM
400      CALLSTART
410      PRINT!SUM1
420      UNTIL FALSE
```

Lines 140–160 stop the loop being entered if (NUM) = 1.
Lines 170–250 compute the $(X + 1)$th term (Xth term + X).
Lines 270–350 add the $(X + 1)$th term to the sum for X terms to get the sum for $(X + 1)$ terms.

2.

```
10 TERML=&70:TERMH=&71:SUM1=&72:SUM2=&73:SUM3=&74:
   STOTAL1=&75:STOTAL2=&76:STOTAL3=&77
20 DIM START 100
30 FOR I%=0 TO 2 STEP 2:P%=START
40     [OPTI%
50     LDA #0
60     TAX
70     STA SUM2
80     STA SUM3
90     STA TERMH
100    .LDA #1
110    STA SUM1
120    STA TERML
130    .LOOP
140    INX
150    LDA STOTAL1
160    CMP SUM1
170    LDA STOTAL2
180    SBC SUM2
190    LDA STOTAL3
200    SBC SUM3
210    BCC FINISH
220    STX MEMLOC+1
230    CLC
240    LDA TERML
250    .MEMLOC
260    ADC #0 Dummy operand
270    STA TERML
280    BCC NOCARRY
290    CLC
300    INC TERMH
310    .NOCARRY
320    LDA TERML
330    ADC SUM1
```

```
340      STA  SUM1
350      LDA  TERMH
360      ADC  SUM2
370      STA  SUM2
380      BCC  LOOP
390      INC  SUM3
400      BCS  LOOP
410      .FINISH
420      RTS:]NEXTI%
430 CLS:REPEAT
440      INPUT"Maximum total",!STOTAL1
450      PRINT((USRSTART AND &0FFFFFFF)MOD &10000) DIV &100
460      UNTIL FALSE
```

As question 1 except that lines 150 and 160 are replaced by 150–210.

3.

```
10  TERML=&70:TERMH=&71:SUM1=&72:SUM2=&73:SUM3=&74:
    STOTAL1=&75:STOTAL2=&76:STOTAL3=&77
20  DIM START 100
30  FOR I%=0 TO 2 STEP 2:P%=START
40      [OPTI%
50      LDA  #0
60      TAX
70      STA  SUM2
80      STA  SUM3
90      STA  TERMH
100     LDA  #1
110     STA  SUM1
120     STA  TERML
130     .LOOP
140     INX
150     SEC
160     LDA  STOTAL1
170     SBC  SUM1
180     STA  MEMLOC1+1
190     LDA  STOTAL2
200     SBC  SUM2
210     STA  MEMLOC2+1
220     LDA  STOTAL3
230     SBC  SUM3
240     BCC  FINISH1
250     .MEMLOC1
260     ORA  #0 Dummy operand
270     .MEMLOC2
280     ORA  #0 Dummy operand
290     BEQ  FINISH2
300     SBC  SUM2
310     LDA  STOTAL3
320     STX  MEMLOC+1
330     CLC
340     LDA  TERML
```

```
350    .MEMLOC
360    ADC #0 Dummy operand
370    STA TERML
380    BCC NOCARRY
390    CLC
400    INC TERMH
410    .NOCARRY
420    LDA TERML
430    ADC SUM1
440    STA SUM1
450    LDA TERMH
460    ADC SUM2
470    STA SUM2
480    BCC LOOP
490    INC SUM3
500    BCS LOOP
510    .FINISH1
520    DEX
530    .FINISH2
540    RTS:]NEXTI%
550 CLS:REPEAT
560    INPUT"Maximum total",!STOTAL1
570    PRINT((USRSTART AND &0FFFFFFF)MOD &10000) DIV &100
580    UNTIL FALSE
```

As question 1 except that lines 150 and 160 are replaced by 150–310 and 360 by 510–530.

Exercise 6.1

When an early part of the new locations overlaps a later part of the old locations.

Exercise 6.2

1.

```
10 INPUT"HOW MANY BYTES",NUMBER
20 DIM ARRAY NUMBER-1:DIM START 50
30 FORI%=0 TO NUMBER-2 STEP4:!(ARRAY+I%)=RND:NEXTI%
40 FLAG=&70:TEMP=&71
50 FORI%=0 TO 2 STEP 2:P%=START
60    [OPTI%
70    .BEGIN
80    LDX #NUMBER-1
90    LDA #0
100   STA FLAG
110   .LOOP
120   LDA ARRAY,X
130   CMP ARRAY-1,X
140   BCS OVER
150   STA TEMP
```

```
160    LDA ARRAY-1,X
170    STA ARRAY,X
180    LDA TEMP
190    STA ARRAY-1,X
200    LDA #1
210    STA FLAG
220    .OVER
230    DEX
240    BNE LOOP
250    LDA FLAG
260    BNE BEGIN
270    RTS:JNEXTI%
280 CALL START
290    FOR I%=0 TO NUMBER-1: PRINT?(ARRAY+I%),:NEXT
```

(a) By reversing the comparison we gain space and time since only one branch instruction is necessary.

(b) Usually, we put values into storage locations so that we do not need to reassemble the program every time that we change the values concerned. In this case, however, we will want to change the base address of the array (that is, ARRAY) and this will require reassembly. We will see a way round this in the next chapter.

2.

```
10 INPUT"HOW MANY BYTES",NUMBER
20 DIM ARRAY NUMBER-1:DIM START 50
30 FORI%=0 TO NUMBER-2 STEP4:!(ARRAY+I%)=RND:NEXTI%
40 TEMP=&70
50 FORI%=0 TO 2 STEP 2:P%=START
60     [OPTI%
70     LDY #0
80     .BEGIN
90     STY MEMLOC+1
100    LDX #NUMBER-1
110    .LOOP
120    LDA ARRAY,X
130    CMP ARRAY-1,X
140    BCS OVER
150    STA TEMP
160    LDA ARRAY-1,X
170    STA ARRAY,X
180    LDA TEMP
190    STA ARRAY-1,X
200    .OVER
210    DEX
220    .MEMLOC
230    CPX #0 (Dummy operand)
240    BNE LOOP
250    INY
260    CPY #NUMBER-1
```

```
270    BNE BEGIN
280    RTS:]NEXTI%
290 CALL START
300  FOR I%=0 TO NUMBER-1: PRINT?(ARRAY+I%),:NEXT
```

Notice that this is less efficient since we require an extra CPY.

3.

```
10 INPUT"HOW MANY BYTES",NUMBER
20 DIM ARRAY NUMBER-1:DIM START 50
30 FORI%=0 TO NUMBER-2 STEP4:!(ARRAY+I%)=RND:NEXTI%
40 TEMP=&70
50 FORI%=0 TO 2 STEP 2:P%=START
60    [OPTI%
70    LDY #1
80    .BEGIN
90    STY MEMLOC+1
100    .MEMLOC
110    LDX #0  (Dummy operand)
120    .LOOP
130    LDA ARRAY,X
140    CMP ARRAY-1,X
150    BCS OVER
160    STA TEMP
170    LDA ARRAY-1,X
180    STA ARRAY,X
190    LDA TEMP
200    STA ARRAY-1,X
210    .OVER
220    DEX
230    BNE LOOP
240    INY
250    CPY #NUMBER
260    BNE BEGIN
270    RTS:]NEXTI%
280 CALL START
290  FOR I%=0 TO NUMBER-1: PRINT?(ARRAY+I%),:NEXT
```

Exercise 6.3

1. The flowchart is in figure 6.7.

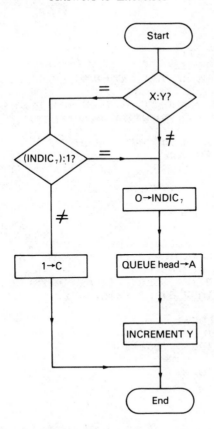

Figure 6.7: Flowchart for withdrawing an item from a queue

```
 10  DIM START 50:VDU14
 20   DATUM=&70:INDIC=&71:DIM BASMEM 255
 30  FOR I%=0 TO 252 STEP4:!(BASMEM+I%)=RND:NEXTI%
 40  DIM TEST 256
 50  X%=0:Y%=0:?INDIC=&80
 60  FOR I%=0 TO 2 STEP2:P%=START
 70     [OPTI%
 80     STX MEMLOC+1
 90     .MEMLOC
100     CPY #0 (Dummy operand)
110     BNE OK
120     LDA INDIC
130     BMI OK
140     SEC
150     RTS
160     .OK
170     LDA #0
180     STA INDIC
190     LDA BASMEM,Y
```

```
200     INY
210     CLC
220      RTS: JNEXTI%
230 FOR I%=0 TO 256
240      !&404=USR(START):X%=?&405:Y%=?&406:
         ?(TEST+I%)=?&404
250      IF (?&407 AND 1) =1 THEN PRINT"ERROR AT
         "STR$(I%+1)"TH WITHDRAWAL":GOTO270
260      NEXTI%
270 PRINT'"      WITHDRAWAL   QUEUE"'
280 FOR I%=0 TO 255
290    PRINT ?(BASMEM+I%),?(TEST+I%):NEXTI%
300 VDU15
```

2.

```
10 DIM START1  50:DIM START2 50:VDU12
20   DATUM=&70:INDIC=&71:DIM BASMEM 255
30 X%=128;Y%=0:?INDIC=&80
40 FORI%=0 TO 124 STEP4: !(BASMEM+I%)=RND:NEXTI%
50 FOR I%=0 TO 2 STEP2:P%=START1
60     [OPTI%
70     STX MEMLOC+1
80     .MEMLOC
90     CPY #0 (Dummy operand)
100    BNE OK
110    LDA INDIC
120    BPL OK
130    SEC
140    RTS
150    .OK
160    LDA #&80
170    STA INDIC
180    LDA DATUM
190    STA BASMEM,X
200    INX
210    CLC
220     RTS: JNEXTI%
230 FOR I%=0 TO 2 STEP2:P%=START2
240    [OPTI%
250    STX MEMLOC+1
260    .MEMLOC
270    CPY #0 (Dummy operand)
280    BNE OK
290    LDA INDIC
300    BMI OK
310    SEC
320    RTS
330    .OK
340    LDA #0
350    STA INDIC
360    LDA BASMEM,Y
370    INY
380    CLC
390     RTS: JNEXTI%
```

```
400 REPEAT
410   INPUT' "DATA",?DATUM
420   IF ?DATUM<128 THEN !&404=USR(START1) ELSE !&404=
      USR(START2)
430   X%=?&405:Y%=?&406
440   IF (?&407 AND 1) =1 THEN PRINT"ERROR"
450   IF X%>Y% THEN LGTH=X%-Y% ELSE IF X%<Y% THEN LGTH=
      256-Y%+X% ELSE IF ?INDIC = 0 THEN LGTH=0 ELSE
      LGTH=256
460   PRINT"HEAD   "?(BASMEM+Y%)
470   PRINT"TAIL   "?(BASMEM+X%-1)
480   PRINT"LENGTH"LGTH
490   UNTIL FALSE
```

Exercise 6.4

Note that all programs should begin in the usual way, defining labels as necessary.

1.
```
50        LDX   #0
60        JSR   OUTPUT2
70        RTS
80        ·OUTPUT2
            .
            .
            .
            .
150       .TEXT: ]NEXT
160       $TEXT  =   "This is question one"
```

or

```
150       .TEXT
160       EQUS "This is question one"
170       EQUB 13:] NEXT
```

2.
```
50        LDX   #0
60        JSR   OUTPUT1
70        RTS
80        .OUTPUT1
            .
            .
            .
            .
```

```
160              .TEXT:]NEXT
170              $TEXT  =  "This is question two"
```

or

```
160              .TEXT
170              EQUS  "This is question two":] NEXT
```

3.   50   JSR   OSNEWL
       60   RTS:]

4.   50   JSR   OSNEWL
       60   LDX   #0
       70   JSR   OUTPUT1
       80   RTS
       90   .OUTPUT1
               .
               .
               .

```
170              .TEXT:]NEXT
180              $TEXT  =  "This is question four"
```

or

```
170              .TEXT
180              EQUS  "This is question four":]NEXT
```

Exercise 6.5

1.

```
10 OSWRCH=&FFEE:OSNEWL=&FFE7
20   DIM START 50
30 FOR I%=0 TO 2 STEP2
40    P%=START
50    [OPTI%
60    LDA #ASC("?")
70    JSR OSWRCH
80    JSR &BC05
90    LDX #&FF
100   .LOOP1
110   INX
120   LDA &700,X
130   CMP #13
140   BNE LOOP1
150   CPX #0
```

```
160    BEQ NOSTRING
170    .LOOP2
180    DEX
190    LDA &700,X
200    JSR OSWRCH
210    CPX #0
220    BNE LOOP2
230    .NOSTRING
240    JSR OSNEWL
250    JMP START:]NEXTI%
260 CALL START
```

2.

```
10 OSWRCH=&FFEE:OSASCI=&FFE3
20    DIM START 50
30 FOR I%=0 TO 2 STEP2
40     P%=START
50     [OPTI%
60     LDA #ASC("?")
70     JSR OSWRCH
80     JSR &BC05
90     LDA &700
100    CMP #ASC("*")
110    BNE NTSTAR
120    LDA &701
130    CMP #13
140    BEQ FINISH
150    .NTSTAR
160    LDX #&FF
170    .LOOP
180    INX
190    LDA &700,X
200    CMP #ASC(" ")
210    BEQ LOOP
220    JSR OSASCI
230    CMP #13
240    BNE LOOP
250    BEQ START
260    .FINISH
270     RTS:]NEXTI%
280 CALL START
```

3.

```
10 OSWRCH=&FFEE
20    DIM START 250
30 FOR I%=0 TO 2 STEP2
40     P%=START
50     [OPTI%
60     LDA #TEXT MOD 256
70     STA &37
80     LDA #TEXT DIV 256
```

```
 90     STA &38
100     LDA #ASC("?")
110     JSR OSWRCH
120     JSR &BCOD
130     LDX #&FF
140     .LOOP1
150     INX
160     LDA TEXT,X
170     CMP #13
180     BNE LOOP1
190     CPX #0
200     BEQ NOSTRING
210     .LOOP2
220     DEX
230     LDA TEXT,X
240     CMP #ASC(" ")
250     BEQ LOOP2
260     INX
270     LDA #13
280     STA TEXT,X
290     .NOSTRING
300     RTS
310     .TEXT:]NEXTI%
320 CALL START
330 PRINT"New length is ";LEN($TEXT)
340 PRINT'"Another?"
350 A$=GET$:IF A$="Y" THEN320 ELSE IF A$="N"
    THEN END ELSE 350
```

Exercise 6.6

(a)

```
 10 DIM NUM1(3),NUM2(3),RESULT(3)
 20 DIM START 50
 30 P%=START
 40 FOR I%=0 TO 3:NUM1(I%)=&70+I%
 50    NUM2(I%)=&74+I%:RESULT(I%)=&78+I%
 60    GOSUB140:NEXTI%
 70 [OPT2
 80 RTS:]
 90 REPEAT
100    INPUT"Numbers to be added",!NUM1(0),!NUM2(0)
110    CALLSTART
120    PRINT!NUM1(0)+!NUM2(0),!RESULT(0)
130    UNTIL FALSE
140 [OPT2:LDA NUM1(I%):]
150 IF I%=0 THEN [OPT2:CLC:]
160 [OPT2:ADC NUM2(I%)
170 STA RESULT(I%):]
180 RETURN
```

(b)

```
10 DIM NUM1(3),NUM2(3),RESULT(3)
20 DIM START 50
30 REPEAT
40    PRINT"Add or subtract  (A/S)?";
50    REPEAT: A$=GET$
60       UNTIL A$ ="A" OR A$="S"
70    P%=START
80    FOR I%=0 TO 3:NUM1(I%)=&70+I%
90       NUM2(I%)=&74+I%:RESULT(I%)=&78+I%
100       GOSUB170:NEXTI%
110    [OPT2
120    RTS:]
130    INPUT'"Numbers",!NUM1(0),!NUM2(0)
140    CALLSTART
150    PRINT!NUM1(0)+(A$="S")*!NUM2(0)-(A$="A")
      *!NUM2(0),!RESULT(0)
160    UNTIL FALSE
170 [OPT2:LDA NUM1(I%):]
180 IF I%=0 AND A$="A" THEN [OPT2:CLC:] ELSE IF I%=0
    THEN [OPT2:SEC:]
190 IF A$="A" THEN [OPT2:ADC NUM2(I%):] ELSE [OPT2:
    SBC NUM2(I%):]
200 [OPT2:STA RESULT(I%):]
210 RETURN
```

Exercise 7.1

1. !NEWLOC < !OLDLOC or !NEWLOC ≥ !OLDLOC + !NUML.

2.

```
10 CLS
20 NUM=&70:OLDLOC=&72:NEWLOC=&74
30 DIM START 100
40 FOR I%=0 TO 2 STEP 2:P%=START
50    [OPTI%
60    LDA OLDLOC
70    CLC
80    ADC NUM
90    STA OLDLOC
100    LDA OLDLOC+1
110    ADC NUM+1
120    STA OLDLOC+1
130    DEC OLDLOC+1
140    LDA NEWLOC
150    CLC
160    ADC NUM
170    STA NEWLOC
180    LDA NEWLOC+1
190    ADC NUM+1
200    STA NEWLOC+1
210    DEC NEWLOC+1
```

```
220    LDY #&FF
230    LDX NUM+1
240    BEQ LOLOOP
250    .LOOP1
260    LDA (OLDLOC),Y
270    STA (NEWLOC),Y
280    DEY
290    CPY #&FF
300    BNE LOOP1
310    DEC OLDLOC+1
320    DEC NEWLOC+1
330    DEX
340    BNE LOOP1
350    .LOLOOP
360    LDX NUM
370    BEQ FINISH
380    .LOOP2
390    LDA (OLDLOC),Y
400    STA (NEWLOC),Y
410    DEY
420    DEX
430    BNE LOOP2
440    .FINISH
450    RTS:]NEXTI%
460 INPUT"How many bytes will be moved",!NUM
470 INPUT"Starting address of memory to be moved",A$:
    !OLDLOC=EVAL(A$)
480 INPUT"Starting address of new location",B$:!NEWLOC=
    EVAL(B$)
490 CALL START:PRINT"Memory moved. Checking now."
500 A=EVAL(A$):B=EVAL(B$)
510 FOR I%=0 TO 256*?(NUM+1)+?NUM-1
520   IF ?(A+I%)<>?(B+I%) PRINT "Error at move"I%+1:END
530   NEXTI%
540 PRINT"Check OK":GOTO460
```

This works if !NEWLOC > !OLDLOC or !OLDLOC ≥ !NEWLOC + !NUML.

Listing 7.3 is more efficient.

3. (i) No provision for (NUM + 1) = 0. Put

     65   BEQ NOHIGH and 175   .NOHIGH

(ii) In the move of the (NUM) residual bytes, a major fault occurs. For example, if !OLDLOC = &9400, !NEWLOC = &4000 and !NUM = &1040, when the residual bytes are to be moved !OLDLOC is &A400, !NEWLOC is &5000 and X = &40. The first move is &A440 to &5040 and the last &A401 to &5001. &A400 to &5000 has been missed out, and &A440 has been moved erroneously.

This is not correctable without reverting to the method in listing 7.3. The fault is obscured if (NUM) = 0, or if (NUM + 1) = 0 and the correction in (i) is not made.

(iii) The routine fails if !NUM ≥ 33K or if !OLDLOC − !NEWLOC < 256. Neither of these is correctable.

Exercise 7.2

```
 10 NUMBER=&70:FIRST=&72:SECOND=&74:TEMP=&76:RECLENGTH=
    &77:KEYSTART=&78:KEYEND =&79:BASE=&7A:LOOPCOUNTH=&7C
 20 DIM START 150
 30 FOR I%=0 TO 2 STEP 2:P%=START
 40    [OPTI%
 50    LDA BASE
 60    STA SECOND
 70    LDA BASE+1
 80    STA SECOND+1
 90    LDX #0
100    STX LOOPCOUNTH
110    .BEGIN
120    LDY KEYSTART
130    LDA SECOND+1
140    STA FIRST+1
150    LDA SECOND
160    STA FIRST
170    CLC
180    ADC RECLENGTH
190    STA SECOND
200    BCC LOOP1
210    INC SECOND+1
220    .LOOP1
230    LDA (FIRST),Y
240    CMP (SECOND),Y
250    BCC NEWRECORD
260    BNE SWAP
270    INY
280    CPY KEYEND
290    BCC LOOP1
300    BEQ LOOP1
310    BCS NEWRECORD
320    .SWAP
330    LDY RECLENGTH
340    .LOOP2
350    DEY
360    LDA (FIRST),Y
370    STA TEMP
380    LDA (SECOND),Y
390    STA (FIRST),Y
400    LDA TEMP
410    STA (SECOND),Y
420    CPY #0
430    BNE LOOP2
```

```
440   .NEWRECORD
450   INX
460   BNE NTZERO
470   INC LOOPCOUNTH
480   .NTZERO
490   CPX NUMBER
500   BNE BEGIN
510   LDA LOOPCOUNTH
520   CMP NUMBER+1
530   BNE BEGIN
540   DEC NUMBER
550   BEQ LOWZERO
560   LDA NUMBER
570   CMP #&FF
580   BNE START
590   DEC NUMBER+1
600   BPL START
610   .LOWZERO
620   LDA NUMBER+1
630   BNE START
640   RTS:]NEXT
650   CLS:INPUT"What is the record length",R:
      ?RECLENGTH=R+1
660   INPUT'"What are the limits for the key",
      ?KEYSTART,?KEYEND
670   INPUT'"How many records",N:!NUMBER=N-1
680   DIM B ?(RECLENGTH)*N: !BASE=B
690   PRINT'"Setting up strings now"
700   FOR I%=0 TO N-1:FOR J%= 0 TO R-1:?(B+I%*(R+1)+J%)
      =RND(26)+64:NEXTJ%:?(B+I %*(R+1)+J%)=13 :NEXTI%
710   PRINT"Sorting now.":CALLSTART:PRINT"Checking."
720   FOR I%=0 TO (?RECLENGTH)*(N-2) STEP (?RECLENGTH):
      IF MID$($(B+I%),?(KEYSTART)+1,?KEYEND-?KEYSTART+1)
      >MID$($(B+I%+(?RECLENGTH)),?(KEYSTART)+1,
      ?KEYEND-?KEYSTART+1) THEN PRINT "ERROR
      AT"STR$(I%):END
730   NEXT:PRINT"O.K.":END
```

The reasons for this considerable increase in complication when dealing with more than 256 records will be discussed in section 10.3.

Exercise 7.3

```
10 NUMBER=&70:FIRST=&72:SECOND=&74:TEMP=&76:
   BASE=&77:LOOPCOUNT=&79
20 DIM START 150
30 FOR I%=0 TO 2 STEP 2:P%=START
40    [OPTI%
50    LDA BASE
60    STA SECOND
70    LDA BASE+1
80    STA SECOND+1
90    LDA #0
```

```
100     STA LOOPCOUNT
110     STA LOOPCOUNT+1
120     .BEGIN
130     LDY #0
140     LDA SECOND+1
150     STA FIRST+1
160     LDA SECOND
170     STA FIRST
180     CLC
190     ADC #4
200     STA SECOND
210     BCC NOCARRY
220     INC SECOND+1
230     .NOCARRY
240     LDX #4
250     SEC
260     .LOOP1
270     LDA (SECOND),Y
280     SBC (FIRST),Y
290     INY
300     DEX
310     BNE LOOP1
320     BVC NOOVFLOW
330     EOR #&80
340     .NOOVFLOW
350     EOR #0
360     BPL OVER
370     DEY
380     .LOOP2
390     LDA (FIRST),Y
400     STA TEMP
410     LDA (SECOND),Y
420     STA (FIRST),Y
430     LDA TEMP
440     STA (SECOND),Y
450     DEY
460     BPL LOOP2
470     .OVER
480     INC LOOPCOUNT
490     BNE NTZERO
500     INC LOOPCOUNT+1
510     .NTZERO
520     LDA LOOPCOUNT
530     CMP NUMBER
540     BNE BEGIN
550     LDA LOOPCOUNT+1
560     CMP NUMBER+1
570     BNE BEGIN
580     DEC NUMBER
590     BEQ LOWZERO
600     LDA NUMBER
610     CMP #&FF
620     BNE START
630     DEC NUMBER+1
640     BPL START
650     .LOWZERO
```

```
660    LDA NUMBER+1
670    BNE START
680    RTS:]NEXT
690 CLS:INPUT"How many numbers",N: !NUMBER=N-1:
    DIM B 4*!NUMBER: !BASE=B
700 FOR I%=0 TO N-1:!(B+4*I%)=RND:NEXTI%
710 PRINT"Numbers assigned.  Sorting now":CALLSTART:
    PRINT"Done.  Checking now. "
720 FOR I%=0 TO N-2:IF  !(B+4*I%)>!(B+4+4*I%)  THEN
    PRINT"ERROR AT "STR$(I%):END
730   NEXTI% :PRINT"Checking O.K.":END
```

Exercise 7.4

Identical to changes made in exercise 7.2, with LOOP4 and LOOP3 instead of BEGIN and START respectively. The pointer allocation in line 20 will need to be increased also.

Exercise 7.5

1.

```
        CMP    #&61
        BCC    OVER
        CMP    #&7B
        BCS    OVER
        SEC
        SBC    #&20
OVER    JMP    E0A4
```

2.

```
        LDA    #ASC("?")
        JSR    OSWRCH
        JMP    &DEC5
```

Exercise 8.1

1. Box 1   becomes $0 \rightarrow$ RES
$0 \rightarrow$ RES+1
$0 \rightarrow$ RES+2
$0 \rightarrow$ RES+3

Box 2   becomes   Shift (MULTER+1; MULTER) right

Box 3   becomes   (RES+3; RES+2) + (MULTED+1; MULTED) $\rightarrow$ RES+3; RES+2; RES+1; RES) right

Box 4   becomes Rotate (RES+3; RES+2; RES+1; RES) right

```
 10 MULTER=&70:MULTED=&72:RES=&74
 20 DIM START 50
 30 FOR I%=0 TO 2 STEP2:P%=START
 40    [OPTI%
 50    LDA #0
 60    STA RES
 70    STA RES+1
 80    STA RES+2
 90    STA RES+3
100    LDX #16
110    .LOOP
120    LSR MULTER+1
130    ROR MULTER
140    BCC ZERO
150    LDA RES+2
160    CLC
170    ADC MULTED
180    STA RES+2
190    LDA RES+3
200    ADC MULTED+1
210    STA RES+3
220    .ZERO
230    ROR RES+3
240    ROR RES+2
250    ROR RES+1
260    ROR RES
270    DEX
280    BNE LOOP
290    RTS:]NEXTI%
300 CLS:REPEAT
310    INPUT"Numbers to be multiplied",A,B:!MULTF
       =A:!MULTED=B
320    CALLSTART
330    PRINTA*B,16777216*?(RES+3)+65536*?(RES+2)+
       256*?(RES+1)+?RES
340    UNTIL FALSE
```

The accumulator is used for the multiple precision add in lines 160 to 210 so it cannot be used to store part of the result.

2.

```
 10 MULTER=&70:MULTED=&71:RES=&72
 20 DIM START 150
 30 FOR I%=0 TO 2 STEP2: P%=START
 40    [OPTI%
 50    LDY #0
 60    LDX #0
```

```
 70     LDA MULTER
 80     BPL PLUS1
 90     INX
100     EOR #&FF
110     CLC
120     ADC #1
130     STA MULTER
140     .PLUS1
150     LDA MULTED
160     BPL PLUS2
170     DEX
180     EOR #&FF
190     CLC
200     ADC #1
210     STA MULTED
220     .PLUS2
230     TXA
240     BEQ PLUS
250     LDY #1
260     .PLUS
270     LDA #0
280     STA RES
290     LDX #8
300     .LOOP
310     LSR MULTER
320     BCC ZERO
330     CLC
340     ADC MULTED
350     .ZERO
360     ROR A
370     ROR RES
380     DEX
390     BNE LOOP
400     STA RES+1
410     TYA
420     BEQ ANSPL
430     SEC
440     LDA #0
450     SBC RES
460     STA RES
470     LDA #0
480     SBC RES+1
490     STA RES+1
500     .ANSPL
510     RTS:]NEXTI%
520 CLS:REPEAT
530     INPUT"Numbers to be multiplied",A,B
540      IF A<0 THEN C=256+A ELSE C=A
550      IF B<0 THEN D=256+B ELSE D=B
560       ?MULTER=C:?MULTED=D:CALLSTART
570     PRINTA*B,
580     IF ?(RES+1)>127 THEN PRINT(?(RES+1)-255)*
        256+?RES-256 ELSE PRINT?(RES+1)*256+?RES
590     UNTIL FALSE
```

The details are

50	Flag for sign of result
60	Indicator for each sign
70–130	Check if multiplier negative, and if so increment X and obtain two's complement of multiplier
150–210	Check if multiplied number is negative, and if so decrement X and obtain two's complement of multiplied number
230–250	If X is not zero, result will be negative. Set flag in Y
270–400	As listing 8.3
410–490	If result is to be negative, form two's complement of result by subtracting from zero

3. There are many possible solutions, one of which is to use listing 8.3, but the following is shorter and quicker. It does the computation by evaluating $256 * Y + X - 6 * Y$. It is often the case that knowledge of the multiplier can allow quicker routines than the general-purpose listing 8.3, and this is such a case.

```
10 RES=&70
20 DIM START 50
30 FOR I%=0 TO 2 STEP 2
40     P%=START
50     [OPTI%
60     STY MEMLOC+1
70     STY RES+1
80     TXA
90     LDY #6
100    .LOOP
110    SEC
120    .MEMLOC
130    SBC #0 Dummy operand
140    BCS NOBORROW
150    DEC RES+1
160    .NOBORROW
170    DEY
180    BNE LOOP
190    STA RES
200    LDY MEMLOC+1
210    RTS:JNEXTI%
220 CLS:REPEAT
230    INPUT"What are X and Y",X%,Y%
240    CALLSTART
250    PRINT250*Y%+X%,256*?(RES+1)+?RES
260    UNTIL FALSE
```

Lines 70 and 80 compute $256 * Y + X$ (with X in the accumulator).
Lines 90 to 180 subtract Y six times, giving $250 * Y + X$.

It is possible to use TEMP to save Y, instead of the internal location MEMLOC, but while this saves 2 bytes it costs 4 cycles of time (see appendix 1).

Exercise 8.2

Put 193   DEC NUMBER+1
  196   BPL BACK

and change ?NUMBER to !NUMBER in line 400.

Exercise 8.3

1. The REPWHILE loop executes infinitely. Put BEQ MISTAKE at 75, where MISTAKE is some error-handing routine (see listing 8.8).

2.

```
 10 DVID=&70:DVIS=&72:QUOT=&74
 20 DIM START 50
 30 FOR I%=0 TO 2 STEP 2:P%=START
 40    [OPTI%
 50    LDX #0
 60    LDA #0
 70    STA QUOT
 80    STA QUOT+1
 90    LDA DVIS+1
100    BMI LOOP
110    ORA DVIS
120    BEQ FINISH
130    .REPWHILE
140    INX
150    ASL DVIS
160    ROL DVIS+1
170    BPL REPWHILE
180    .LOOP
190    LDA DVID
200    CMP DVIS
210    LDA DVID+1
220    SBC DVIS+1
230    BCC LESS
240    INC QUOT
250    LDA DVID
260    SEC
270    SBC DVIS
280    STA DVID
290    LDA DVID+1
300    SBC DVIS+1
310    STA DVID+1
320    .LESS
330    DEX
340    BMI FINISH
350    LSR DVIS+1
360    ROR DVIS
370    ASL QUOT
380    ROL QUOT+1
```

```
390    JMP LOOP
400    .FINISH
410     RTS:]NEXTI%
420 CLS:REPEAT
430    INPUT"Dividend",DD
440    INPUT"Divisor",DS
450    !DVID=DD:!DVIS=DS
460    CALLSTART
470    PRINTDD DIV DS,DD MOD DS
480    PRINT256*?(QUOT+1)+?QUOT,256*?(DVID+1)+?DVID
490    UNTIL FALSE
```

3. The following code should be inserted after line 390 in the listing in question 2, replacing BEQ or BMI FINISH in lines 120 and 340 by BMI ROUND. Alter lines 460 and 480 accordingly.

ROUND	LSR	DVIS+1	
	ROR	DVIS	Divide divisor by two.
	BCC	NOFRAC	If there is a half,
	INC	DVIS	then round up.
	BNE	NOFRAC	
	INC	DVIS+1	
NOFRAC	LDA	DVID	
	CMP	DVIS	Compare remainder (in DVID)
	LDA	DVID+1	with half the divisor (in DVIS).
	SBC	DVIS+1	
	BCC	FINISH	
	INC	QUOT	
	BNE	FINISH	If remainder is at least half
	INC	QUOT+1	the divisor round up.
FINISH	RTS		

4.

```
10 DVID=&70:DVIS=&71:QUOT=&72
20 DIM START 150
30 FOR I%=0 TO 2 STEP 2:P%=START
40    [OPTI%
50    LDY #0
60    LDX #0
70    LDA DVIS
80    BPL PLUS1
90    INX
100   EOR #&FF
110   CLC
120   ADC #1
130   STA DVIS
```

```
140     .PLUS1
150     LDA DVID
160     BPL PLUS2
170     DEX
180     EOR #&FF
190     CLC
200     ADC #1
210     STA DVID
220     .PLUS2
230     TXA
240     BEQ PLUS
250     LDY #1
260     .PLUS
270     LDX #0
280     STX QUOT
290     LDA DVIS
300     BEQ ANSPL
310     .REPWHILE
320     BMI LOOP
330     INX
340     ASL DVIS
350     BPL REPWHILE
360     .LOOP
370     LDA DVID
380     CMP DVIS
390     BCC LESS
400     INC QUOT
410     LDA DVID
420     SEC
430     SBC DVIS
440     STA DVID
450     .LESS
460     DEX
470     BMI ROUND
480     LSR DVIS
490     ASL QUOT
500     JMP LOOP
510     .ROUND
520     LSR DVIS
530     BCC NOFRAC
540     INC DVIS
550     .NOFRAC
560     LDA DVID
570     CMP DVIS
580     BCC SIGN
590     INC QUOT
600     .SIGN
610     TYA
620     BEQ ANSPL
630     SEC
640     LDA #0
650     SBC QUOT
660     STA QUOT
670     .ANSPL
680     RTS:]NEXTI%
690 CLS:REPEAT
```

```
700    INPUT"Dividend",A:IF A<0 THEN C=256+A ELSE C=A
710    INPUT"Divisor",B:IF B<0 THEN D=256+B ELSE D=B
720    ?DVID=C:?DVIS=D:CALLSTART
730    PRINTA/B
740    IF ?QUOT>127 PRINT ?QUOT-256 ELSE PRINT?QUOT
750    UNTIL FALSE
```

The details are

50–250   Virtually identical to first half of solution for question 2, exercise 8.1
270–500   Identical to listing 8.7 (with the addition in question 1)
520–590   Equivalent to question 3 for 8-bit numbers
610–660   Identical to last part of question 2, exercise 8.1

Exercise 8.4

```
10 DVID=&70:DVIS=&72:QUOTH=&74:OSWRCH=&FFEE
20 DIM START 100
30 FOR I%=0 TO 2 STEP 2:P%=START
40    [OPTI%
50    LDA DVIS
60    ORA DVIS+1
70    BEQ MISTAKE
80    LDA #0
90    STA QUOTH
100   LDX #16
110   .LOOP
120   ASL DVID
130   ROL DVID+1
140   ROL A
150   TAY
160   ROL QUOTH
170   CMP DVIS
180   LDA QUOTH
190   SBC DVIS+1
200   BCC LESS
210   TYA
220   SBC DVIS
230   TAY
240   LDA QUOTH
250   SBC DVIS+1
260   STA QUOTH
270   INC DVID
280   .LESS
290   TYA
300   DEX
310   BNE LOOP
320   RTS
330   .MISTAKE
340   LDA #ASC("?")
350   JSR OSWRCH
```

```
360    LDA #7
370    JSR OSWRCH
380    RTS:JNEXTI%
390 CLS:REPEAT
400    INPUT"Dividend",A
410    INPUT"Divisor",B
420    !DVID=A:!DVIS=B
430    !&403=USRSTART
440    PRINTA DIV B,A MOD B
450    PRINT256*?(DVID+1)+?DVID,256*?QUOTH+?&403
460    UNTIL FALSE
```

The details are

50–70	Output error message if (DVIS+1; DVIS) is zero
120–160	Shift left (DVIS+1; DVIS) one bit into (QUOTH; A) saving the accumulator temporarily in Y
170–200	Compare (QUOTH; A) to (DVIS+1; DVIS)
210–270	If quotient not less than divisor, retrieve the accumulator, subtract (DVIS) (the carry must already be set), save the accumulator in Y, subtract (DVIS+1) from (QUOTH) with any borrow, and increment the dividend by one
290–320	Retrieve the accumulator, loop 16 times, and then return
340–380	If a division by zero occurs, output a query sign and a short beep, and return

The program is shorter and quicker.

Exercise 9.1

1.

```
10 OSWORD=&FFF1:OSWRCH=&FFEE
20 DIM START 100
30 !&80=&FFFFFF9C:?&84=&FF
40 FOR I%=0 TO 3 STEP 3:P%=START
50    [OPTI%
60    .SETCLOCK
70    LDA #4
80    LDX #&80
90    LDY #0
100   JSR OSWORD
110   RTS
120   .ENTRY
130   STA &FC
140   PHA:TXA:PHA:TYA:PHA:PHP
150   LDA &FC
160   CMP #5
170   BNE FINISH
```

```
180    LDA #7
190    JSR OSWRCH
200    JSR SETCLOCK
210    .FINISH
220    PLP:PLA:TAY:PLA:TAX:PLA
230    RTS:]NEXT
240 ?&220=ENTRY MOD 256:?&221=ENTRY DIV 256
250 *FX14,5
260 CALL SETCLOCK
```

2.

```
 10 OSWRCH=&FFEE:OSWORD=&FFF1
 20 DIM START 500
 30 FOR I%=0 TO 2 STEP 2
 40    P%=START
 50    [OPT I%
 60    LDA #TEXT MOD 256
 70    STA &80
 80    LDA #TEXT DIV 256
 90    STA &81
100    LDA #19
110    STA &82
120    LDA #&41
130    STA &83
140    LDA #&5A
150    STA &84
160    .BEGIN
170    LDA #ASC("?")
180    JSR OSWRCH
190    LDX #&80
200    LDY #0
210    LDA #0
220    JSR OSWORD
230    BCC CR
240    RTS
250    .CR
260    LDA &80
270    ADC #20 \ Carry already clear
280    STA &80
290    BCC BEGIN
300    INC &81
310    BCS BEGIN
320    .TEXT:]NEXT
330 CALL START
```

Exercise 9.2

1.
```
              PHP
              PLA
              ORA   #&C0
              PHA
              PLP
```

2.

```
                    SEC
                    PHP
        LOOP1       PLP
                    LDA     (SECOND), Y
                    SBC     (FIRST), Y
                    INY
                    PHP
                    CPY     #4
                    BNE     LOOP1
```

The first is more efficient in memory space, since fewer bytes are used; and more efficient in time in that the loop here contains two excess instructions.

Exercise 9.3

1.

```
                    TAY
                    TXA
                    PHA
                    TYA
                    TAX
                    PLA
```

2. (i)

```
                    PHA
                    STX     MEMLOC+1
                    SEC
        MEMLOC      SBC     #0          Dummy
                    TAX
                    PLA
```

(ii)

```
                    PHA
                    TXA
                    STY     MEMLOC+1
        MEMLOC      ADC     #0          Dummy
                    TAX
                    PLA
```

Exercise 9.4

```
10 COLUMNS=&70:ROWS=&71:COLCOPY=&72:LIMIT=&73:
   BEGINCONTROL=&74:HIBYTE=&75:LOCATION=&76:
   STORE=&78:OSWRCH=&FFEE:OSBYTE=&FFF4
20 FORI%=0 TO 2 STEP 2:P%=&D01:RESTORE
30   [OPTI%
40   LDA #3
50   STA LIMIT
```

```
  60    LDX #0
  70    JSR CONTROL:LDA #2:JSR OSWRCH
  80    LDX #4
  90    LDA #&85
 100    JSR OSBYTE
 110    STY MEMLOC+1
 120    LDA #&84
 130    JSR OSBYTE
 140    STY HIBYTE
 150    .MEMLOC
 160    CPY #0 Dummy operand
 170    BNE ZEROMODE
 180    LDA #7
 190    STA LIMIT
 200    LDA #3
 210    STA BEGINCONTROL
 220    LDA #40
 230    BNE FOURMODE
 240    .ZEROMODE
 250    LDA #11
 260    STA LIMIT
 270    LDA #7
 280    STA BEGINCONTROL
 290    LDA #80
 300    .FOURMODE
 310    STA COLUMNS
 320    LDA &322
 330    STA LOCATION
 340    LDA &323
 350    STA LOCATION+1
 360    LDA #32
 370    STA ROWS
 380    .BEGIN
 390    LDA COLUMNS
 400    STA COLCOPY
 410    LDX BEGINCONTROL
 420    JSR CONTROL
 430    .LOOP1
 440    LDY #7
 450    .LOOP2
 460    LDA (LOCATION),Y
 470    STA STORE,Y
 480    DEY
 490    BPL LOOP2
 500    LDY #8
 510    .LOOP3
 520    LDX #7
 530    LDA #1
 540    JSR OSWRCH
 550    .LOOP4
 560    ASL STORE,X
 570    ROR A
 580    DEX
 590    BPL LOOP4
 600    JSR OSWRCH
 610    DEY
```

```
620    BNE LOOP3
630    LDA LOCATION
640    CLC
650    ADC #8
660    STA LOCATION
670    BCC NOCARRY
680    INC LOCATION+1
690    .NOCARRY
700    DEC COLCOPY
710    BNE LOOP1
720    LDA #1
730    JSR OSWRCH
740    LDA #&0D
750    JSR OSWRCH
760    LDA LOCATION+1
770    BPL OVER
780    LDA HIBYTE
790    STA LOCATION+1
800    .OVER
810    DEC ROWS
820    BNE BEGIN
830    LDA #13
840    STA LIMIT
850    LDX #11
860    JSR CONTROL:LDA #3:JSR OSWRCH
870    RTS
880    .CONTROL
890    LDA #1
900    JSR OSWRCH
910    LDA TABLE,X
920    JSR OSWRCH
930    INX
940    CPX LIMIT
950    BNE CONTROL
960    RTS
970    .TABLE:]NEXTI%
980 FOR I%=1 TO 13
990    READ ?P%
1000   P%=P%+1:NEXTI%
1010 DATA27,65,8,27,75,64,1,27,76,128,2,27,50
```

The details are

40–130	As listing 8.6
140	Only the high byte of physical screen memory is required to be saved
150–310	As listing 8.6, 160–320
320–350	Store start of actual screen memory (that is, taking into account changes due to scrolling) in LOCATION
360–750	As listing 8.6, 330–720
760–790	If we go beyond &7FFF, the high byte becomes negative, and we replace it by the high byte of the start of physical

screen memory (that is, the start of actual screen memory when there has been no scrolling)

800–1010   As listing 8.6, 730–930

Notice that this program is longer; so if we know that there will be no scrolling (typically so when using the high-resolution graphics), listing 8.6 is the better choice if memory is at a premium.

Index

318

Details of Cassette

A software cassette is available to accompany this book. This cassette is obtainable through all major bookshops, but in case of difficulty order direct from

Globe Book Services
Houndmills
Brunel Road
Basingstoke
Hampshire RG21 2XS
ISBN 0–333–38267–6

The cost of the cassette is £9.00 (including VAT). This price applies to the United Kingdom.